into the never-never

into the never-never

travels in australia

Brian Johnston

MELBOURNE UNIVERSITY PRESS

Melbourne University Press
PO Box 278, Carlton South, Victoria 3053,
Australia

First published 1997

Designed by Guy Mirabella
Typeset by Melbourne University Press
in 10 pt Sabon
Printed in Australia by McPherson's Printing
Group

National Library of Australia Cataloguing-in-
Publication entry

Johnston, Brian, 1966– .
    Into the never-never: travels in Australia.

    ISBN 0 522 84807 9.

    1. Johnston, Brian, 1966– —Journeys—
Australia. 2. Australia—Description and
travel—1990– . I. Title.

919.40465

To my sister Nicola

who encouraged most of these travels
and made them so pleasant

contents

note to the reader

When I made the travels that are the subject of this book I had never before been to Australia, and I looked on the country through foreign eyes, from a European perspective. I made notes on the assumption that, if they were ever written into a book, it would be published in Britain, and I therefore wrote for the benefit of non-Australians. Halfway through my task I found myself an Australian resident and, with one book already published in Australia, it seemed likely this one would be as well.

As a result some of my material was rewritten into the book as it stands now, because I was well aware that, while there were many things I had said that might interest foreigners, they would have struck Australians as rather obvious. The balance is a fine one, and I hope it has worked: I have certainly benefited both through seeing Australia with fresh eyes as an outsider, and having had the time to reconsider my views in more depth and detail, and perhaps more sympathy, as an insider. I have, however, resisted the urge to change all that I wrote on reconsidering the country with greater intimacy. The book remains a traveller's view of the continent, rather than a resident's.

I would like to thank my sister Nicola for her spirit of adventure and equanimity in the face of all obstacles; without her I would certainly never have managed such extensive travels in the Australian outback. It was not the first of our adventures together, and I certainly hope it will not be the last. I also appreciate her good humour in letting me write about her—and sometimes poke fun at her—in these pages.

Mike Kirk was a very agreeable companion, not to mention an invaluable car mechanic, from Darwin to the Blue Mountains. As for my brother Simon, he came to Australia several years before I did, and was instrumental in my making the decision to visit the continent in the first place, so it is really to him that I owe a new life in Sydney. Their views on Australia have also contributed to this book.

I would also like to mention the other members of my family who, at one stage or another, read the manuscript and offered both advice that improved it and opinions that boosted my confidence in the writing of it. My mother and father in particular have always offered me a great deal of support, and a first draft of this book was written under their roof.

Teresa Pitt, the commissioning editor at Melbourne University Press, has once again provided invaluable help and encouragement. Other members of the publishing staff are, of course, unsung heroines who work enthusiastically on the book before and after publication: their contribution has not gone unnoticed.

Jenny Lee corrected errors of fact and interpretation with breathtaking erudition, and followed up with scrupulous copy-editing. Her suggestions have greatly improved the text.

Needless to say, it is the large number of Australians who appear in these pages to whom I owe the greatest appreciation, for without them there would have been nothing to write about. Although I make fun of Australia and criticise some aspects of its society in this book, I have a great respect and admiration for this wonderful country. I am now immensely happy to call Sydney home and myself an Australian. I hope this book may be seen as an expression of my thanks for the privilege.

Life consists of choice. The perpetual reservations of judgement, and the perpetual choosing.

Lawrence Durrell, Balthazar

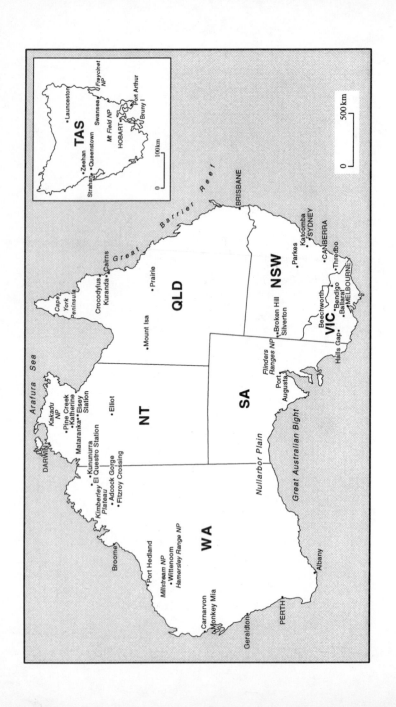

prologue: arrival

For hours the plane had been travelling over the Australian continent, its bare rocks, exposed thousands of feet below, as timeless and haunting as the skeletons of insects preserved in amber. The bones of worn-down mountains protruded painfully from the eroded red flesh of the earth, scarred with patches of brown and ochre. The land below me reminded me of the body of a Stone Age man I had once seen in the British Museum, a body eerily preserved for centuries in peat bogs by humic acid: the same parched tautness and painful deformity, the same stained roughness in tans and blacks, melancholy relic of a time when there was more life. Below, as the Qantas jumbo headed almost imperceptibly south towards the Great Australian Bight, I could see huge stones sticking up like yellowed teeth through the purple gums of the plains. The great lazy arteries of dried-up river-beds meandered across the desiccated countryside as if bewildered, before dwindling into a fine network of shrivelled veins that vanished into stone and sand.

The passing landscape did not change as we ate lunch, fell asleep, woke up again: hours and hours of hostile emptiness under a clear, unpolluted sky. Australia was a red country, red like the dried-up rust on scrap metal that had been abandoned for years; red the colour of clotted blood, dark and old. Sometimes it was orange in great slashes cutting across the earth, and sometimes hills rose up, purple in the early afternoon light, dark shadows of great rocks in a weary land. Strange colours, smeared across the earth by an apocalyptic

1

painter, violating all that was familiar to me: no greens or blues, only raw redness and violet and cadmium yellow.

The pilot had been keeping his passengers informed along the way: the Alps, the Black Sea, Bombay, Singapore, the island of Bali. Over Australia he fell silent, as if overawed by the unrelieved vastness of his own country. There was nothing to point out here: no cities, no rivers, no mountain ranges, no lakes. It was hard to believe the flight attendants (hosties, the Australians called them comfortably), with their honey-coloured hair and ready smiles, their tidy blue uniforms, came from this barren land. I peered down, daunted by the endless uninhabited expanse. I had come to travel this outback and, though I had not yet formulated exactly how I would make my journey, I intended to wander thousands of kilometres across the top of Australia, from the lush rain-forests of north Queensland on the east coast to the remote Kimberley Ranges in the west, and from there down the western coast and back across the wilderness of the interior to Sydney and then—who knows?—south to Tasmania. Now, as I stared out through the oval window, mesmerised and astounded by this vast continent, I thought my ambition bold and even foolish. A city-dweller, coming from a Europe of tamed countryside and intimate distances, I was appalled by the immensity and barrenness of this Australia seen from an aeroplane. It was a merciless landscape, without compromise or familiarity.

'Very big,' said the Taiwanese gentleman sitting beside me. He goggled down over my shoulder, aghast at the landscape below him. He did not drink, but swirled whisky around his plastic cup before glancing back at the whisky-coloured desolation of Australia. He sighed and muttered and took an electronic translator from his pocket, punching at the buttons. The liquid-crystal display flashed up in front of my eyes: *Intimidating*. I smiled my agreement. As if to reassure himself, the Taiwanese turned his back on the oval window and began showing me the wonders of his miniature equipment.

'Many many thousand words,' he grinned happily, tapping in samples in Chinese and holding up the translations for my approval. I took the dictionary, not much larger than a calculator, and with curiosity typed in: *Taiwan*.

The screen remained blank and the Taiwanese took his toy back in confusion. *Taiwan.* He tried again. Excitedly, I snatched the translator back and tried *Australia.*

'Don't know these words,' confessed the man unhappily, looking embarrassed at the blank display. He seemed to shrink in his seat, dismayed at the shortcomings of his Taiwanese gadgetry. I smiled to myself: I secretly enjoyed the failure of this instrument that pretended language was so easy to understand, so mechanical. But later I felt guilty as I watched the Taiwanese stare down at the untamed landscape below him, as if bewildered.

After a while he asked me why I was going to Australia.

'For a holiday,' I said vaguely. But my answer was deceptive. I did not really know why I was going to Australia: to travel, yes, and because my brother lived in Sydney, and because my sister was travelling there and my mother wanted a first-hand report on her strange adventures. These were not the real reasons. I was not going but leaving: leaving a job and a country where I no longer felt I belonged. Growing up in Switzerland, I had always been a foreigner, and when I returned there after almost three years in China I felt rootless, suffocated, restless living with my parents, horrified at the prices, the materialism, frustrated at the apathy of the Swiss to the world outside, to different societies and concepts of life. I did not like my office job, I did not know what I really wanted to do, and the easiest way of dealing with these weighty questions was to flee them all. And so I fled, attracted by the vast emptiness of Australia, the youthfulness of its culture, the cosmopolitanism of its cities.

I could not say all this to the Taiwanese sitting beside me: his was an innocent and casual question, and he neither expected nor wished to hear me harangue him about the directions of my life. I muttered a few banalities about meeting my sister and travelling the outback, before staring once more out of the window, feeling helpless.

Some time later I added, hopefully: 'And I'm going to Australia to find the Chinese.'

And I was. My years in China had given me a fascination for oriental culture and people in general and the Chinese in particular. I knew, rather vaguely, that there was a sizeable

Asian community in Australia; that Australia was attempting to become politically and economically a part of Asia; and that the Chinese had had a long involvement in Australia's history.

'China?' said the Taiwanese, misunderstanding. 'Is Australia good producing of china?' I said I did not know if Australia was good producing of china, but that I meant the Chinese people, not teacups.

'For that you should go to Hong Kong,' said the Taiwanese in puzzlement. 'Or the People's Republic.' But I had been there already, and now the overseas Chinese I thought could be particularly interesting, bridging as they did East and West, not to mention somehow being a symbol of my own confused views and my own rootlessness.

'There are no Chinese in Australia,' observed the Taiwanese, glancing down once more at the barren wastes below as if to confirm it.

'I think there are.' In fact, I knew the Chinese had been snooping around here for a long time. Old Chinese maps depicted the Australian continent, and there was no doubt the Chinese had sailed these waters perhaps a thousand years before the first Europeans, although they had settled here permanently only in the last 150 years.

'No.'

'Yes. Many.'

'I do not think that you are in the correct thinking.'

'Maybe not,' I conceded politely. 'But at least there will be you. Why are *you* going to Australia?'

The Taiwanese looked embarrassed and muttered to himself —perhaps he was smuggling drugs or, who knows, heading for the flesh-pots of Kings Cross on a leave of absence from his wife? Now he looked even more unhappy, no doubt imagining himself in this unknown country, pinned between hostile outback and aggressive Westerners with their rude questions and bizarre purposes.

The long afternoon was already dying as the plane, having banked over the corner of the continent, turned towards Sydney. After sailing across the Pacific, Captain Cook had first sighted land here on this south-east coast of Australia, forewarned by the appearance of an errant butterfly, then a gannet, on his ship. Poor weather and unfavourable winds, however, had prevented him from making landfall. Perhaps, had he seen my vision from the window of an aeroplane, he might have turned tail and fled from this hostile continent. Instead, he sailed the *Endeavour* north along the coastline and finally cast anchor in a sheltered harbour he was to name Botany Bay.

Although his voyage of discovery was remarkable, James Cook could not have been wholly surprised to find land here in the vastness of the Southern Ocean. The thought of such a continent had haunted and intrigued Europeans since the time of the ancient Greeks, when its existence had first been conjectured: such a land mass was needed to act as a counterbalance to the vast weight of Europe and Asia. In the second century Ptolemy postulated a southern land mass that stretched from Africa to South-East Asia, roughly covering the area of what is now known to be the Indian Ocean, while Plato located the lost continent somewhere beyond the Pillars of Hercules, which form the entrance to the Mediterranean. Naturally, this mysterious land abounded in riches—gold, gemstones, precious metals, sandalwood and incense surpassing the legends of El Dorado. The lost continent was believed to be a strange and mysterious place where the sea was as thick as treacle and the heat so fierce that humans would combust. It was inhabited by grotesque creatures, including a tribe whose members each had one massive foot, under which they could shelter from the furious rays of the sun.

A real urge to go and find such a wondrous place probably began with the travels of Marco Polo. According to him, about 700 kilometres south-west of Java was a great country which he named Locach or—perhaps appropriately, given its centrality to Australian culture—Beach. But it was not until the seventeenth and eighteenth centuries, with developments in navigational and shipbuilding technology, that several attempts were made to find this Terra Australis Incognita. From 1606 onwards the Dutch mapped Australia's northern and western coasts, as well as southern Tasmania. Then, in 1770, Cook managed to place Australia firmly on the Anglo-

Saxon map by charting the eastern seaboard and claiming
the land for Britain, bringing a new beginning to this continent that had slumbered, almost unchanged, for millennia.
To Cook too fell the honour of discovering Australia in the
popular imagination, although the Macassans and Dutch—
and possibly the Portuguese and even the Chinese before that
—had already done so.

What sense of impatience, of incipient discovery, of excitement and maybe of terror might have surged in the minds of
those first sailors on the *Endeavour*, confronted with an alien
land straight out of legend, as they warily hugged the
coastline, waiting for the winds to change? I could not
imagine the state of mind of these early explorers. I too was
arriving on foreign shores and yet, despite my astonishment
over the country's barren immensity, they were shores already
somehow known, anticipated, my arrival presaged by the
reality of maps, television documentaries and soap operas,
family photos, the novels of Patrick White and Peter Carey,
Australian friends, my brother in Sydney. By such threads
was I connected to this far-flung corner of the planet, already
visited in mind if not in reality. In the modern world so little
was truly new, truly a discovery, and on this aeroplane there
was no adventure, no sudden, exhilarating sighting of unexplored land, but only a weary wish to arrive: an expected
arrival announced by the clicking of seat-belts and a sudden
reanimation in the faces of the flight attendants. Nor were
there any butterflies, let alone gannets, on this sterile modern
tube as we headed towards Botany Bay, descending sharply
over rolling heath land dotted with eucalypts. Modern travel:
a reconstruction of preformed ideas and images, perhaps (for
we too have our legends and El Dorados); certainly not a
genuine voyage of discovery. A rearrangement, a journey
into one's own perceptions and attitudes and preconceived
notions, never truly a fresh beginning.

The jumbo roared down towards the ocean. *The coast
here resembles the scraggy hips of an old cow*: so wrote
Joseph Banks, the *Endeavour*'s botanist, in an apt description of a parched land of yellowed grass and thin soils
stretched over protruding rocks, crumbling over the cliff edge

into the swell of the rolling Pacific breakers. Only minutes from landing was the emptiness abandoned, to be filled by container terminals, industrial smoke-stacks, houses with red roofs, a golf course sprawling on the sea's edge. Suddenly, as if by sleight of hand, Australia's empty vastness became domesticated by control towers, passenger terminals, airport corridors, and I was back in the landscapes of normality as I steered my way through baggage claim, here on the opposite side of the world, with the boredom of familiarity.

'Do you have any artefacts?' The customs official's accent was the only indication I was now in the Antipodes: a long, lazy drawl, the words as eroded as the Australian landscape. The woman beside him scowled at me professionally. (So too had a couple of Aboriginal Australians greeted Captain Cook, grimacing and brandishing spears at the absurd menace of white gentlemen in frock coats.)

'Any wooden artefacts? Animal products, vegetable matter? Anything made from animal products? Seeds? Anything made from grasses? Flowers? Soil samples?' The customs officer rattled the list off like a machine-gun burst. When I claimed that I did not possess any such goods he stared at me suspiciously.

'Leather goods? Bone or ivory? Fresh foods?' Beside him his companion fixed me with an ancient mariner's gimlet eye.

'*Cut flowers?*' The official snapped the words out triumphantly as if he had penetrated my guilty secret.

'I don't have any cut flowers,' I said firmly.

Having satisfied himself that my baggage was of sufficient sterility to be imported into Australia, the customs official seemed to relent. 'Have a nice day,' he drawled, even though it was almost night. He smiled after me as I tottered on through the green channel, already glancing about desperately for signs to the domestic terminal. I was very late for my connecting flight.

'Two dollars fifty, mate,' observed the driver of the bus linking the two terminals.

'I don't have two dollars or any dollars,' I retaliated, outraged. ('And I'm not your mate,' I felt like adding.) 'I've just arrived and my flight to Cairns is leaving in twenty minutes!'

The driver gave a boyish grin as if perpetrating a practical joke. 'Two dollars fifty, mate, that's the regulation.'

I staggered back into the terminal, wrenching traveller's cheques from my money-belt and thrusting one of them through the window at the exchange booth. Then I pounded back to the bus and collapsed heaving in a seat.

'The plane to Cairns has just departed,' said a woman, also smiling brightly, when I finally arrived at the Qantas desk in the domestic terminal. Departed, I thought: a curiously formal word, hinting at death. Our dear departed and much missed plane flight . . .

'When's the next one?'

'Well there isn't another one tonight. The next one would be tomorrow morning. But we can put you on a flight to Brisbane now—'

'Brisbane?' I did not like to admit that I had only the haziest of ideas about the location of Australia's third-largest city. '*Brisbane?*'

'—and from there there's still another flight to Cairns this evening.' She smiled, a big, broad Australian smile in the interests of customer relations, before driving home the final barb. 'But that flight is actually *full*, so you'd have to rely on a stand-by seat.'

I had been travelling for thirty hours. My eyes stared out redly at the woman behind the desk and I grimaced back at her from parched lips. Perspiration trickled down my back in the heat, but inside I felt as dry as the bog man in the British Museum. Taking my desperation for assent, the woman began tapping at her computer keyboard, and then I was running down another endless corridor like a character from some nightmarish post-modernist film, and being shoehorned into another aeroplane.

I gazed out for what seemed like hours at a black coastline as we headed north to Brisbane. I felt fuzzy, almost as if I were floating above my own body, disoriented in time and space, and lights winked and glimmered below like reflections of the misplaced southern stars that gleamed above. Bony fingers of moonlight grasped at the ocean. I wondered, as the plane shrieked down towards a runway like a vulture on a carcass, if the flight attendant had laced my Coca-Cola with hallucinogens.

'The flight to Cairns is full . . .' smirked another official in Brisbane airport. I had emerged from my trance not in Brisbane but, it appeared, in the middle of a jungle. The airline representative was half hidden behind a potted fern. Half the Queensland rainforest was lined up against the vast glass expanses of the airport lounge, and ferns and ivy dripped from the light fixtures.

There was a pause, and then the man added cryptically, making it sound like a threat: 'But you can *wait and see*.' He fiddled with his hair, and twirled his finger in his ear when he thought I wasn't looking.

I did wait, as passengers—relaxed, holidaying passengers bound for the Barrier Reef with confirmed seats and a happy air of assurance—boarded the aircraft. The ground staff shuffled papers and boarding passes like tarot cards, counting and recounting to determine my immediate future. Finally, almost with regret, they ushered me on, slamming the aircraft door behind me.

I sank wearily into my seat.

'Going to Cairns?' the woman beside me enquired brightly. She pronounced it *Khens*, through her nose. Mid-forties, bursting with Antipodean energy, with healthy skin and windswept auburn hair and a voice full of confidence and curiosity: the last person a barely conscious traveller would want sitting beside him.

'As long as the pilot knows how to get there, I suppose,' I grunted rather uncharitably, shrugging.

'English?'

'No,' I replied firmly.

The woman hesitated before deciding to battle on with her conversation. 'Been in Australia long, then?'

'I've just arrived. A few hours ago. Sydney airport. Brisbane airport.' Gathering up my last shredded remnants of sociability I told her I intended meeting my sister in Cairns and travelling for several months through the outback.

The woman dug her husband in the ribs, delighted. 'Get the man a drink, Paul. He's just arrived in Australia.'

I grimaced at her husband as he emerged from behind his in-flight magazine, but he must have mistaken it for a smile. 'Good on ya,' he said laconically.

When the flight attendant came around the husband ordered three Fosters. ('Not that the *Australians* actually drink Fosters,' he added mysteriously.) He tipped his plastic glass in the air, waving it in my direction.

'Welcome to Australia, mate,' he said affably, drawing out the last two words in a great yawn of diphthongs.

And after the first cool, refreshing gulp I relaxed, and we talked, and I ordered three more Fosters, and I warmed to the Australian couple, who generously said I should come and visit them near Melbourne where they lived, and gave me their address scribbled on the back of a Qantas place-mat. And in no time at all we were descending into the voluptuous blackness of a tropical night in Cairns, and my journey had begun.

barrier reef one

While still at home in Switzerland, where I was then working and where my parents lived, I had received a postcard from my sister Nicola telling me she was working on a hippy farm in South Australia. Although details were lacking, my mother seemed half-convinced that her only daughter had become entrapped in the brainwashing excesses of some obscure pseudo-Christian cult. One line of the postcard in particular roused my mother's suspicions. *The people on the hippy farm are left-wing, middle-class professionals with short hair*, my sister had innocently written. This was enough to condemn them. There seemed little point in being a qualified professional in order to spend one's days growing fruit in the wilderness. My mother also expected these hippies to have long hair; somehow it was even more sinister that their hair was short. Short, cropped, shaved: from here it was easy to extrapolate to banging tambourines and strange robes and maybe even sexual perversions.

Nicola had been wandering the world, in the company of her boyfriend Mike, since her graduation from university over a year previously. Such a long period away from civilisation and responsibility, it appeared, was finally encroaching upon her sanity and judgement. She also claimed to have no money left, and her retreat to a hippy farm—at least in my mother's eyes—seemed to smack of desperation, perhaps even of the sordid poverty one might find among lost Americans on an Indian ashram. And when was Nicola coming home? What were her plans? And what exactly was happening with her relationship? Vague hints from obscure destinations around Australia, funnelled through my brother in Sydney or casually scribbled in letters home, had suggested all was not well. Now Nicola had come to Cairns on her own, deserting Mike somewhere in the Red Centre—this last piece of information dropped into a shouted and brief phone conversation with my mother from a booth somewhere in the wilderness.

I was an odd emissary to send on a quest to bring my sister back into the fold of civilised behaviour (job, boyfriend—or better fiancé—and Sunday tea with my mother), but there was no one else to do the task. My brother—he was in Sydney, couldn't he rescue my sister? But Simon was a research scientist, an occupation that seemed to disqualify him from dealing with emotional crises. Less than three weeks after receiving the suspicious postcard about the hippy farm, my mother bundled me on to a plane before I could think of any more excuses.

I did not know what I expected to find at Cairns airport: my sister in a robe perhaps, ashes on her forehead; or maybe just dressed normally but with a glazed and distant look in her eyes. As it happened, I was somewhat disappointed to find she looked perfectly natural, in a T-shirt and shorts, much thinner than when I had last seen her, but with no sign of abuse or malnutrition. The blueness of her eyes, always startling, was accentuated by her healthy-looking tan.

Now I asked her, hiding my suspicion under a casual tone: 'How was the ashram?'

'What ashram?' said Nicola, frowning.

'The hippy farm,' I said, not caring to admit that her family had imagined her kidnapped by freaks. 'Were they ... I mean, was it a ... a religious establishment?'

'No. Not that I ever noticed. I suppose they might have been Church of Australia? If there is such a thing? Anglicans?' My sister frowned vaguely, without interest. I felt myself deflating.

'But they did have shaved heads?' I muttered feebly.

'Shaved heads!'

'You said in a postcard they had shaved heads!'

'I did not!'

'Well, were they hippies or weren't they?' I snapped.

'No, that's just what we called the place, Mike and I. The hippy farm. I mean I suppose their *ideas* were quite hippyish, but they didn't *look* like hippies. There were five families, lawyers and midwives and university tutors and things. They lived in a commune. It was an alternative way of living.'

I felt glad she hadn't written this on her postcard, leaving our mother free rein to interpret what an alternative life-style might be.

'The farm was called Cennednyss, which means New Beginning.'

I snorted. 'In what language?'

My sister shrugged. 'Don't be so scornful. It was all harmless enough.'

I reluctantly agreed that I supposed it might have been. There didn't seem to be anything else to say, except maybe that postcards were cryptic and misleading things. My confusion seemed an inauspicious beginning to a trip across the world's emptiest continent. I did not think there was much wrong with my sister, apart from a typical restlessness and inability to conform to accepted, traditional pathways that seemingly went with being young in the 1990s. Nicola did not know what she was doing in Australia, and she did not know what she was going to do when she left it; but neither did I. I lapsed into silence, and it was apparent my sister felt the topic closed, for she did not mention the hippy farm again. My mother worried at the subject in subsequent letters and then fell silent. She realised I was in Nicola's camp now, and she had lost me too to Australia.

Cairns is a modern town of whitewashed buildings and houses built in traditional Queensland style, on stilts with wide, shaded verandas—this is what I wrote to my mother on a postcard, taking an uncontroversial line. It had a well-cared-for air, dotted with impressive palm trees and great swathes of bougainvillea and other tropical blossoms. Gaudy flocks of parakeets in bottle-green and red squawked among the trees in the pedestrian shopping zone.

'Mere sparrows to the Queenslanders,' commented Nicola carelessly, sweeping past the parakeets with the full indifference of one already months in the country. I marvelled at the noise they were making. 'Probably disease-ridden,' Nicola added.

'Psittacosis?'

But Nicola—concentration was not her forte—was already talking about something else, heading towards the post restante like a homing pigeon towards its favourite nesting box. She carried off a pile of mail to the nearest café, leaving me to my own amusements.

Cairns was a well-known tropical holiday destination, yet a rather unusual seaside resort: it stood on a tidal river, and I was surprised to find it had no beach. Ironically, there were once sands here, but they had been destroyed by a harbour built to attract tourists. Now, as I watched the tide go out, expensive cream yachts were left bogged down in grey mud, tilting over on their sides as if in disappointment. Pure white ibis stalked through the mire, probing deep with their long curved beaks for tasty morsels below the murky surface. The mud oozed and burped, casting up strange smells as the sea retreated out towards the Barrier Reef.

Cairns had changed its name several times since its settlement: first Thornton, then Dickson, both after colonial government officials. It was renamed Cairns in 1876 after William Wellington Cairns, the Governor of Queensland. The name had finally stuck, but Cairns still had a problem with its identity. It seemed to me a town without much character, indeed a town without even a true centre: merely a collection of bland hotels and restaurants and souvenir shops surrounded by brief suburbs where cheap bungalows hid behind the jacaranda trees. Only the tourists gave the town its energy, a transient energy oscillating with the seasons and the foreign exchange rate. Japanese couples flew into Cairns for romantic weddings in the tropics, hiring Rolls-Royces and tail-coats and even bridesmaids: elaborate ceremonies without much meaning that seemed to encapsulate the spirit of the town. Besides, nobody actually came to *Cairns* for their holidays— rather they came to swim on the Barrier Reef, or to see the rainforest, or to take a trip on the scenic railway to Kuranda. Cairns supplied them with their food and relieved them of their money, but the real activities were happening elsewhere.

Cairns, I soon decided, had the same atmosphere as any town dependent for its existence on tourism: a vaguely hysterical air of living on the edge; a scarcely hidden greed driving it to make money before the good times ran out; the same crowded but unlived-in feeling as an international airport (or, indeed, the post restante), where people merely passed through, living their real lives elsewhere. There was a man I spotted repeatedly in Cairns, walking the length of the shopping mall with a sandwich-board over his shoulders. *Are you a real Christian? I'm a Presbyterian*, it said on the front in virulent neon green, yellow and orange, the colours of young teenager disco-goers. *I'm a fool for Jesus!* it proclaimed across his back. On the Sabbath an additional paper was pinned to the bottom of the board: *It's Sunday—are you going to Church?* It seemed a forlorn hope. There wasn't much soul in Cairns, and I had only seen one church, a tiny stone edifice crushed between Hibiscus Holiday Homes and a swimming pool.

Tourism was the religion on the Queensland coast: not a private, soul-seeking philosophy but an unthinking religion of numbers and shared experience. Japanese coaches stopped outside souvenir shops that had paid the tour companies thousands of dollars for the privilege, and long crocodiles of tourists were ushered inside by their high priests to spend money on knick-knacks that were half the price in the empty shops around the corner. Sermons on entertainments and the local attractions were intoned through microphones on coaches and boats bound for the tourist meccas of Queensland. Personally I could not see the attraction of such holidaying, but I no longer looked down on the tourists who journeyed with such well-planned itineraries and superficial speed. They were busy people with limited time, searching for excitement but wary of too much novelty; wanting value for their hard-earned money; looking to relax and let others do the organising.

Besides, the Japanese reminded me of my quest for orientals. The Japanese themselves did not really count, for they were only transients, but I thought the way they were treated rather interesting: with ill-concealed impatience mostly and, behind their backs, a certain hostility, for Japanese companies owned a huge slice of the Queensland tourist industry.

'They only shop in the Japanese-run shops. They're brought there by their tour leaders,' said one shopkeeper to me, smiling nastily before adding, absurdly: 'And they can't speak English.'

On the other hand, Australia to these Japanese was a sort of Disney World, a place of reef visits, jumping dolphin shows and cheap souvenirs, and they did not care to see it as a real country, with real people: this could well be good cause for some resentment.

Now I asked my sister: 'Have you seen any Chinese?'

'Yes, there's one on the promenade. The sweet and sour pork is pretty good and it was only five dollars fifty,' said Nicola, hurrying me along the street to what she called the 'cheap Barrier Reef ticket-selling place', as if one could buy chunks of the reef at discount prices.

'I meant people-from-China Chinese, only not from China but Australians.'

'I don't know what you're talking about,' said Nicola impatiently. 'How can they be Australians if they're from China?' It was barely a question, more a statement.

'Ha! That's the whole point. They *are* Australians but at the same time they're not.' Somehow I felt the argument was slipping away from me, and I did not really know what I was talking about.

'You don't know what you're talking about. Now here's the cheap Barrier Reef ticket-selling place.'

And my oriental research was temporarily put on hold while we sorted out which ticket was the best value to the best place on the reef, and for the longest time.

'*Noah's Ark*,' said Nicola. 'The boat's called *Noah's Ark*. Not tomorrow's boat but the day after's. There should be some Chinese on that. A pair of them.'

And smugly she marched out into the street.

It is because of the Barrier Reef—as well as the nearby rainforests of northern Queensland—that Cairns is renowned, for the reef is closer to the coast here than at any other easily accessible point along its 2000-kilometre length. Trinity Opening off Cairns is also one of only two recognised shipping passages through this extensive congregation of corals, so complex and labyrinthine that its exact extent has not yet been accurately mapped. *Unexamined but Considered*

Dangerous to Navigation, it says on some of the charts of the region, and one pictures sea-monsters or sirens rising from the deep to waylay the unwary mariner.

'A Reef such as is here spoke of is scarcely known in Europe,' Captain Cook recorded in his journal on 16 August 1770. 'It is a wall of Coral Rock rising almost perpendicular out of the unfathomable Ocean.' In fact the sea here is far from unfathomable, for the water around the coral is never more than sixty metres deep, and in places the coral is often exposed at low tide for a few hours. But this only makes navigation the more difficult. Cook himself almost came to permanent grief on the Barrier Reef when his ship ran aground, and hundreds of other vessels have since been wrecked along its length.

'The HMS *Pandora* was one of them,' announced the disembodied commentary on board the pleasure craft that was taking us out to Green Island. 'It struck the reef in 1791 on its way to England from Tahiti with the mutineers from the *Bounty*. Thirty-five lives were lost, although ten of the fourteen mutineers managed to survive. They were caught again, returned to England and court-martialled at Portsmouth.' It was potted guided-tour information that bored me, unenthusiastic and riddled with dates and numbers, and I wandered out on to the deck.

The boat was crowded with Australian, European and Japanese day-trippers. Green Island was an easy place to see the reef: you could swim—or indeed just wade—right among the corals a stone's throw from its beaches, or view them from glass-bottomed boats or mini-submarines. Most of the Australian passengers were middle-aged couples or yuppies in a hurry, up from Brisbane or Melbourne for a long weekend. They leaned over the railings, snapping photos of themselves against expanses of glittering ocean.

'Funnily enough,' said Geoffrey, an Australian man beside me with whom I had fallen into conversation, and to whom I had expressed disappointment with the commentary, 'the story of the *Pandora* has strange links with another pretty amazing sea journey.'

This was information that I liked. In what must have been one of the most truly remarkable sea journeys of all time, as Geoffrey explained, Mary Bryant, with her husband, children and seven other convicts, had managed to commandeer a small boat, and had sailed thousands of kilometres north-wards from the penal settlement at Sydney Harbour, up the east coast of Australia and on to Timor in Indonesia. Bryant's was only the second boat to navigate this coast after Captain Cook's *Endeavour*, and her life became tangentially involved with those shipwrecked from the *Pandora*.

'Mary Bryant came from Cornwall and was transported for seven years for stealing a cloak or coat or something,' said Geoffrey. 'It seems she led the escape, but her husband was a fisherman, so he was used to boats, and they had a rough chart of these waters.'

Even so it must have been a dangerous journey, I thought, especially considering what it meant in terms of distance and the unknown. Most of the convicts had probably never been outside the boundaries of their own shire before they were shipped out to Australia; and in the 1790s Australian waters had barely been charted.

'Too right,' agreed Geoffrey. 'At one point, they were blown way out to sea by bad weather and never made it to shore for three weeks. They couldn't light a fire, of course, and lived off handfuls of raw rice. At other times they caught fish and collected wild berries, and once they caught a turtle somewhere here on the Barrier Reef.

'They were chased by hostile Aborigines, not to mention by cannibals in rigged canoes out in the Arafura Sea. Two months after leaving Sydney they finally arrived in Timor. Where the Dutch governor had them jailed!'

Ironically enough, an English captain turned up in Timor at this time, which was where the *Pandora* came in. Captain Edwards had been shipwrecked in the *Pandora* on the Bar-rier Reef and had made it to Timor with other survivors in small boats. Edwards took charge of the escaped convicts, along with the *Bounty* mutineers who had also survived the *Pandora* wreck, and returned with them in a passing English ship to London.

'Where the mutineers were court-martialled,' I remem-bered.

'Yep. And Mary became briefly famous in the newspapers as the Girl from Botany Bay.'

Mary Bryant, surprisingly enough, escaped being re-transported; there was a great deal of public sympathy and admiration for her, and she was pardoned. She returned to Cornwall and disappeared from public attention, although, in an interesting titbit of history, she was given an annuity by James Boswell, who was moved by her bravery and her plight.

'Her husband and two children had all died on the sea journey between Timor and London,' added Geoffrey. 'Not unusual in those days, but pretty ironic considering what they had already survived.'

And I wondered about Mary Bryant, back in England, her family lost, about the sharp brutality of her convict life and the heady but desperate romance of her escape. One of those truly remarkable people who fascinate me, nobodies from history with fierce spirits and tormented lives. What did she think, the Girl from Botany Bay, I mused, as she grew old, alone among the windswept, haunted hills of Cornwall?

I was still wondering about her when the boat docked and I disembarked at Green Island with the gulls shrieking overhead.

If tourism in Cairns was almost a religion, the Barrier Reef was its Jerusalem, its Mecca, and visiting it did not fall far short of a mystical event. To snorkel or scuba-dive on the Barrier Reef was almost like being born again: the discovery of a universe of startling colour and shape and strangeness hidden beneath the water. By the time we returned to Cairns, my sister and I were dizzy with euphoria. There were the angel fish, greeny-yellow, flecked with blue, with pouting marigold lips and black eyes; orange-and-white clown-fish that lurked among the waving tentacles of anemones; Moorish idols with their thick stripes and long, streamer-like dorsal fins pirouetting like dancers between the banks of coral. The bright neon colours, triumphantly brash, dazzled with their cunning displays, designed both to attract and confuse. Small, brightly coloured yellow butterfly fish had a false eye spot near their tails to mislead predators, concealing their true eyes in a broad black band; coral trout were pink, dappled with white spots like a fashionable sofa, blending in perfectly against the corals; damsel-fish, unashamed extroverts in bold blue and yellow, called out for attention.

Next day, on *Noah's Ark* (no Chinese, one Japanese in a ragged sarong and nose-stud, hair dyed rust brown), the reef did not seem so inviting. 'Don't worry about the reef sharks. They're not usually dangerous,' said Nick, one of the diving instructors, thereby calling them to our attention and throwing us into instant anxiety. I did not like the sound of the word *usually*. Nor did the other novice divers. A Canadian woman asked in a quavering voice if there were other kinds of sharks too.

'White-tip sharks, silver-tip whalers and grey reef whalers on the outer reef,' replied Nick. 'They're much bigger than reef sharks, are known to be aggressive towards divers and have killed people in the past. But that's out in the open ocean and we're not going there. On the inner reefs you can come across black-tip whalers, sometimes known to attack even in very shallow water.' He smiled charmingly. 'But I don't think anyone has actually been *killed* by a black-tip. You might just get your leg bitten off . . .'

There was a ripple among the dozen passengers, either of amusement or horror according to their characters.

'But you're very unlikely to see any of these sharks, except grey reef sharks, which as I have mentioned are not usually dangerous. As a matter of fact they're rather inquisitive and you'll probably have a chance to see them up close, maybe even touch—'

'What size are they?' I demanded suspiciously.

'Quite small,' said Nick. 'Maybe about as long as you or a bit longer, but you should treat them with caution. On no account should you panic if one approaches you.'

We digested this advice in silence. As Nicola pointed out, I was hardly a dwarf, and anything a bit longer than me would measure a full two metres. It did not seem easy to remain sanguine if a two-metre reef shark swam up and peered through one's mask.

We were heading towards the outer Barrier Reef. *Noah's Ark* was a small craft, a converted fishing boat with none of the luxuries of the bigger cruise launches that took tourists out to Green Island and other locations. Its advantage was that it carried just a dozen passengers and was one of only two boats serving Michaelmas Cay and Hastings Reef: a good way to escape the hordes. Its crew of three, all diving instructors, were relaxed and informative and managed to imbue the proceedings with a sense of adventure, as if we were the first boatload of intrepid explorers ever to have sailed out of Cairns.

Michaelmas Cay, although treeless, supported the largest colony of birds on the Barrier Reef, swooping and shrieking indignantly over their small hump of sand in the middle of the ocean. I could not wait to get my head under water again to view the reef, and this time to try my hand at scuba-diving.

'I would say sharks are the least of your worries,' said Nick as we prepared to take the plunge. 'I must warn you very seriously about two other creatures. On no account must you touch them: they're both extremely dangerous.

'The first is the cone shellfish. They produce conotoxins that prevent the post-synaptic membrane from receiving the acetylcholine manufactured by the nervous system.' The patter came out with a smoothness born of endless repetition, and although none of us understood a word we were riveted.

'In ordinary language that means you'll be overcome by numbness, slurred speech, blurred vision and eventually paralysis. They shoot their poison out through a dart which pierces the victim's skin. The trouble with cones is that they have patterned shells very attractive to divers. My advice to you is not to go souvenir hunting: apart from the fact that they are also protected species, you may be picking up something that will do you no good at all.

'The other pretty little creature of the Barrier Reef is the blue-ringed octopus, which also produces a poison, TTX. TTX induces numbness around the mouth, spreading to the cheeks and face, followed by stiffness, slurred speech, vomiting and in severe cases complete paralysis. A victim will eventually recover, but artificial respiration would need to be maintained for some time.'

'Charming!'

'Bloody hell!'

'What does it look like?'

When the babble of voices had subsided, Nick answered: 'Small, usually dull yellow or maybe grey, but if it feels threatened, blue rings emerge on its skin with a surprising vivid neon colour, hence its name. Unfortunately that's precisely when it appears most attractive and interesting for a good old poke.'

It seemed to me, though I did not say so, that one should not go poking around anywhere near the Barrier Reef. And yet here I was in wet suit and flippers, with an oxygen tank on my back, preparing to descend into the shark- and octopus-infested waters beneath. Nicola had already dropped over the side. I spat into my mask like a professional, smearing the saliva across the glass and then rinsing it to prevent it from clouding over under the water. Then with a mental shrug of my shoulders I went after her.

That is how it must be to step through the looking-glass, through a magic door into another time or place. One moment the sun was glaring overhead and birds wheeling in the familiar sky, and I was a clumsy creature with a heavy tank strapped to my back, staggering across the deck in my outsize flippers. ('Fins,' Nick had said. 'Call them fins. Flipper is a dolphin.') Then, quite suddenly, I was almost weightless, I was flying, surrounded by deep blue, like the birds flying in that other place, and fish in bewildering colours were floating all around my head like a drug-induced fantasy. Grey and carbuncled on the outside, the shells of giant clams opened to reveal a flesh of startling beauty: soft purples and mauves dotted with electric blue and emerald and the palest yellow. They were surrounded by corals, nearly as varied and multi-coloured as the fish that swam among them. Yet where the fish were flamboyant and vivid, the corals had soft pastel and watercolour shades: cream and ivory, pink, fuchsia, primrose, lavender, peach and salmon.

There were no words for this loveliness. It was a strange and unusual place, a fantasy indeed, an improbable landscape of improbable creatures. Returning to the surface was like returning to reality, and only in terrestrial descriptions could one come to terms with the underwater world. The living creatures were called brain and mushroom and staghorn corals, tiger cowries, bat fish. Angel fish had fins sweeping back like saintly wings, parrot fish were as dazzling as the birds that tumbled in the tropical trees around Cairns, and zebra fish, striped black and white like their namesakes, floated through savannas of weed. To scuba-dive among this abundance was to end up, like Alice in a new wonderland, inside some endless kaleidoscope of spots and stripes and bands, creating optical illusions, teasing, endlessly fascinating with its thesaurus of colours. Many fish, with darker backs that merged with the colours of the sea bed from above, darted away with a uniform flash of brightness, showing the paler underbellies that camouflaged them in the sea when observed from below. It was one of those moments of pure magic on the reef, of which I never tired: I would shoot out a hand, as if to grasp those glittering jewelled fish, and see them flash away, hundreds of tiny creatures shimmering always just out of reach.

One minute I was floating languidly in a blue heaven; the next I was surrounded by four sharks, moving up silently, sleek and streamlined.

Don't panic, I said to myself. I sucked a big lung-full of air from my tank, hovering immobile above the coral. The leader was easily my length, though smaller in bulk. For some reason I was astonished to find them looking so classically shark-like: those distinctive tails and fins, the broad gills along their sides, the sinister greyness. They had big grins: not broad, amiable smiles but menacing, self-satisfied smirks. They turned slowly in the water, propelling themselves with indolent flicks of their tails, perfectly balanced. I floated slowly, mesmerised by their grace and power and control, until they vanished among the banks of coral as silently as they had come.

'It's time for boom-netting!' bellowed Nick happily as we headed back towards Cairns. 'A great Australian sport!'

I had not been in the country long, and Australia to me was still a place of stereotypes. I thought boom-netting like many of the Australian pastimes of my imagination: simple in concept and fundamentally violent in nature, the sort of thing all-Aussie males might have dreamed up after a few bottles of lager in order to impress the sheilas.

'It's perfectly easy,' explained Nick—misleadingly as it turned out—as he gathered us in the back of the boat. He lashed some ropes attached to a net on to the sides of the boat. Then he tossed the net over the railings into the foaming water of the boat's wake.

'All you have to do is jump or dive over the side of the boat into the water from *there*—' he pointed up at the roof of the cabin '—and then grab the end of the net as it passes and *cling on*. And then make your way up the net and back into the boat.'

It was an Australian who, by popular acclaim, took the first leap in demonstration: let a native test out the merits of this Australian sport. He jumped with flailing arms off the roof of the cabin, vanishing under the water and reappearing just in time to clutch the last rope of the net.

'Just don't miss it,' said Nick to the rest of us. 'You'll have a long float. It'll take us ten minutes to turn the boat and pick you up again.' He paused, and then added reflectively: 'If the sharks haven't got you in the mean time.'

The Australian began to inch his way slowly towards the boat, tossing in the white foam of the wake, sometimes disappearing under the water before popping to the surface again with the violence of a cork out of a champagne bottle. By the time he reached us he was gasping, pulling the air into his lungs in long, unsteady gulps. He hauled himself over the side.

'Ace!' he gasped, and then lay down on the bottom of the boat as if unconscious, water streaming out of his wet-suit.

Nicola was smirking in my direction. 'Your turn next.'

There is something exhilarating and yet frightening in plunging off a moving boat into the open expanse of the Pacific Ocean in the hope of grabbing on to a short net. As I felt myself come up for air and my hand close over the rope I suddenly realised the Australian's breathlessness was due more to the adrenalin rush than the physical exertion. I had to admit it was also quite enjoyable in a terrifying kind of way, this aquatic roller-coaster. I clawed my way up the net, banging up and down violently in the waves, which washed into my face and pummelled my body like a Swedish masseuse bent on vengeance.

Suddenly there were people all around me, leaping off and hanging on to the net and spluttering and grinning like maniacs. And I was grinning too. The net flapped up and down, tossed on the waves as if it were weightless, its catch of humans a tangle of whirling arms and legs.

Clinging on to a net in the Pacific Ocean with the sun in my face, laughing into the foam, I felt free, accountable to no one. In such pure moments does the Australian dream of sun, sea and leisure time become reality.

Reality hit me on the return to Cairns—literally, in the form of a metal fan whirling at high speed on the ceiling of my backpacker's room. Unused to such contraptions, I had clambered on to the bed to tie up a string on which to hang our wet swimwear. Before I was aware of it a blade had smacked me across the top of the head and knocked me flat.

I sat on the edge of the bed contemplating my stupidity and finally noticed blood was splattering across my knees and on to the floor. My hair was thick and sticky. I finally realised that if I sat there much longer I would bleed to death, so I staggered up and outside (not before shoving my wallet and passport down my shorts—traveller's reactions not yet slowed) in search of my sister.

In the communal kitchen two girls stared at me aghast. 'Are you all right?' they said. By this time the blood was dripping down my face, through my hands and down my shirt, and this seemed like a peculiar question.

'Yes,' I said. 'But I'm looking for my sister. She's in the shower. If you could just get her . . .'

One of the girls hurried off and the other held my head over a sink. I wondered vaguely at her foolishness; one wasn't supposed to touch other people's blood these days. Nicola came flapping out of the shower and goggled at me, silenced for once.

'Why do they put the fans so bloody low?' I said in explanation.

'Why didn't you hear it?'

'Hear it?'

'Making a sort of whooshing noise in your ear before impact.'

'Well I didn't. It whooshed into my head and nearly decapitated me.'

Minutes later Nicola was dressed and we were heading towards the hospital in the hostel's pick-up van.

'Funny thing, standing on your bed under a ceiling fan,' said Luke, the driver, reflectively.

'Yeah, well. I'm a foreigner. I don't expect ceiling fans.'

'Although you might have *heard* it coming,' my sister reminded me.

'Anyway, happens all the time. Not the first time, not the last,' added Luke. 'Just remember this is Queensland, mate.' He said it in a satisfied tone of voice, as if delighted that Queensland possessed such malicious instruments of torture in every room. I thought there was a metaphorical lesson for the traveller here, a reflection on the unexpected, on cultural dislocation, on the symbols and realities of an alien society that would eventually catch up with you and lay you low. But I was beginning to feel dizzy, and such speculation seemed absurd.

The hospital emergency room was like something from *ER*. (That *ER* was actually something like a hospital room didn't seem to occur to me; American television always seemed to have been there first.) Recumbent figures were being wheeled in and out trailing plastic tubing, anxious parents flicked through magazines, and people in blue dashed about with stethoscopes dangling from their necks. A harassed nurse said I would have to wait until someone had time to see me, since my case was not urgent.

'Not urgent? My head's bleeding. Flowing with blood, actually.'

She shrugged and moved off, and we sat there for the next two hours, my sister and I, as they brought in drunks and overdoses, a boy with a broken leg, another man with his head cut by a ceiling fan ('How dare he,' I thought in annoyance), an alcoholic whose heart had almost stopped and who was dragged in arms first by two police officers to be thrown on a wheeled stretcher. This was another side to Cairns, the holiday paradise.

Finally my head was shaved and stitched and I was released. That evening I wrote another postcard to my mother. 'Shaved my head,' I wrote. 'Just like those people on the hippy farm.' I didn't tell her I had also had my now half-bald head tattooed in the shape of a ceiling fan.

'You look like a freak,' said Nicola sociably. And I thought to myself: the tables have been turned. *You* were the one who was supposed to be the freak, and that is why I came here.

I went to bed in a sulk, the ceiling fan whooshing overhead.

Scuba-diving was not recommended for people with stitches to their cranium, but Cairns provided a more sedate form of entertainment in the scenic railway to Kuranda, up in the Atherton hills. It was one of those small-town tourist attractions that are relentlessly advertised, so that the anticipation ends up far greater than the reality. The old railway cars were pleasant enough, with their sliding wooden window frames and cream-and-brown coachwork, as were the minute, pretty country stations, with their deep verandas and baskets of hanging ferns. The train crept through fields of sugar cane—this was like something from *The Thorn Birds*, I thought to myself. No foreigner could escape the influence of Australian soap operas for long: frighteningly, our whole view of the country was coloured by them. Not that *The Thorn Birds* had even been filmed here; it had been shot on location in California with the help of mechanical kangaroos —but what did that matter? Illusion was all in television, and counted for much in tourism too. The scenic railway was famous, famous for being scenic, and so tourists leaned out of its windows as we started to climb up into the tablelands, taking pictures. There was the odd glimpse of the coastal plain, with its scattering of houses and the glitter of the sea, the brief passing of a scenic waterfall, even the occasional view of the back of the train as it curved around the sweep of the hillside. But most of the time I couldn't see much, except the back ends of camera-toting Germans as they leaned out of the windows, and expanses of tall monotonous grass that lined the railway tracks to the height of a grown adult.

Kuranda was also an illusion, a place that existed thanks only to the tourist trade. It had just 600 inhabitants but dozens of restaurants and shops, a butterfly farm, a noctarium, an Aboriginal theatre, an information centre, and an enormous market milling with thousands of people. There was no doubt that the market's customers were not the locals: it sold candles in outrageous colours (puce spotted with blue and crimson) and shapes (a naked couple entwined, a bulbous octopus), incense burners, Indian rugs, Balinese batik skirts and other trappings of the New Age. There was also a stall selling crystals in small baskets: quartz and agate, alexandrite and amethyst, garnet and moonstone. I fingered some rose quartz, polished smooth and pink and smoky. *Soothing influence. Friendship*, said the sign on the basket in Gothic script.

The stall owner descended on me like a vampire, draped in black garments and vast purple eye shadow, her face pierced in unusual places with metal rings, and a knitted shawl over her head like an Irish peasant woman during the famine.

'I see you're interested in the rose quartz,' she purred as if pronouncing a spell. I wasn't, except in the texture, but I did not say so.

'It responds well to people's emotions. It's a very sympathetic stone on an emotional level.'

'Really.'

'It stimulates friendship and love and tender feelings for everything around you,' said the vampire encouragingly.

'Hm. Nicola, you could do with one. Improve your love life.'

Nicola glared at me and the vampire said: 'You might wear it on a necklace. It should be worn over the heart.' She was now staring hopefully at my sister.

'Not today,' said Nicola in a huff, and dragged me off.

In the middle of the market was a clearing containing a muddy pond and overhung by a crane. Here another occult ceremony was being performed: people were flinging themselves shrieking from the crane's topmost platform towards the mud below, only to be prevented from breaking their necks by an elastic strap wrapped around their ankles, which merely dislocated their knees. It seemed a highly expensive and dangerous way to spend two seconds of one's life, although there was no charge if you volunteered to do it in the nude (no one came forward, alas, while Nicola and I waited). Here it was again, that analogy between television and tourism. Television, especially the news, loved the short, sharp thrill: the politician's quote, the three-second wars, the one-shot famine in Africa, so that by the end of the programme you felt you knew what the world was all about, packaged and made simple. Just like tourism, and the two-second bungee jump: that was what people remembered of Queensland. They went back to Europe or Japan and three weeks of holiday were distilled into minutes of excitement: the dive through air, the dive under the water, and the stone with its sympathetic vibes that would solve your love life.

That was what Australia was all about to a foreigner, I thought: an image projected artificially on the screens of their minds, while behind it all the reality and complexity went ignored. As for myself, I did not like neat packages and cosy answers. I revelled in the unexplained, in vast complexities, in enigmas and puzzles to which, maybe, there *was* no answer.

I didn't know why I was in Kuranda (except that the tourist brochures had told me to come here); I didn't even know why I was in Australia, where I was going, what I would do, what it all meant.

And as we descended back into the evening of Cairns, the sun setting fire to the sugar-cane fields, I knew that was just the way it should be.

In the shelter of the bay the sun had long gone, and small waves lapped against the wooden pylons of the jetty. I stood with my sister staring out to a dark sea.

'You should be standing closer together,' urged a hoarse voice in my ear. A scrawny hand shot out and grasped my arm, pushing me in the direction of Nicola. It was late evening, and we were both standing down on the pier, doing nothing but looking at the vast spread of stars and watching the play of moonlight on the water.

'Closer together!' repeated the voice. 'The stars being so romantic, you know!' Nicola and I turned around and found ourselves confronted by an Aboriginal Australian, tall and thin with a wrinkled face and hair gone white at the edges.

'She's my sister,' I said, inexplicably feeling foolish. The man's face cracked into a wide grin.

'Not much good looking at the stars with your sister,' he commented. I did not reply. In general I might have agreed with him, but at this moment I was enjoying Nicola's company.

'You should join the party,' said the Aboriginal man. 'Hear the music?' Now that he had mentioned it I could hear it, drifting across the harbour from the shopping mall, mingled with people's voices and clinking glasses.

'I'm not sure I like big parties,' I said to him equably.

'I love 'em. Nothing like dancing.' He began to hop across the wooden boards of the pier like a cockatoo after a seed, wiggling his hips. 'I won a competition once. A dancing competition. I did a strip-tease.' He cackled again, and I realised he was very drunk.

'What did you win?' said Nicola.

'A prize! A prize!' He peered at us out of the dark. 'You don't believe me! Let me show you.' The man began to gyrate slowly in front of us, shimmying back and forwards suggestively. Nicola was staring at him as if hypnotised. He now had his eyes closed and was stamping on the wooden boards in time with the distant music. He did indeed, I could see, have a grasp of rhythm and a casual grace. He made as if to pull off his shirt and then abruptly let it go, screeching with laughter.

'Thought I was going to take it all off, didn't you! Nah, too old for that. I'm seventy-two now.'

'When did you win this competition?' asked Nicola.

'Last year. But I didn't take all my clothes off, you know. Didn't want to frighten the ladies.' He gave a Monty Python-esque leer at Nicola, closing one eye in an exaggerated wink. Then he turned to me.

'So she's your sister, eh? Travelling with your sister?'

I said that I was.

'I've got twelve sisters, mate. No brothers. Twelve sisters, though two of them are dead now. Keep me in order, you know, always telling me what to do.' He looked cheerful at the thought.

'They all live in Cairns?'

'Nah, Brisbane. Don't really live here myself. Just come and go up and down the coast. Good fishing. Off to Magnetic

Island soon.' He turned his gaze on my sister once more. 'Got a boyfriend?'

'Yes. He's in Darwin.'

'Not much use in Darwin now, is he?' the Aboriginal man cackled. Privately I agreed with him. Reading between the lines, I had concluded some days ago that Mike and Nicola must have fallen out with each other somewhere between the hippy farm and Ayers Rock. It seemed appropriate, if sad, to arrive at a parting of the ways in the barren wastes of the Red Centre.

'We're going there soon,' said Nicola with unexpected decision.

'On his pat in Darwin then?'

'Sorry?'

'Alone, is he?'

Nicola seemed to hesitate. 'Yes.'

The man sank into a silence. He muttered a little about Darwin and Magnetic Island. Then suddenly, without a farewell, he ambled off along the pier, disappearing into the night, leaving behind only the slap, slap of his bare feet on the wood.

'Going to Darwin to meet Mike?' I speculated. I found Mike's supposed lack of interest in the Barrier Reef inexplicable. My sister told me he had gone to Darwin 'to think' —though about what was unclear. She had phoned him once and returned to our room with a face like tropical thunder. I was surprised we were going to Darwin at all.

'Yes,' Nicola answered defiantly, daring me to question her further. 'Aren't we?'

I shrugged non-committally. 'Might as well. I want to visit the rainforests north of here first, though. We could book our tickets before that.'

'Tickets? Why don't we just hitch to Darwin?' said my sister, as if contemplating getting a lift to the next village to visit her grandmother for afternoon tea. I guessed she was thinking sadly of her scanty remaining supply of traveller's cheques.

'Thumbing? To Darwin?'

'The Australians don't thumb exactly. They wave the flat of their hand up and down at arm's length and—'

'Oh, please, spare me the scientific details.'

I had been scrutinising the map of Australia I had bought upon arrival in Cairns. It was the size of a bed sheet. There were vast patches of brown emptiness clear across the top half of the map between Cairns and Darwin. If I remembered correctly, only a single straggling red line of unnerving thinness connected the two towns.

'It's thousands of kilometres,' I now commented. 'It's not just halfway across a country, it's halfway across a *continent*.'

Nicola was unimpressed. 'So what? I hitched with Mike all the way up through the centre of Australia from Melbourne to Ayers Rock.'

'Well, if you think so . . .' I returned uncertainly. 'After the rainforest we could double back through Cairns, go southwards down the coast. Then we'll turn inland at Townsville and stop at Charters Towers . . .' I jabbed my finger along the railing of the jetty, tracing my finger down an imaginary map, pointing out a town on the edge of Queensland's interior where the outback began. Gold had been discovered in the area by a stockman searching for a stray horse. Charters Towers had sprung up on the site, becoming in its heyday the second-largest city in Queensland: it might be a pleasant place, I thought.

After that my voice trailed away. After Charters Towers I knew that the road was devoid of sizeable towns for hundreds of kilometres.

'From Charters Towers there's no need to stop,' added Nicola firmly. 'Direct to Darwin. Where we'll meet Mike,' she added, staring me in the eye. 'Then we'll plan some serious outback travelling.'

'The three of us? Together?'

'Together.' My sister seemed quite definite on this point.

'Then why not go by coach if we want to go direct?' I said, and then added wildly: 'Or plane?' I had an abhorrence of long journeys that had as their sole purpose arriving somewhere else.

'Pathetic,' said Nicola witheringly, peering at me with contempt.

I knew then that I would have to hitch all the way to Darwin with her or my family reputation would be in tatters.

Secretly, although traditionally the footloose family member, I had never thought of myself as a particularly adventurous traveller. If I did not follow the beaten track, the paths I frequented were at least fairly well trodden. Nicola, an eternal optimist, seemed much more sanguine in the face of adventure: to her the byways always appeared to be highways. I was never sure if this was the result of impressive self-confidence or appalling naivety, but I envied it all the same. I looked at Nicola curiously now, through the dark, startled at the revelation that she was a woman in her twenties with her own confidence, her own character: not just the kid sister I had seldom seen in the last few years.

I contemplated the stars and wondered what Nicola envisaged when she thought of serious outback travelling. After our side-trip to the rainforests north of Cairns, and if we ever made it thumbing—or flat-handing—to Darwin, it seemed I would surely find out.

rainforest *two*

Australian telephone directories make interesting reading. In Cairns I had noticed that Marine Stinger Emergencies were listed along with other telephone numbers for use in the event of disaster. The number—008 079909—was a free call from anywhere in Australia. I had the impression from television advertising that 008 numbers were used by businesses in order to attract enquiries at no cost to the caller. I thought it curious that victims of marine stingers should be equated with the customers of mail-order services and financial counselling.

A sign on the beach north of Cairns had the telephone number emblazoned across the top. Underneath it gave advice in the event of severe stings. *Flood sting with vinegar!* it suggested in red lettering. There was a box providing a bottle of ordinary household vinegar, which deactivated stinging cells. Below that was the more sinister instruction: *If breathing stops give artificial respiration!* The last line sounded almost desperate and very final: *Give closed chest massage if heart stops!* Decorating the sign was a cartoon picture of a swimmer entangled underwater in the tentacles of a jellyfish of improbable size. This was the marine stinger.

Despite the fanciful diagram, the jellyfish in question is actually quite small—about the circumference of a plate. A delicate, transparent creature, it has neither the dimensions nor the strength to drag a man underwater in its tentacles and drown him. There was nothing fanciful about the written warnings, however. These jellyfish, properly known as chironex, have tentacles covered in nematocysts with as many as a thousand poisonous threads in an area the size of a pinhead. They are one of the most dangerous creatures in Australia, and have actually killed more people in tropical inshore waters than crocodiles and sharks combined. There is only one way to avoid them, as the sign concluded in enormous scarlet capitals, finally abandoning its recurring exclamation marks as if to reinforce the seriousness of its advice: DO NOT SWIM IN THESE WATERS BETWEEN OCTOBER AND MAY.

And so it was that this beautiful tropical beach, a long sweep of crystal sands between two magnificent headlands covered in lush vegetation, was completely deserted. The sea, crested by small waves and glinting invitingly under the hot Queensland sun, was a death trap. Fortunately for Australian tourism, chironex are found only in season along the coast of northern Australia, and then only in inshore waters, which makes the Barrier Reef a safe haven.

'Unless a jellyfish gets swept out to sea in an unexpected storm,' our minibus driver commented comfortably.

We were heading north out of Cairns on the Captain Cook Highway. The road hugged the coast, a dramatic and relatively undeveloped chain of sea-cliffs and golden sands, where the palms crowded down to the water's edge and parrots swooped overhead in the trees, splashes of vivid green, red and turquoise. Sir George Bowen, Queensland's first governor, had dwelt with rapture on the scenery of the area when he came here on a cruise aboard HMS *Pioneer* in 1862, saying that it reminded him of the famed attractions of southern Italy and Greece, the outlying islands of the Aegean and Ionian seas. Presumably Sir George had never actually been to those places and his classical romanticism had got the better of him. There seemed little to remind me of Europe here.

Our bus driver, taking us to the rainforests of Cape Tribulation, was also giving us a little guided tour on the way. Nicola and I had not wanted to go with a tour group, but there was no other way of getting to the Cape—even hitching would have been uncertain. In any event we were enjoying the trip. Ken, the driver, was a mine of local information. He had chatted into his microphone all the way up from Cairns and had stopped at this beach to give his ten passengers a leg-stretch.

'The effect of the stings only lasts about half an hour,' Ken explained. 'But if you're severely stung you'd probably be dead by then, unless given artificial respiration. The reaction can happen very quickly, even before you manage to struggle out of the water. If you swam into a chironex and got the tentacles right in your face, you'd probably be dead before you knew what had happened.'

Ken took a sip of coffee from his polystyrene cup. His tone was light and bantering, in the style of all entertaining tourist guides. He might have been imparting information on the dimensions of the Sydney Opera House or the cost of the parliament building.

'You would survive lesser stings. But the pain is supposed to be unbearable—victims scream uncontrollably and become totally irrational, which makes first aid difficult. The tentacles leave your skin blistered and you'd probably have scars for the rest of your life.' Ken sighed dramatically and then offered us a charming smile as we clambered back into the van. 'Stick to the swimming pool in the summer, mate!'

The road, tarred only as far as Daintree, some hundred kilometres to the north of Cairns, hugged the coastline, offering impressive views of an aquamarine ocean and the rolling hills of the Atherton Tableland, tumbling into the sea in a froth of palm trees. As the highway's name suggested, we were following Captain Cook's trail. Heading north after a few days in Botany Bay, Cook had sailed unwittingly through the Whitsunday Passage, avoiding the coral banks of the Barrier Reef, and entered tropical waters, following this very coastline. It was in Queensland that his sailors saw their first kangaroo and dingo, as well as an animal 'about as large as a one-gallon keg, as black as the devil and with wings and two horns on its head'—a flying fox. The existence of the Barrier Reef was finally brought to the attention of Captain Cook after the *Endeavour* ran aground on it, puncturing the hull; he named this part of his newly drawn map Cape Tribulation because of the mishap. Fortunately the crew managed to repair the damage, continuing northwards, and on 22 August 1770 a flag was planted and the east coast of Australia claimed for Britain in the name of King George III.

'Luckily for his crew, people didn't really swim for enjoyment in those days,' said Ken. 'Not that there would have been any marine stingers in August, but there are plenty of other potential dangers in the sea. Sharks, of course, blue-ringed octopus, cone shells.' As we headed north he gave us a quick run-down on their appearance, lethal potential and effects on unsuspecting victims. His patter came out as smoothly and entertainingly as Nick's aboard *Noah's Ark*. Both men were dedicated to propagating the image of a dangerous country to wide-eyed tourists, eager for their trips to seem adventurous; both, to their credit, succeeded, perhaps because they were as enthralled as the visitors with this image of Australia.

'And then of course there are stone-fish too, considered to be the most poisonous fish known,' Ken was saying as we swung around another headland. 'And then you think it's safe to stay on land! But the place is crawling with venomous snakes and spiders, cane toads, you mention it.' Ken was well into his stride now, outlining improbable scenarios in which the unwary traveller might be poisoned, driven to hysteria by pain, eaten alive, clawed apart. Ken was a friendly man. He seemed to be relating his stories to his captive audience not out of a lust for horror but out of a genuine fascination and respect for the wildlife that surrounded him. His passengers listened, enthralled but uneasy, to his fluent wit and vivid descriptions.

'The worst are the crocodiles, of course. Famous for them up around here. I saw a photograph once of the biggest croc ever shot in Australia—with thirty people sitting along its back. Talk about crocodile shoes, you could have made boots for an entire army out of that monster! They're protected species now, though. I suppose the average male is twice as long as I am: maybe three and a half metres. They grab their prey at the water's edge, see. They leap out of the water using their tails, pulling the animal down in their jaws and drowning it. They spin around with incredible force to tear off flesh—wrench out an arm or a leg, no problem. Call it the death roll. Some people say they have a taste for rotting flesh and keep their prey impaled under water for weeks, in a kind of larder, eating it piece by piece. Can't say if that's rightly true, though.' He pursed his lips doubtfully, glancing back at us in the rear-view mirror.

'There was a woman eaten on the Daintree River, where we're heading now, in 1985. She was called Beryl, a local store-owner, so she knew all about the dangers of crocs. But she was having a Christmas party, right, and after a couple of drinks some of them decided to cool off by having a dip in the river.

'Of course some of the other guests tried to dissuade Beryl, but, well, she wouldn't hear of it. Off she went to skinny-dip with two men. She just disappeared underwater with barely a ripple and no time to scream—her friends just caught sight of the croc vanishing into the river. Crocs always go for the smallest prey, of course, which is why this one got Beryl first. They always say, if you really have to go down to the water in these parts, to bring a dog with you.

'Anyway there was a terrible reaction in northern Queensland after that. The locals just went on the rampage, killing all the crocodiles they could find for weeks afterwards . . .'

Ken gave an artful pause. His passengers all waited, sensing there was more to come.

'About three weeks later her husband shot a crocodile over five metres long. They found the remains of Beryl in its stomach—nothing much left except a few rings, bones and some fingernails. The nails still had red polish on them from the party!'

There was a silence after this as we all contemplated the story of Beryl and the crocodile. Nicola heaved a sigh in my ear as if overcome by the tragedy.

'It must have been very resistant nail polish,' she said.

At the Daintree River we were loaded into a small boat for three-quarters of an hour of crocodile-spotting. The water swirled slowly seaward, muddy brown, fringed by mangroves and dense tropical forest. The mangrove roots reached deep into the water as if dredging for unseen treasure in the thick mud of the river banks. White egrets roosted in the trees, shifting uneasily as the boat passed by underneath them.

'Don't lean out,' I cautioned my sister. I plucked at her sleeve as she aimed her camera lens out into the trees.

'I'm not leaning out!'

'Crocodiles jump up at their prey,' I retorted furiously. 'Don't expect me to pull you back in if one grabs you by the arm and wrenches you overboard in a death roll.'

'You'd already be cringing at the far end of the boat by then,' Nicola retorted sarcastically. But she retreated slightly from the railings; Ken's stories had put us all slightly on edge.

There did not seem to be any crocodiles that day on the Daintree River—and why should there be? They had probably retreated from the endless moan and hum of outboard motors, the clicking of cameras, the muffled shouts of tourists disturbing their sleep as they lay supine in the mud of the river banks. We cruised slowly up and down, seeing imagined reptiles only in the shadows of the mangrove swamps. Finally we came across a young female crocodile, sitting with jaws agape on the mud of the bank, the interior of its mouth pink as a shell. It did not move as we swung by within metres of it.

'I bet it's stuffed,' I whispered to Nicola in disappointment. 'It's the one they show tourists on the off-days.' But my sister was too busy whirring her lens in and out to answer.

Later, at the ferry crossing, there was another sign. WARNING, it proclaimed, *Crocodiles inhabit most rivers, swamps and lagoons throughout Cape York Peninsula.* Unlike the marine stinger sign it did not suggest abstinence from swimming, but a cartoon picture of a gaping reptile with teeth the size of garden shears made the suggestion unnecessary. We had not seen anything remotely resembling such an aggressive beast, but we took photos of the sign in compensation, with a little *frisson* of horror.

Cape York Peninsula, stretching 800 kilometres northwards, pointed its long finger towards Papua New Guinea. It was one of the most remote regions of Australia, requiring a four-wheel drive and a good knowledge of outback survival to explore it. Nicola and I were only penetrating its southern reaches, intending to stay at a place in the rainforest called Crocodylus. Cape York truly began on the other side of the ferry crossing, where an unsurfaced road of red dust cut like a scar through the trees. To reach it, we boarded the ferry, a rusting, flat-bottomed metal boat that held a few cars at a time, its dilapidated appearance against the dense forest that crowded to the water's edge recalling scenes from *Heart of Darkness*. 'An empty stream, a great silence, an impenetrable forest. The air was warm, thick, heavy, sluggish,' wrote Conrad in the story. Here the water swirled in our slow wake in great, spreading ripples of brown mud, concealing melancholy and danger. Against the loud chugging of the ferry's engine I thought of one of Conrad's infamous lines: 'It was the stillness of an implacable force brooding over an inscrutable intention.' What did it mean? I had made fun of it at university, memorised it for use on unsuspecting victims, but now it seemed wholly apt, wholly comprehensible.

Not that the silence was entirely great, nor the forest entirely impenetrable, though perhaps some of the Japanese tourists, if one believed in stereotypes, were inscrutable as they took photos of themselves with fingers held up in the victory salute against a background of river. The ferry alone made over a hundred crossings of the river a day, and some sixty tour operators had licences to operate in the Daintree. Twenty years ago there had been no road north of Cape Tribulation and only a handful of adventurers; now some 250 000 tourists a year charged through the area, generating a substantial income for the locals. This was a region where the interests of tourism and local residents met environmentalism head on. There were those who argued that the Daintree, a unique World Heritage Area where coast and rainforest met, should be preserved intact and undisturbed, but meanwhile slices of the forest were up for sale as private lots for around $40 000 a hectare. A property developer had levelled an entire hillside and divested it of trees to leave a better view for the houses he was building.

'That car there's in trouble,' said Ken, breaking into my thoughts as the ferry made its short crossing over the crocodile-infested waters. 'It's a rented car, see. Probably drove up from Cairns. But the rental agreement stipulates that no dirt-road driving is allowed.' He grinned mischie-vously. 'The ferry attendant marks down the date, time and number-plate of every rented car that crosses the Daintree. He works for all the rental companies, right? Reckon they pay him ten dollars a car. That driver's going to find he's lost his deposit when he returns his vehicle in Cairns!'

We made slow progress along the road, leaving a towering plume of red dust in our wake. The forest crowded in closely on either side, blocking out a surprising amount of the hot tropical sunshine. As we climbed upwards we could catch, down on our right, glimpses of flat wetlands, strips of sand and the bright blue of the Coral Sea. On the left was evi-dence of clearings in the forest, side tracks to private lots, even bright yellow estate agents' signs. We drove on, deep into the rainforest, pausing only for lunch before arriving at Crocodylus. Here Ken deposited us at the side of the road; he was returning directly to Cairns with more passengers. His van sped off in a cloud of dust, and we were abandoned to our own adventures, our heads full of tales of woe.

'Beware of the melomys,' said the manager of Crocodylus as if quoting the witches in *Macbeth*. Instead of a warning, he made it sound like a curse. 'Don't leave any food in your backpacks.' He leaned back on his chair after this pronounce-ment, as if observing what effect it might have on us. None of us knew what melomys were. We did not shake in our shoes, but Ken's stories had already made us apprehensive, and a vague rustle of disquiet spread among us. Melomys!

'They're rodents,' said the manager after a theatrical pause. I was beginning to recognise the style and the banter. 'A little like rats, only smaller, and they live all around Crocodylus. They have an unerring nose for food and an incredible gnawing capacity. If you have chocolate in tinfoil, wrapped in a plastic bag and buried in the middle of your backpack, you could well find it gone in the morning. You'll have a hole clean through the nylon, plastic, tinfoil and anything else that gets in the way. This is where you should leave any food.' We all trooped after him and peered into the kitchen.

'Put it in one of these bins'—he waved towards a row of heavy metal containers—'and then at night we lock the kitchen door.' He banged the mosquito screen shut and then, in demonstration, the heavy wooden door, which was lined as far as the keyhole with metal. The kitchen was solid stone —unlike the wood most of the other buildings were made from—with metal window-frames and a corrugated-iron roof. The windows were covered by iron grilles. It looked like a terrorist-proof Northern Irish police station.

'I don't need to remind you of the dangers of snakes and spiders,' continued the manager with true Australian relish. 'A great many of them are poisonous and we advise you to leave them alone. Any spider with a body larger than the nail on your smallest finger is potentially dangerous. Don't brush them off your clothes with your bare hands, and make sure there's nothing in your shoes before you put them on in the morning.'

Nicola was gesticulating to me silently behind the manager's back. She pointed up into the low wooden rafters. Across one corner stretched a spider's web of dimensions only seen in horror movies. In the centre of it sat a spider that looked not only larger than my fingernail but at least the size of a saucer.

'There are also crocodiles around here, so don't go swimming in any local rivers or waterholes unless you ask us first whether they are safe,' intoned the manager calmly. 'I'd also advise you to familiarise yourself with the stinging plant we have over here in that cage. Don't touch it or any similar bush or tree you may see in the rainforest. Brushing against it is excruciatingly painful and causes a red rash and agonising swelling; a more general irritation can last for months afterwards. Possibly it could kill you if you fell into a big bush.'

We all stared dutifully at the fatal plant behind its metal fence. It had large leaves shaped like the spades in a pack of cards, covered in fine stinging hairs, apparently tipped with silica and laced with a noxious mixture of chemicals.

'There is no reason to be paranoid,' lied the manager after he had concluded his pep talk, designed to instil paranoia in us all. 'But a certain amount of caution and common sense is necessary . . . I hope you enjoy yourself in Crocodylus.'

There was a moment's uncertain silence. No one wanted to be the first to penetrate the wall of trees a stone's throw from the hostel. We all wondered what dangers might be lurking there. The small group of new arrivals shuffled their feet and pretended to busy themselves by splashing liberal quantities of Jungle Formula repellent on their exposed flesh. In twos and threes we wandered off towards our allocated huts, lugging our backpacks now emptied of food.

Crocodylus was affiliated with the International Youth Hostel Federation and was run along the same Spartan lines. It had its own generator for electricity—there was no national grid north of the Daintree River, and the only public telephone box I had seen, sitting on the side of the road between dirt track and jungle, had been powered by solar energy. The generator provided a vaguely comforting rumble, falling quiet at night, when Crocodylus was taken over by the almost threatening silence of the deep forest.

The chalet-style sleeping quarters were roofed with green canvas, and the whole community blended in against the background of the jungle, which hemmed us in closely on every side. Spiders and frogs and creepers had taken over the new surroundings. The visitors here maintained a church-like quiet, as if deferring to the superiority of the nature that so closely surrounded them. There were no shops, discos, televisions nor any other entertainment: just a few trestle tables in the open air under a central wooden roof. At night bandicoots—pointy-nosed marsupials not much larger than a rabbit—shuffled myopically around the benches, searching hopefully for scraps of food, while the visitors wrote in diaries already going mouldy in the damp climate. The bandicoots were still fundamentally wild animals, snapping with sharp teeth at any fingers that strayed too close towards them: there was none of the cuddly tameness of the tourist-park koalas here.

A few kilometres by dirt track from the youth hostel lay the sea, fringed by palms: as the tourist blurbs repeatedly pointed out, the only stretch of coast in Australia where the rainforest met the Barrier Reef, here closely hugging the shore. Mangroves, the haunt of crocodiles, hid the river banks in deep, sinister shadows. The shore was criss-crossed with the cryptic markings of scuttling crabs and birds and the odd human footprint, although there were few enough people on these remote acres of golden sand. Swimming was out: although chironex had last been seen here two weeks ago, nobody could be really sure if the jellyfish season had ended yet. Between jellyfish and crocodiles, the coastline was a dangerous place.

The jungle was violent too. There were the unseen terrors of poisonous snakes and spiders, salt-water crocodiles that sometimes strayed far upstream, dangerous birds and toads, plants that might sting the unwary: a place of savage competition, where nature was red in tooth and claw. Mosquitoes whined in fierce clouds among the damp undergrowth, tiny jet-fighters among the lumbering bombers that were finger-length hornets, bent on destruction. There was also the more visible violence of the plants: the giant creepers that looped from branch to branch, throttling the trees, the thorns and hooks and spikes that stuck and ripped and jabbed at the passer-by, the giant trees that ruthlessly blocked out the sunlight and left the forest floor in perpetual gloom. Fig seeds lodged in the branches of other trees, sending down long roots that, when they finally reached he ground, enabled the fig to grow on top of its supporting host, eventually strangling it. There was no mercy in the rainforest. I knew it was highly unlikely that I would encounter a crocodile or a venomous snake, and I did not feel physically threatened. But I found the rainforest's silence, its pressing humidity, its hidden energy, even its lushness, almost terrifying.

It was easy to become disoriented here: the sun was hidden, the forest floor a maze of pools and trickling streams that seemed to flow in every direction, the thick wall of trees offering little by way of distinguishing features. With this in mind the management of Crocodylus had built an Orange Rope Walk. This was a looped track through the forest, several kilometres long, marked along its length by orange nylon. It was a lifeline to civilisation, nothing more: the walk was still a struggle under fallen trees, through dense undergrowth, across streams and through pools of mud. Nicola and I struggled around it twice a day, intent on seeing a cassowary or python. Most of the time the rain dripped down through the interlaced branches overhead. We saw few creatures, and were menaced mainly by the black clouds of mosquitoes that hovered under the immense palm leaves by the riverside, ignoring the Jungle Formula. Despite the heat and humidity I had long trousers tucked into my boots, and a long-sleeved shirt: the mosquitoes clustered on my hands and the back of my neck, which was swollen and blotched with clusters of stinging red bites.

Ten minutes in the rainforest had already taught me it was no paradise. Unlike the Edens of television advertisements with their sun-drenched coconut palms, the rainforest dripped water most of the time. I would see brilliantly coloured parrots and hibiscus and bougainvillea in towns throughout Australia, but the rainforest seemed for the most part monochrome, devoid of tropical flowers and animal life. The waterholes we swam in, picturesque among the trees, their banks cushioned in emerald-green moss, had refreshing water, cooled by being long underground. But away from the advertising clichés they were host to thousands of mosquitoes and other biting insects. There was no time here for my sister to lounge in a sarong, with a hibiscus blossom tucked behind her ear, enjoying Bounty Bars or recommending Tahiti shampoo. She lurked in the water away from the insects, submerged up to the ears like a hippopotamus, and then scrambled out, throwing on her clothes in a burst of speed, shaking repellent all over her socks, dancing and leaping from rock to rock like a dervish, flapping and waving her arms.

I could find it amusing until it was my own turn to emerge. Then, perspiring profusely once more, we would struggle through the trees, untangling ourselves from thorns and tripping over tree roots, gasping in the humidity, keeping an eye out for snakes. Paradise, it was obvious, had its price.

I was disgruntled to find it was raining in the rainforest. I felt that I had come a long way to see it, and did not deserve to be rained upon. I wanted big shafts of tropical light to come slanting through the fronds of the giant trees, lighting up the gloomy under-canopy like the nave of a cathedral and hopefully even spotlighting a suitably exotic tropical creature.

But it did not stop raining. It was not just rain, but an all-pervasive damp that hovered like a mischievous poltergeist, waiting to pounce on my biscuits, shoes, sleeping-bag or camera lens. Once it had ensconced itself, it clung with a tenacity that defeated any attempts at drying out. The rainforest was a place where I squelched in smelly boots that had been wet for days; where I pulled on the least damp shirt in the morning. The rain dripped down my forehead, washing insect repellent into my eyes. Water glistened on giant spiders' webs and trickled down palm leaves and churned the ground into mud.

'Of course it rains in a *rain*forest,' Nicola said at frequent intervals, flapping at frogs bathing themselves in the puddles that had formed in our bedroom. I imagined she had never thought at all about what happened in a rainforest until this very week, when she had invented her phrase to provide some benign, logical explanation for the perversity of the weather. She would say it with a monumental female calm that drove me to thoughts of murder. But after a few days I noticed with satisfaction a hint of irritation creeping into her voice, a mounting hysteria at the continuing deluge.

On the evening of our night walk it was raining heavily.

'A tropical downpour,' said my sister, rolling the words out smugly, as if revelling in the exotic sound after years of announcing grey European drizzle. And then she said to me, as if offering words of comfort, 'Of course it's *raining*, this is the *rain*forest.' She wrapped herself in a yellow knee-length sou'wester and put a hard hat on her head, complete with miner's lamp. Runnels of water poured down her plastic garb and gathered in her boots. She looked as if she had been caught in a gale-force wind on a small fishing-smack in the North Sea.

'Maybe we'll see a python,' she said.

The night walk had seemed a good idea at the time—a guided evening's stroll, for a modest sum, through the forest with its variety of nocturnal creatures: bandicoots, possums, flying squirrels. Now in the pitch black our lights wavered uncertainly, bobbing up and down as we stumbled in single file over roots and slipped through mud. My eyes were stinging with insect repellent. I doubted I would see a python until it had wrapped itself around my throat.

'Victims are either strangled or suffocated,' shouted Jamie, our local guide, out of the darkness as we crashed through branches and soggy foliage. 'The theory about holding on to the python's tail so it can't tighten its coils is an old wives' tale, I'm afraid. It grips tighter every time its victim exhales, whether you're holding its tail or not. The only thing you could do would be to stop breathing.' He chuckled over the roar of the rain at this no-win situation.

I was sweating under the heavy mackintosh, so that it felt as clammy inside as it was outside. The lights of our small group danced like Shakespearian fairies through the undergrowth, pin-pointing bizarre segments of leaf and plant and the odd gaping amphibian in a surrealistic slide-show. Even over the tumult of the rain I could hear my sister crashing along the narrow path, through the tangle of rainforest, like a wounded brontosaurus in a blindfold. Her light careered wildly in the air, somewhere up in the canopy, sweeping back and forwards down the trees like anti-aircraft lights seeking the enemy. Nicola was still searching for the pythons Jamie had said preferred the forks in tree trunks.

It was mostly insects we saw: green or black prehistoric monsters in miniature, glistening in the rain; and spiders the size of my hand immobile at the hubs of their universes of spun thread, strung out with water droplets like cheap plastic beads on a necklace. Then there were the lizards, frozen briefly in our spotlights and as soon vanishing with their distinctive sideways wiggle under the palm leaves that dwarfed them.

'Cane toad,' said Jamie, pointing his light down on the leaf litter. I peered down at the fallen vegetation rotting on the forest floor, and saw nothing but a uniform khaki camouflage of mottled colours. Jamie stooped down and in one swift movement picked something up from among the browns: a misshapen leaf that suddenly transformed itself into a toad of impressive size, struggling violently and sending a spurt of liquid into the air.

'Have to be careful of that,' said Jamie, holding it for our inspection. Then we left the toad behind and continued on through the rain, along narrow winding paths of mud, shrouded close on either side by dripping trees and undergrowth. With uncanny skill Jamie used his light to pick out birds, huddled together in the trees with their eyes firmly closed against the rain: little brown bundles of feathers almost invisible among the branches. He brought us to a great hollow tree that he told us was the burrow of a wild pig, warning us to be silent and to do nothing to disturb the animal if it was at home. In the dark I could see the beast sleeping, a vast mound of solid muscle, a snout and two tusks curved as scimitars: I could hear its rasping breath and its snuffling grunts over the sound of my own wildly beating heart. I crept away from the burrow backwards, keeping my eye on the boar. This nature in the raw frightened me.

'What we're going to do now is have our own personal experience of the rainforest,' said Jamie after an hour, having herded us together in a little group. His beard was sodden and his eyes glinted fanatically under his yellow hat. He looked like a mad prophet about to abandon his flock to a terrible ordeal.

'I shall take you in twos and leave you alone for ten or fifteen minutes. I want you to turn off your lights at that point and listen to the sounds of the forest.'

There were murmurs of New Age delight at this announcement. Jamie marched Nicola and me into the undergrowth and then vanished into the darkness with the remains of the group. If Nicola thought it perverse to stand abandoned in a rainforest in the middle of the night during a tropical downpour she did not say so.

'Maybe we'll see a python now,' she merely said with her eternal optimism, and promptly turned off her light and mine, plunging us into absolute night.

I was silently hoping we would not see a freshly awakened wild pig. I could hear my sister breathing heavily, harumphing and shuffling on my left. I knew that if Jamie did not come back we would be lost for ever in this jungle. The darkness was like a physical weight. The rain roared overhead in the tree tops and trickled down all around us in a steady stream. Gradually I could hear other sounds emerging: leaves brushing and shivering against each other, branches cracking overhead. A sudden violent rustling noise in the leaf litter at our feet.

'Put the light on,' screeched my sister in my ear, lunging for my arm. 'A python!'

'Jeez, you scared the hell out of—'

'The light—'

'It didn't sound like a—'

'PUT THE LIGHT ON!'

I did not know if she was excited or terrified. My own heart was pounding. As I scrabbled at the switch on my battery, Nicola's light snapped on and its thin beam swung through the trees before righting itself and focusing on the ground around our feet. A small, furry animal with a quivering pointed nose and bright red eyes was pinned horrified in its light for a split second, before vanishing into the rain.

'A rabbit,' I said bitterly. I thought I was going to faint.

'I don't think so.'

'That's what they call a personal experience in this rainforest. A bloody rabbit!'

'Not a *rabbit*,' said Nicola. 'One of those Australian things, a marsupial. A possum or bandicoot or kangaroo or something.'

'A kangaroo the size of a rabbit?' I snapped.

'There are little kangaroos that climb trees,' returned my sister serenely. It sounded so improbable that I could not give her credit for making it up, and I was stunned into silence.

When we were finally reunited with our group it was to discover that no one else had seen a python either. Despite this I felt chastened by my personal experience of the rainforest. In the face of unknown natural powers, in what appears to be a great chaos of darkness and water and danger, one cannot help a steadily rising feeling of insignificance. When you are abandoned in a black jungle in the pouring rain, the trappings of civilisation and culture suddenly seem not only inadequate but ludicrous, and my helplessness was both a thrill and a kind of nightmare.

I tramped on through the night, chastened, following the flickering lights and low talk of my companions.

How then had the Chinese felt in the last century, arriving on this demented coastline, freshly off boats from the familiarity of Shanghai and Canton? I could not conceive of their horror and bewilderment. They had come in search of gold for, as the 1886 *Picturesque Atlas of Australasia* put it, 'the far-resounding cling and clang of the sacred metal was heard throughout the world, and even China heard the echo. Hordes of short, sturdy men, oblique of eye, yellow-complexioned and with plaited hair-lock, invaded the colony . . . like a plague of locusts.' It was only one of the very many derogatory references to the Chinese in Australia at this time. They were frequently called 'orientals' or 'celestials', but more often, inaccurately, 'Mongols', 'Mongolians' or 'Tartars'. Such terms were nearly always preceded by insulting adjectives: 'infernal celestials', 'heathen Chinese', 'vermin Mongols', 'yellow-skinned mummies of the Celestial Empire'. As individuals they were referred to as 'Chink', 'Chinkie', 'Chow', 'Dink' or 'John Chinaman', their real names considered too difficult and too outlandish—or possibly too unimportant—for the white settlers to remember.

Gold had been discovered on the Palmer River not far north of Crocodylus in the 1870s, provoking a surge of immigration from China; by 1876, 7000 mining licences had been issued to Chinese, much to the anger of competing white miners, themselves also immigrants. Notices appeared: 'Any Chinese past this point will be shot'—and some were, but the next year 10 000 more arrived, until 20 000 in all had passed through the disembarkation points at Cooktown. The Chinese numbered some 35 000 in Cooktown itself, although the town has now fallen into obscurity, with only the Chinese shrine in the local cemetery paying tribute to the hopeful immigrants who once thrived here. At the turn of the century their numbers were already falling swiftly. Rumours spread that the Chinese planned a takeover, and the Queensland government moved to restrict their entry.

Bigots and shootings, government decrees and insulting words: the Chinese had survived all these, and no doubt pythons and crocodiles too. But there was another danger here in the rainforest, searching for gold, as I discovered when I asked Jamie if he knew of any Chinese still living hereabouts.

'Not that I know of,' he said. 'Maybe up in Cooktown. Likely the Aborigines polished them all off.'

'Meaning?'

'The Aborigines round here favoured Chinese flesh,' said Jamie.

'I didn't know Aboriginal Australians were cannibals.'

'Some tribes in far north Queensland were. They developed a taste for the "long pork" or human flesh of the Chinese, thinking it better-flavoured and less tough than that of the Europeans. I've heard that those who were caught were tied from the branches of trees by their pigtails until ready for roasting,' added Jamie, smiling mirthlessly.

This silenced me; it also seemed to exhaust Jamie's interest in the Chinese, for later he confessed he knew little about their history in this region. It was already becoming apparent to me that, although it seemed the Chinese had come to Australia in large numbers and played a part in its settlement history, there was little knowledge of their role. Much later, combing the local library, I confirmed the story of the race riots and hostility in the mining areas around Cooktown; but they were passing references, these 20 000 Chinese and their diligence in pursuit of gold. As for the claims about Aboriginal cannibalism, it appeared that evidence for it was far too tenuous to be taken seriously—though that did not prevent it from being reported in various documents and newspapers of the time, and repeated in accounts ever since. Hearsay, sensationalism and a misunderstanding of various ceremonies such as funerals probably gave rise to the rumours. Accusations of cannibalism would also have provided a convenient rationale for occupying indigenous lands and labelling the dispossessed people as inhuman savages.

My hunt for the Chinese in Australia was not going well: in fact, I had yet to see a Chinese. Now I plodded on behind my sister and Jamie and the other travellers, looking instead for pythons. 'I used to catch pythons around here,' Jamie was now relating flippantly, those citizens of the Celestial Empire forgotten. He had remained seemingly undaunted by his surroundings. We had come out on a wide dirt road and were heading back towards Crocodylus. The rain had almost stopped now and I could see a full moon tossing on black clouds.

'Had some mighty struggles,' recounted Jamie. 'Normally when catching a snake you'd grab it by the tail and hold it out at arm's length. But it's no good grabbing a python by the tail, because unlike other snakes, pythons can twist themselves around and latch on to you, even bite you, anyway. They've got sharp teeth that can give you quite a serious injury.' He paused. I knew he wanted someone to ask him how, in that case, you *did* catch a python, and Nicola obliged. So entranced was she that, as she told me later, she did not think to ask *why* he should be catching pythons.

'You grab it just behind the head. I remember one night I was driving along here, the weather a bit like this, black as the ace of spades. Up in front of me in the headlights I could see something lying right across the road. Thought it was the branch of a tree, but as I slowed down I realised it was a python. Don't think I'd ever seen such a big one, must have been all of four or five metres long. It stretched clear across the road and into the bushes. So I lifts a sack and hops out of the car and grabs it by the scruff of the neck, as it were.

'I was on my own, right, which was probably a mistake. Soon as I got a hold of it and started trying to get the coils into a sack it started thrashing around, mad as a hornet in a bottle. That was one powerful beast. Reckon I struggled with it for about an hour and a half, I was nearly done for. Every time I got a few metres into the sack it just seemed to wriggle and heave itself out again, I just couldn't hold on to all the coils at once. I knew if it got a good hold on me I would have to kill it fast with my knife or I'd be a goner.

'Towards the end I was weak as anything,' claimed Jamie. He had a grin like a small boy on his tall, broad frame of solid Australian muscle. 'But the python had almost given up too. Finally got it all into the sack and tied it up. You should have seen the thing lashing about even then, the sack shuffling across the road with a life of its own!' He shook his head in wonderment.

'A real battler, that python. A real battler.'

And as we continued on up the track towards Crocodylus, though I still hadn't seen a snake, I seemed to share in Jamie's adventures, and could almost imagine wrestling with a python on a lone path in the rainforest: the heavy breathing of the human, the rasping, eerie sweeping noise of the snake's coils as it writhed in the dust, the silent battle of strength and wits.

And I smiled to myself, listening to the sounds of the night in a forest dimly lit by the moon. I shook the rain from the folds of my sou'wester and sloshed happily through the mud. I liked the rainforest, I decided. I even, perversely, liked the rain.

And anyway, as my sister said, there was nothing one could do. It always rained in a rainforest.

into *the outback*

We were spending my first morning in the Australian outback. It was raining again. The sun, still not far over the horizon, was a large, gloomy disc behind the cover of clouds, burning slowly as if rehearsing for its final extinction. The rain was not heavy but persistent, falling thinly from a flat, grey cardboard sky. Neither my sister nor I had a raincoat, nor indeed any clothes of particular warmth. We stood by the side of the road in our shorts, smelling of damp, shivering, our Barrier Reef tans looking pasty in the poor light. It was cold. The slight sigh of wind that blew in from nowhere made the hairs on my legs prickle. I hunched my neck down inside the upturned collar of my sweatshirt like a nervous tortoise inside its shell. The outback was not meant to be like this.

I was standing with Nicola by the roadside in Prairie, a place I was sure did not figure in my atlas, nor indeed anywhere except in the minds of those who lived here. On the other side of the road, facing us, was the town. Town, village, hamlet—such terms merely lent a spurious dignity to what was a random collection of a dozen buildings strung out along the highway. The hotel was the only one half-heartedly turning a well-presented face to the travellers passing through: a pleasant enough building with a deep veranda hung with baskets of ferns. The other buildings were shabby, concrete nonentities: a garage with two petrol pumps and a mechanic's yard, ill-advertised by two ruins that looked as if they would never drive again; a tiny shop selling dusty tinned food; a couple of cottages in anaemic grey. There were no people to be seen. A horse, gazing over the picket fence of a nearby field, was the only sign of life.

Behind our backs as we stood waiting on the road was a defunct building that once served as a public toilet. Its roof of corrugated iron was rusted to a mottled blood-red, and what remained of the doors—peeling green wooden boards clinging on to sagging hinges—creaked mournfully in the breeze. A faint smell of long-forgotten urinating passers-by hung in the air. Behind the building was a haphazard, straggling fence, three strands of barbed wire dragging across the landscape. On the other side there was a railway track, and then nothing but a vast expanse of stunted grass and bushes that faded flatly, without the slightest distinguishing feature, into the distant grey horizon.

It was about ten days since we had left Crocodylus, returning to Cairns with Ken and then, on Nicola's continued insistence, hitch-hiking down the coast to Townsville and (after some days on Magnetic Island) westwards a brief hop to Charters Towers. We had left Charters Towers that morning, accepting a ride 200 kilometres into the interior in the direction of Darwin.

'This is the worst place to be waiting for a ride,' observed my sister, squatting down and hugging her bare knees against her chest for warmth. 'They say you should never accept a ride to a small place, even if it's on the right road. It's better to wait for a good lift to somewhere you really want to go.'

'Oh, great. We would have been waiting for ever in Charters Towers for a lift to Darwin. It's 3000 kilometres away, you know.'

'Not to Darwin,' said Nicola impatiently. 'But somewhere big, on the way.'

'There's nowhere big between here and Darwin except Mount Isa and Katherine.' It was hard for a European mind to comprehend, this emptiness in a State bigger than European countries: the populations of the twenty largest outback towns in Queensland, lumped together, would produce a town about the size of Cambridge in England.

'Anyway, it's too late for your grand theories on hitching. We're here now.'

An hour later the fact that we were still there began to weigh heavily on us. In that time only two cars had passed along the road in our direction. The first, a blue Ford, had contained a middle-aged couple who had looked in the opposite direction as they passed us, staring fixedly out over the soggy, empty fields as if seeing visions. We cursed them as they vanished into the all-absorbing outback. The couple in the second car, more infuriatingly, glared straight at us, as if daring us to flag them down. They continued looking as they swept by on hissing wet tyres within a metre of us, the woman craning her neck around and watching us with an inquisitive but inhospitable face. We wondered what she was thinking as we stood there beside our knobby backpacks. Our hitching sign was running in the rain. MOUNT ISA it said in black capitals, smeared down the paper like mascara on the face of a weeping woman.

'Here comes the coach,' I said to my sister some time later. 'Must have left Townsville early this morning.'

The bus appeared out of the rain like our salvation, *Ansett Pioneer* painted in welcoming letters along its side, *Darwin* glowing in illuminated letters across the top of the windscreen like the answer to a prayer.

'We could always flag it down,' I muttered half-hopefully.

'I suppose we could,' said Nicola in a voice that suggested she would rather fling herself down in front of its wheels and be run over. 'But we've only come a few hundred kilometres . . . Can't give up *yet*.'

I did not like the way she stressed the *yet*. I felt an overwhelming despondency at the thought of standing in Prairie all day. The bus was nearly on us: I could see the uniformed driver pinned behind a steering-wheel big as a Dutch cheese. Then the bus was travelling past us. In my anxious imagination it seemed to slow down, tauntingly. It crept by in slow motion. Through the windows, trickling with raindrops, I could see passengers, comfortable, warm, dry passengers: Japanese with their earphones on, listening to music and staring in vague surprise at two hitch-hikers standing in the rain in the back of beyond.

Then the bus was gone. I could see its tyre marks on the wet road, slowly fading like the grin of the Cheshire Cat. The smell of exhaust hung in the air before it too vanished.

Minutes later there was a sign of life in Prairie. A woman came out of one of the houses and climbed into her car. She started the motor and I could hear the handbrake being released. She drove over the pot-holes and on to the road, turning in our direction. She roared past us without a glance. It seemed unlikely in any case that she was going very far.

'Only one per cent of Australian women say they would pick up a hitch-hiker,' observed my sister phlegmatically. 'I read that in an old *Cleo* in the backpackers' at Cairns. A survey,' she added, just to make sure it was fixed firmly in my mind. 'Of Australian women.'

'I see,' I said ungraciously. What I saw was that virtually half of the entire Australian population wouldn't stop to pick us up. The other half were not, at this moment, passing through Prairie. I could feel drops of rain gathering on the end of my nose. Queensland was, according to car number-plates, the Sunshine State. *Queensland, sunshine state! Beautiful one day, perfect the next*, the Queensland Tourist Board's jingle claimed on television without the faintest hint of irony. The refrain circulated through my head with irritating insistence. My hands were freezing.

Our salvation arrived in the form of a beige VW camper-van. It came bumbling out of the rain like a happy bee, its engine droning richly. It stopped down the road from us at the garage. A man with a beard got out. As he stood putting petrol into his tank my eyes bored into the back of him, sending desperate messages. You're going to get back in that van and you're going to stop . . . And he did. At the last moment it looked as if he might just drive on by, but then the van shuddered to a halt.

'G'day, where ya going?'

'Darwin,' shouted Nicola boldly. 'But Mount Isa or any-where along the road will do.'

'I'm going to Katherine,' the bearded man replied. 'That's only a few hundred kilometres from Darwin. It'll take two days, but I'll bring you all the way if you like.'

Without pausing to consider the strange generosity of his offer, we slung our packs into the back, scrambled into the front of the van, and drove thankfully out of Prairie.

I have noticed that people who pick up hitch-hikers always talk about three things. They are always at great pains to stress that you are the only person they have ever picked up. They warn you how dangerous hitching is, usually relating ghoulish tales of recently strangled local hitch-hikers to back up their claim. And they talk about sex, a subject with which they seem even more preoccupied than the average person. The speed at which Peter, the driver of the campervan, launched into all three topics was astonishing.

'I wouldn't hitch-hike in Queensland if I were you,' he said as soon as the common courtesies were dealt with, pursing his bearded lips and peering out through the windscreen.

'Why not?'

'Dangerous!' he almost shouted in my ear, making me jump. 'Illegal, too. Not allowed to hitch-hike in Queensland.'

'In what way dangerous?'

'Well, you never know who might pick you up, right, mate? Could be a criminal. Could be a sex maniac!' He leered out between his flashing windscreen wipers at the thought. 'There were two girls out here not long ago, car broke down. One of them hitched a lift, but she never got to the next road-house.'

'Yes?'

'She was found lying with her throat cut. She'd been raped. Happens all the time. Hitching in Tasmania is OK. Victoria, that's OK. Hitching in Western Australia, that's fine.' He shook his head mournfully. 'Not Queensland, mate. Hitching in Queensland's bloody dangerous.'

'Are you from Queensland?' I asked, trying to be casual. I hadn't noticed his registration.

'Yes. From Brisbane, mate. Started off from home yester-day, been driving all night as a matter of fact . . . Course, it's not always the passengers that get done for, right? This guy a couple of months back, in Collinsville, must have picked up a hitcher. Found in his car with his head bashed in.' Again the lips pursed like those of an old woman over a teenager's delinquency. A shake of the head. 'Not in Queensland, mate.'

'And yet you picked us up,' said Nicola, breaking out of her stunned silence. 'We're two and you're only one.'

'Yeah, well, you looked OK. Never picked a hitcher up before, mind, but I thought, they look all right, and I could do with some conversation. It's a long way to Katherine. Road's bloody boring. Bloody outback.'

'Well, I see you've got a TV with you, anyway.'

'Usually stop at a camp-site so I can plug it into the mains. I like watching TV. There's a programme on Thursday night I'd like to see. It's a series about sex, see. It's on every week on Channel Nine, but this Thursday they're going to show an erection, right—' I could feel my sister shifting in the seat beside me '—and I thought, have to watch that. I mean, this guy's going to sit there and show you his erection. I mean, how's he going to get it up at the right time, in front of all the TV cameras? Sitting in the studio with Sophie Lee! Suppose if he's a porn actor he could do it OK—used to it, mate. Maybe he's going to show you how to put on a condom or something.' Peter shook his head in disbelief.

'Educational, of course. That's what they claim, right? All you ever wanted to know about sex but never dared ask your mother—or even your girlfriend! Caused quite a row, of course, people complaining. Whingeing Christians and wowsers and that. But how do they know what it's like unless they watch it themselves? Glued to it every week, just like everyone else, only too pious to admit they enjoy it. Educational my eye, just an excuse for sensationalism. What's educational about an erection, eh?'

I did not have an answer to this question, so I stared out of the window instead. The rain had stopped now and the tarmac was dry. There was nothing to be seen on the road or surrounding savanna, except the odd water-tower piercing the monotony of the spear-grass and marking a distant cattle station. As we drove westwards these gave way to windmills, pulling water up from deep below the surface of the ground: prosaic, Australian windmills of steel, like electricity pylons topped by narrow blades of silvered metal. The grass was yellowed with heat and age, the ground red as a gash along each side of the road, the road itself shimmering black in the heat. The clouds had cleared and the sun had driven away the cold with a vengeance. This was now the outback as I imagined it, the heat bouncing in relentless waves off the road surface and the van's roof and windows, sending oily coils of air upwards like the fumes from a heated chip-pan. There was nothing to be seen, not even a cow in this cattle-raising interior supposedly supporting a good quarter of Australia's herds.

Peter had lapsed into silence. He drove on through the Queensland flatness, hunched over the driving wheel, peering out through the windscreen as if he were driving along a particularly difficult obstacle course. But the road was empty, marked only along the verges by the bodies of dead kangaroos with a regularity that made them seem like a grotesque adaptation of the milestone. They hardly looked like animals, dried up taut and hollow in the sun like bizarre plastic models; or still limp, indeterminate humps of flesh and fur. I marvelled at their numbers. It was to be a recurring picture in the next few months, for thousands of kilometres clear across northern Australia, kilometres marked by a petrified series of pathetic bodies, struck down by passing vehicles. And I could almost hear the jackeroos talking to one another, *Yair, mate, only three dozen dead kangaroos to Coolabah Station; Darwin now, that's a long way, coupl'a thousand dead roos away, mate.*

'I haven't actually seen a kangaroo yet,' I remarked to Peter. 'I mean a *live* one. Which is a bit strange, seeing how many there are by the edge of the road.'

'Actually, they're mostly wallabies. They come out at dusk,' said Peter. Come out of where? I thought to myself, squinting against the fierce sun at the flat, dry grasslands. 'But you don't want to see them at dusk, believe me. Bloody dangerous animals. Stupid as hell.'

'Dangerous?' Nicola said, perplexed.

'They come on to the road at night because it's still warm on the tarmac, see, and the grass along the road edge is greener, because of run-off from dew. And then a car comes along and they get blinded by the headlights. And they're so bloody stupid that instead of jumping off the road they jump straight for the lights. As big as you, right, and a bit heavier, leaping at fifty kilometres an hour towards your car. The big trucks are OK, they've got huge metal roo bars across the front. But they can cause quite a dent in an ordinary passenger car. Crash!' He bashed his fist down on the dashboard in front of him, making the van rattle.

'Can't you, well, see them on the road ahead?'

'No hope, mate, not in the twilight. They're just grey against the grey road. Haven't got Buckley's. Don't see them until your bonnet's been smashed in around your legs,' said Peter with gloomy satisfaction. 'Don't drive in the outback at night.'

I looked out at the crumpled bodies at the roadside, seemingly so defenceless. I imagined driving along the road and suddenly, with a wet thud, hitting a crazed kangaroo and skidding out of control in the dark night of outback Australia.

'That's not the worst of it. Sometimes they jump high and come right through the windscreen. They've got bloody powerful legs and great claws like daggers. I reckon you've had it if one of them comes through the window, kicking and panicking. Rip you to pieces, no problem . . .

'It's not just kangaroos. You could hit cattle, sheep. Wombats. They're just solid muscle. Hit a wombat and it's like going over a boulder. Chances are your car'll be a write-off and the wombat'll just walk on, right as rain. No wombats up around here, though,' added Peter with what I thought was a shade of disappointment.

And we continued on up the road in thoughtful silence, making distance before the coming of the dark and desperate animals.

The outback towns passed in an irregular flow, for the most part as undistinguished as Prairie, a scattering of houses rising up out of the grasslands and as soon disappearing into the dust again: Hughenden, Marathon, Richmond, Julia Creek, Gilliat. As dusk fell we were approaching Mount Isa, my eyes straining ahead for kangaroos leaping through the evening like avenging furies, bringing death and destruction. The town emerged up ahead, chimney stacks and winding gear reaching up through the red dusk like the turrets of a surreal castle, trailing smoke, and I could not help thinking of Dickens' famous description of Coketown from *Hard Times*: 'It was a town of red brick, or of brick that would have been red if the smoke and ashes had allowed it . . . of machinery and tall chimneys . . . and where the piston of the steam engine worked monotonously up and down like the head of an elephant in a state of melancholy madness.'

Behind the town loomed the ridges of the Barkly Tableland, an ancient weathered plateau stained orange and violet in the rays of the dying sun. That was how we entered Mount Isa, with the sky and hills afire with blood and brimstone, the buildings plunged into deep shadows, the river a yawning, bottomless chasm, the few people in the streets casting grotesque, flickering shadows under the pools of yellow thrown out by the street lamps. Months later, in a Sydney cinema, I was to recognise this approach to Mount Isa in the lurid, fire-lit sets of *Bram Stoker's Dracula*: the vast, dark shadows flickering against the violent sunset that stained the sky blood-red; the billowing plumes of smoke; the black angles of factories and steel bridges and smoke-stack battlements moving slowly past the car windows like the two-dimensional designs of a demented cinematographer. The experience of those few dying hours of evening would leave Mount Isa, though only briefly visited, for ever impressed upon my imagination.

Founded in the 1920s, Mount Isa was, more prosaically, one of the most famous mining towns in Australia, the world's largest producer of lead, silver and zinc and also a substantial supplier of copper. Nearly half of its population were newly arrived European immigrants, including the largest community of Finns in Australia; a pioneer town still, with large families (the teenagers away, for most of the time, at boarding schools), few elderly people, a predominance of men.

'They live pretty well,' Peter sighed as we drove through the town that night on the hunt for a camp-site. 'Well paid, plenty of leave. Shopping trips to Adelaide or Brisbane. There's an artificial lake that's been made for recreational purposes, water-skiing and all that.'

It was a strange vision, the thought of Finns water-skiing on a lake in the middle of the Australian desert, in an artificial town pock-marked with great mining holes. In this city the people, the trees, the flowers, whole lawns, swimming pools, the water, the electricity, even the food was all brought in from elsewhere. Only beef was produced locally; milk and butter were imported on refrigerated trains from the fresh green distance of the Atherton Tableland; fish flown in from the Queensland coast; fruit, vegetables, packaged food and beer from Cairns or from Melbourne, 2000 kilometres away.

Still, there was no shortage of beer in Mount Isa, a hard-drinking, masculine city of rough miners trapped in a wilderness stretching hundreds of kilometres in every direction. There was a madness about the city, a feel of raw-edged, suppressed violence and hysteria, frustration, isolation, heat; and always the languid plumes of smoke and ash rising into the red sky, the melancholy roar of machinery, the giant mechanised claws that ripped into the earth and spewed up heaps of ore.

We headed out of Mount Isa early the next morning, leaving the chimneys belching behind us. As we headed across the tablelands the soil was grey, cracking in the sun: great slabs of marine sediment thrown up in the centre of a dry continent. Soon out of Mount Isa we stopped for petrol.

'We're just over halfway on this epic hitch,' I commented to my sister, pointing to a sign painted on the wall. *Darwin 1443 kilometres*, it said, pointing forward. And pointing backward: *Cairns via Townsville 1482 kilometres*. Nicola took a photo.

While we were standing back outside the van, waiting for Peter, Nicola hissed in my ear, 'Have you seen that picture?'

'What picture?'

'There,' said my sister dramatically, pointing into the back of the campervan. There indeed, propped up against the sink amid a jumble of saucepans, plastic mugs and guide books, was an enlarged photo of Peter, holding a pair of tongs and standing behind a barbecue on which sausages were cooking. He was standing face-on to the camera, and was completely naked.

'It doesn't look very safe,' I smirked.

'But how bizarre!' said Nicola, goggling. 'A naked barbecue!'

'Not as bizarre as enlarging a photo of yourself, naked, and propping it up in your car,' I suggested, nodding significantly. I paused. 'And then picking up two hitch-hikers.'

We fell silent at this observation. Nicola, despite a degree in psychology, seemed struck dumb by the erratic behaviour of her fellow humans. We started giggling, but straightened our faces as Peter returned to the van.

Then it was back to the orange and red dust, and the treeless savannas of spear-grass, and the dead bodies of kangaroos. We arrived at the State border between Queensland and the Northern Territory, which was announced by a great billboard on the side of the road. We got out of the van, and in desperation I took a photo, a photo of a black road going nowhere, between red ground and yellow grass under a vast blue sky. Despite the billboard, the Northern Territory seemed no different from Queensland, a straggle of outback towns and road-houses on the highway: Avon Downs, Soudan, Wonarah, Frewena.

'You've done plenty of travelling in Asia, then?' Peter asked suddenly, without great interest, as we continued northwards. 'Plenty of Asians up in Darwin.'

'I think I read it had the highest proportion of Asians of any town in Australia,' I commented, pleased.

'Yeah, too many, I tell you. What do we want all these bloody Asians coming here for these days, taking over our university places and jobs when there's plenty of Australians needing them?'

'I doubt they take over many jobs. Many of them set up their own businesses,' I hazarded, bored. 'Probably find they actually create jobs in the long run.' I was not really interested in this racist conversation, full of trite, common complaints. Besides, it was not only 'these days' that immigrants from various Asian countries were coming to Australia. Aboriginal tradition in Arnhem Land tells of people they called the Baijini, who had golden skins and wore exotic clothes and planted rice. They were probably either Chinese or Malays, who had first come here centuries ago to collect the abundant trepang (sea cucumbers or *bêche-de-mer*), prized in China for its nutritive and medicinal properties. Then too, very early British plans for the settlement of the continent had mentioned the possibility of 'drawing on any number of useful inhabitants of China' (Joseph Banks' words) as the Dutch had done in their colonies in the East Indies to the north, and of using China as a place for reprovisioning the fledgeling colony. Such a scheme was actually included in plans for the establishment of a settlement at Botany Bay, though later discarded. Nevertheless, the Chinese had settled permanently in Australia since the early 1830s, and two hapless Malays living in England had been transported to Sydney on the convict ships.

But Peter did not know this: for him the history of Asians in Australia began with the Vietnam War. 'First it was the Vietnamese and Cambodians back in the seventies,' he was grumbling. 'Now it's all these Honkies, right? Why can't they stay in Hong Kong after the Chinese take over—I mean they're Chinese too, aren't they?'

'Ethnically, yes,' I replied cautiously. 'But not materially or politically, maybe not even culturally. Not like mainland Chinese, at least.'

'Most of them can't even speak English,' said Peter, ignoring both my observation and the quality of Hong Kong's public-school system. 'Should bring back the dictation test, I tell you.'

The notorious dictation test, I knew, had been introduced in 1901 in order to reduce the number of non-Europeans entering Australia. It could also be applied to any Chinese who had been in Australia for less than five years, and they could be deported if unable to pass the test; it was not abolished until the Migration Act of 1958. Even then, non-whites were kept out by a discriminatory quota system until the White Australia policy was phased out from the late 1960s.

I told Peter I did not think much of the dictation test as a way of choosing quality immigrants, though I could see the value of fluency in English. Besides, I said, there were twice as many Greeks as Vietnamese in Australia, and a wholly disproportionate number of immigrants still came from the British Isles.

Statistics did not impress Peter: Vietnamese were noticeable, Greeks were not. 'I was talking to my mate the other day,' he said. 'I said to him, we should send all those Asians out to the Nullarbor, give them picks and shovels, get them to dig an irrigation channel all the way across it.' Nicola and I were later to drive across the Nullarbor, the vast treeless plain between the edge of the Great Victoria Desert and the ocean: a thousand kilometres and more of Western Australian and South Australian wilderness, virtually uninhabited and completely waterless.

'That would create more arable land, solve our unemployment and get rid of them! Trouble is, I says, it's too hot—no
one could survive long out in that place.

'And you know what my mate says? He says, too bad if
they cark it. There's plenty more where they come from and
we could use the dead ones to fertilise the soil out there!'
Peter slapped the steering-wheel, chuckling to himself at the
thought. I glared out the window with repressed fury.

When Peter decided to stop at Elliott instead of pushing
on to Katherine I clambered out of the campervan and said
goodbye with bad grace. I was suddenly tired of his gloom
and tired of the way he said 'mate' in nearly every sentence
he spoke to me, and I hated his narrow racism and purpose-
less, unconstructive whingeing.

My sister thanked him appropriately. He had taken us
2000 kilometres.

We had to wait nearly three hours in Elliott the next morning
before being picked up by a retired couple in a brand-new
campervan. Mary and Richard had sold their house, bought
the van, and started off from Adelaide on a one-year tour of
the Australian outback.

'We've never picked up hitch-hikers before,' Richard said.
'But we thought that you both looked harmless.' I could see
my sister eyeing me ironically, with my torn shorts and
three-day stubble and grubby backpack.

'I think you're both very brave, it's not very safe to hitch-
hike these days,' added Mary predictably. (Had I known
more then about Australia and its backpacker murders, I
would have agreed with her.)

As we headed on up the highway it dawned on us that this
was not going to be the speediest of journeys. The campervan
purred on its new motor up the wide expanse of straight,
empty road, the telegraph poles passing as if in slow motion.
I could feel the tension building up in my sister beside me.

'Is it true that there's no speed limit in the Northern
Territory?' she asked with deceptive innocence.

'That's right. You find cars rocketing past at some speed,
I tell you,' replied Richard placidly. 'Some real hoons around!

But what's the point? There's no hurry. If you just go steady you'll get there eventually anyway, and probably enjoy it all the more. We never go more than eighty kilometres an hour, do we, Mary?' Mary smiled in her husband's direction.

'I see,' said Nicola primly. She looked across at me with anguished eyes. Now that Darwin and her boyfriend were within striking distance, she was becoming restless and rather tense. I did not think the meeting between Mike and Nicola would be an entirely comfortable one; I continued to speculate on the state of their relationship, for Nicola had mentioned Mike but little in the last week.

After we had travelled for less than half an hour, Richard observed that it would be a good time to boil the billy. He hoped we didn't mind. It would be a nice rest.

'Not at all,' I said. I was delighted at this Australianism. I commented that the character in 'Waltzing Matilda', if I remembered rightly, waited while his billy boiled. Nicola glared at me, not wanting to wait for anything.

We pulled up at the side of the road. Mary put a saucepan of water on to boil on the gleaming gas cooker in the back of the campervan. Richard got out brand-new chairs and a table and a packet of Arnott's biscuits. My sister stomped glumly up and down by the roadside, staring at the cars zooming northwards. When the kettle had boiled she accepted a cup of coffee from Mary with strangled politeness.

And then onwards. Forty minutes, mouthed my sister to me with her lips as we finally got going, drawing circles with her finger round and round her watch face. Tranquillity had never been part of her character. When we pulled up again on the dust-red verge she looked as if she was going to cry. She was growing more and more impatient, bored with the long journey now. Mary unpacked her video camera from its case, and then with patient care began to take shots of a bush growing by the side of the road.

'Look at the yellow flowers!' she said in genuine delight. 'You don't see too many flowers around here.'

Nicola and I craned out the window at the stunted bush, covered with thorns and a few mustard-coloured blossoms not much larger than pinheads. And then we were off again,

at a stately eighty kilometres an hour, through the Northern
Territory towards Darwin.

When we turned off the main road on to a dirt track for a
little sightseeing detour I knew Nicola had given up hope.
She said nothing and did not even look at me, but sat hunched
by the window, staring out with unseeing eyes at the acres of
termite mounds.

We were truly into the deep outback. The van bumped and
jolted its way slowly along the rutted dirt track between the
trees, further away from the lifeline of the highway that
linked the tiny, far-flung settlements of the empty Northern
Territory. Heat was the primary element of the outback;
everything physical seemed to be its incarnation, its energy
made reality. Hot red clouds of dust danced in our wake,
rusting the bushes by the roadside so they appeared forged
out of copper. The heat parted reluctantly to let the van
through, sending titillating undulations of air through the
windows, promising relief but bringing only more heat. Under
the twisted gum trees the grass was yellow, crackling like
mown hay, and the termite mounds were silent orange domes
burnt as hard as concrete.

Despite its intimidating physical presence there was something almost imaginary about this landscape. Journeying up
this track was like journeying through Australian history,
through the Australian psyche: if my sister gazed with
unseeing eyes, I knew Richard and Mary were seeing not
only termite mounds but a whole part of what it meant to be
Australian. Nationalism in Australia's history had often been
expressed through legends of the outback, where men were
really men (women remained shadowy), free from the tram-
mels of empire, proudly individualist, pitting their masculine
strength and determination against the elements and against
any potential encroachment by the civilising colonial powers.
In modern times Australia, despite being one of the most
urbanised countries in the world, still looked to the outback
in trying to forge a distinctive identity; and here, in the
purifying heat, the city-dwelling Australians also believed

they could perhaps find an inner self. The bush shimmered like some mirage in the back of Australian minds, brooded with the promise of something different, just outside those tamed Australian cities.

Little wonder that one of the most enduring classics of outback life, by the turn-of-the-century writer Mrs Aeneas Gunn, was called *We of the Never-Never*. The outback, wrote the author, was 'a land that bewitches her people with strange spells and mysteries, until they call sweet bitter, and bitter sweet. Called the Never-Never . . . because they who have lived in it and loved it, Never-Never voluntarily leave it'. This confused unreality struck me as wholly Australian. In some sense Australians, living in the suburbs of Brisbane, Sydney and Melbourne, had never never left the outback, which still wove its mysteries into the national temperament.

We were driving towards Elsey Station now, where Mrs Gunn had lived from 1901 to 1903 as the wife of the new station manager, and which provided her with the background for *We of the Never-Never*. She was one of the first white women to live on a Northern Territory station, and her doing so was strongly opposed by the other European women living in the relative safety and comfort of Darwin. The dour Scot who was chief stockman of Elsey Station also bitterly opposed her presence, putting all manner of obstacles and objections in the way of her travelling there. 'No buggy obtainable', he wired her husband, and then 'No side-saddle obtainable' when it was decided Mrs Gunn would ride instead. Still this did not put her off, and the Scot had to telegraph once more: 'Stockhorses all flash'. Much to his disgust, his efforts to dissuade her were of no avail.

There is nothing left now of the original station buildings in which the Gunns lived. Only the graveyard remains, lost in the gum trees, containing the graves of station workers and passing travellers, as well as that of Mrs Gunn's husband, whose death in 1903 closes her book.

'I thought Never-Never was the place where Peter Pan took Wendy and those other children,' said Nicola when we finally arrived.

'Mm, I don't know. Wasn't that the Neverland or something?' I replied vaguely.

'The only never about this is that we're never, never going to get to Darwin,' shouted my sister huffily. I surmised she was thinking of Mike. 'They might have told us they went so damn slowly. Boil the billy! Yellow flowers!'

Richard and Mary ambled slowly around the graves, pointing out those that belonged to characters from the novel: Mr Gunn, the Chinese cook, an itinerant trader and other anonymous people who had turned up at the station only to die: 'In Memory of an Unknown' read one headstone; and another: 'In Memory of Hughes, a Traveller, Died 1898'. They took photos of the tombstones, mimicked but dwarfed in size by the great red humps of termite mounds scattered among the trees. It was uncannily still, the air motionless, the woods silent.

'There's the grave of William Neeves,' said Mary. 'He's in the book too. He'd been travelling and working around Australia for seven years with a mate, but died here of malarial dysentery.'

'Tell me about the Chinese cook,' I said. Neither Richard nor Mary could recall anything about him: he was just a passing figure. But the history of Australian settlement was a history of passing figures, and the apparent insignificance of their lives fascinated me. What had brought this Chinese all the way here, to Elsey Station, and what did he think each morning as he woke up to the sound of screeching parrots and the snapping of tree limbs in the heat? Many such Chinese had helped to pioneer the outback and open up a great deal of northern Australia, working as storekeepers, market gardeners, railwaymen and importers of foodstuffs. The Chinese pioneered the growing of bananas in Queensland, hops and tobacco in Victoria; in the cities, they were important in the laundry and furniture-making businesses. The *Northern Miner* reported in 1877, way back in Cooktown, that the 'drayman, packer, carter, publican, doctor, aye, shame to say, that even the telegraph messenger is of Chinese extraction'. (Two days later, the same newspaper was calling the Chinese 'human vermin'.)

The Chinese were used as coolies too. The naturalist Samuel White, journeying in Queensland around the same time, noted that Chinese were readily available there for hire. In the end he decided against employing them, for they were 'too meek and averse to shedding blood to make good collectors, and seem to lack the savage pleasure of hunting and taking life which is so strongly shown by the Britishers'. It is one of the few positive remarks about the Chinese made at the time, although whether White intended it to be complimentary is not clear.

'I think a lot of the early shearers and shepherds were Chinese as well,' said Richard. 'The early pastoral industry was very short of labourers and they couldn't convince the English to come out here, so they brought in Chinese instead. Have you heard of Jack Howe?'

'Can't say I have.'

'He was a famous champion shearer. He broke all records some time around the turn of the century by shearing three hundred and twenty-one sheep in eight hours. Anyway, I believe it was a Chinese who taught him the trade, and Howe always spoke very highly of him.'

Mrs Gunn also had good to say about her Chinese cook, I was to read—he was the 'ever mirthful, ever helpful, irrepressible Cheon who was crudely recorded in the station books as cook and gardener', but who was actually a jack-of-all-trades and, more importantly, a companion for the lonely Mrs Gunn. Something approaching a quarter of all station cooks and nearly half of all cooks in country towns were of Chinese origin in late nineteenth-century Australia. The outback town of Wamoon in New South Wales was named after one such Chinese cook, who worked on a nearby station.

At Elsey the Chinese cook was but a headstone in the graveyard, and my search for celestials was being derailed by my sister's low spirits.

'I'm going to scream,' she said, watching Richard and Mary pottering through the trees. I grunted my agreement, but secretly I was quite content in this lost place, happy to let this retired couple discover their past and their literature and the great outback they had grown up with but had not seen until now. I was enjoying, too, the immense and almost suspenseful silence, broken only by the swift screeching of parrots in the trees. I liked the name, Never-Never. The

Northern Territory Tourist Board played on it in their advertising slogan, inviting people with breathless suspense to come and discover the pleasures of the outback: *You'll never, never know if you never, never go*, it said, showing extravagant aerial photos of camel treks and rafting and Aboriginal people dancing by firelight and Ayers Rock at sunset.

Back on the main road there were no Aboriginal Australians or camels. There were none of Australia's millions of cattle or sheep or forty-five species of kangaroo to be seen. I had spotted two emus earlier that day, careering on knock-kneed legs towards the bush, but to my disappointment I still hadn't seen a live marsupial. 'If you imagine that you will see some accommodating kangaroo . . . roaming at large in the bush near the pier at Melbourne you will be disappointed,' noted Edward Kinglake in 1891 in his *Useful Hints to those Intending to Settle in Australia*. There were millions of kangaroos—18 million at the last estimate—sometimes reaching plague proportions in certain areas; but there were also millions of square kilometres for them to hide in, and they rarely ventured out in the heat of the day. The flat countryside still appeared as empty as ever.

'As there's nothing to see,' whispered my sister, gazing across the dried grass and termite mounds, 'I don't know why we have to go so *slowly*.' She was almost sobbing with exasperation. 'Five hours and we've come two hundred and fifty kilometres. *Five hours!*'

I sighed and said nothing. Dusk was beginning to fall as we pulled into Mataranka. It was certainly too late to get to Darwin today. Richard and Mary dropped us off at the petrol station, smiling. They were heading off the track again, to spend the night at Mataranka Springs, a station famous for its picturesque hot pools. I was thankful to see them go; but they were kind people, deriving true interest from the emptiness of their own country. I wished them well.

We spent a dull evening in Mataranka, and the next morning Nicola was up early, determined that we should make it to Darwin before evening and wanting to catch the first travellers on the road. She had cursed and spluttered over Richard and Mary all evening, bemoaning having to spend another night in another outback town. It was still dark when we stumbled outside and up the road: six-thirty, and surprisingly chilly. We threw away our Katherine sign and made a new one. DARWIN, I printed in bold dark letters. And underneath, in a desperate afterthought to woo a prospective customer, *please*. I squatted by our backpacks while Nicola solicited the first trickle of passing cars with mounting hysteria, cajoling them into stopping as they approached, cursing them under her breath as they vanished up the road, or commenting on the reasons for our misfortune: already four in the car, too much baggage, a woman, probably not going far . . .

The light grew brighter, warmer. We peeled off our sweat-shirts as the sun gathered heat and climbed up above the red soil. The hours passed. Nicola kicked moodily at the few blades of tough grass growing by the roadside.

I was relieved, mostly for my sister's sake, when finally we were picked up by a young man in a red Ford. We set off with a screech of tyres, hurtling northwards. I could see Nicola watching the speedometer climbing.

She had a smirk of private satisfaction on her face as the red indicator needle hit a hundred and seventy.

darwin four

The car roared up the road in a surge of power, kicking up a cloudburst of red dust and scattering leaves and magpies. Our backpacks tumbled over in disarray and I felt myself pressed against the seat as if we were about to break through the sound barrier. I watched in horrified fascination as our driver steadied the steering-wheel with his elbows.

'Name's Eddy. Never picked up hitch-hikers before. Have to stop in Katherine to see a man about his dogs,' he yelled, craning his neck around to look at my grinning sister and careering from one side of the road to the other. 'But it shouldn't take long. If you want to wait for me I'm going on to Darwin. Have to buy supplies.'

'Supplies? Supplies for what?' I asked politely, clinging on to the dashboard.

'Store,' he answered laconically. 'I run the store on an Aboriginal settlement west of Mataranka, out near Urapunga.'

'What does it sell?'

'Everything. Tinned food, cassettes, clothes, even cars. And beer. Beer! Booze! Anything they want, I can get it for them. Going up to Darwin now to stock up on cassettes, Walkmans, things like that. Usually get the food in Katherine, but for the other stuff there's more choice in Darwin. Generally go about once a month, drive up one day and back down the next.'

'Surely there's a limit on how many Walkmans you can sell out in the middle of nowhere? The settlement can't be that big!'

'Don't you believe it, mate. The Abos have got money to burn and they're complete deadheads when it comes to modern technology. When the batteries on their Walkman run out what do they do, mate? Damn well throw the thing away and buy a new one! Same with cars. A little accident, a puncture, a flat battery, they just get out of the car and leave it right there by the side of the road. Can't be bothered fixing it. Go walkabout. Next week they're driving around in another brand new Toyota four-wheel drive.'

This did not seem very credible to me, but I was in no position to argue, and I had in fact seen several cars abandoned by the roadside in the Northern Territory. I merely asked, if that were the case, where the local Aboriginal people got so much money from.

'Social security! Unemployment benefit, child care, old-age pension, disability, compensation, mining rights, you mention it. It's all from the bloody government. Nobody knows what's what, see? Claim they have ten children and who knows the difference, the kids get shared out among them, same kid gets signed up a dozen times under different families. Conning the taxpayer, mate, while they sit around in the dust all day. Haven't done an honest day's work in their lives.'

'Well, you must do quite some business, then.'

'You said it,' said Eddy happily. 'See, they can't even be bothered to drive a couple of hours into Katherine to buy things, either. So I do it. Whack on a good profit margin. Cars are the best. Buy them a car, whack on thirty per cent, money for nothing. I'm from Adelaide myself, came up here a couple of years ago without a brass razoo to my name. And I'm saving a fortune! Nothing to spend it on either, see?'

'Must be a bit lonely,' commented Nicola, somewhat wistfully I thought.

'Well, there's a couple of other men out there, a schoolteacher and a doctor. And some of the Abos aren't bad for a laugh. Good drinking partners, half of them are just plonkos anyway—you know, alcoholics,' he added, seeing my baffled look. 'I like the outback now. Funny, hated it when I first came up here. I was going to go back to Adelaide when I'd saved enough, but I guess I want to stay in the Northern Territory now.'

'And do what?' asked my sister. 'You wouldn't want to stay out on the settlement for ever,' she added with female certainty, more as a statement than a question.

'Nah. Open a pub. That would be it. Open a pub in Katherine.' And Eddy drummed the steering-wheel with his fingers, narrowing his eyes speculatively.

Eddy really did want to talk to someone about a dog. He was breeding Rottweilers—another commercial venture. Rottweilers, he explained, were good cattle-dogs, highly thought of among Australian drovers. His friend was waiting for him outside the BP station in Katherine's main street, with a boot full of black puppies, their long ears hanging rakishly over their eyes. After poking and prodding at the dogs, they both disappeared into the nearest pub. Nicola and I bailed out of the car and flung ourselves down on the grass strip that ran up the middle of the street, dividing the road. A group of Aboriginal men sat further along, scratching indolently, stretching and staring with glum vacancy at nothing with enforced inaction, like middle-class fathers on a Sunday afternoon.

Half an hour and (by Eddy's own admission) two cans of beer later we were heading out of Katherine and on to Darwin, now only about 300 kilometres away. Considering we were still driving at what seemed like 200 kilometres an hour, I reckoned it wouldn't be long before we arrived. I had forgotten, however, that the Northern Territory has the highest per capita beer consumption in the world. We stopped briefly at Edith River while Eddy quenched his thirst at the local watering-hole. Not much further up the road, at Pine Creek, he veered off the road and screeched to a shuddering halt by a pub, suggesting that a longer stop might be in order. He called for two drinks.

By my estimation Eddy now had five cans—or tinnies—of beer under his belt. We set off again, and the speedometer crept close to the 200 mark as we rocketed on towards Darwin. I felt uneasy; Nicola, however, seemed delighted that the snail-pace of the retired couple in their campervan was now only a bad memory. Adelaide River passed in a blur of buildings. There didn't seem to be any other settlements, or if there were we missed them. We raced through brown, worn-down hills and across dry river-beds and on to the plains that stretch down to the Timor Sea.

Eddy slowed down as we approached Darwin's suburbs, lifting his foot reluctantly from the accelerator. There were speed limits in the Northern Territory's towns, he observed sadly. Nicola and I grinned at each other triumphantly. We had made it halfway across Australia.

We crept unnoticed into town at a hundred an hour, skipping red lights.

People, it is said, go mad in Darwin. They can't stick the isolation, the continual scrutiny by bored neighbours, the oppressive heat and strangling humidity, the monotonous rains during the wet season, the sea that offers no respite, filled as it is with unseen jellyfish that can kill a grown man with a flick of their stinging tentacles. And so they go mad. Some of them get drunk and beat their wives. Others become increasingly eccentric, grow enormous beards and start muttering to themselves like biblical prophets. Some take row-boats and head out blindly into the ocean, to be rescued off the coast of New Guinea or to vanish for ever into the Arafura Sea. A few run amok in their cars, crashing through shop windows and wrecking traffic signs before shooting pedestrians and themselves with their shotguns. The Northern Territory has by far the highest rates of assault, rape, murder, alcoholism and imprisonment in Australia.

The casual Australians have a pleasant expression to explain this violent behaviour: going troppo. *Troppo* is merely *tropical*. But when I first heard this expression its musical connotation was not lost on me: it means excessive, overdone, exaggerated. Its Greek meaning is also inadvertently fortuitous, for the Greek prefix *tropo* indicates a change or a turning. People in Darwin turn crazy. Who knows what the turning point might be? Just another afternoon of torrential rain, perhaps, bouncing off corrugated iron, loud as bullets over the distant shell-bursts of thunder. It is just something that happens to white men in the tropics. Just another poor bloke gone troppo.

I wondered if Nicola's boyfriend might not be going troppo. Mike had been in Darwin for some weeks. He looked dishevelled and wild-eyed. He wore a pair of horrendous batik trousers with a design of poisonous-looking purple and bottle-green flowers that crept and twisted up his legs as if eventually aiming to strangle him. On his feet he had a pair of black Chinese canvas slippers, which I remembered he had pulled out of my rubbish bin earlier in his world travels, when he and Nicola had visited me in China. One of them had a hole at the front and his big toe poked through it. His hair had blossomed in the lush tropical climate and stuck out in disarray. Part of it hung down his back in a skinny tail, squeezed up in a rubber band. Coloured bracelets made of plaited string hung in tatters from his wrist. Certainly he seemed more the product of a hippy farm than my sister. Perhaps he had come here to think, as Nicola said, but according to his explanations it seemed he had spent more time in Darwin sucking up great quantities of beer and wine, purchased cheaply in silver bags and consumed on beaches while watching the sun set. He boasted that he had swum with a two-metre crocodile in a waterhole somewhere in Kakadu National Park. I thought him demented.

'Let's go,' he had said, without surprise, when he saw us arrive triumphant at his dismal lodgings. He had looked relieved to see us but he had made no attempt to kiss or hug my sister; indeed, they barely exchanged a word but eyed each other cautiously.

'Go where?' Nicola asked. Even in those two words I could feel her deep disappointment and anger.

'Buy a bag of wine. Mindil Beach. Drink. Great sunsets.' Only in his Yorkshire accent it came out: *soonsets*.

'For a change,' I said sarcastically. 'But I don't think the *soon* will be setting for quite a few hours.'

'Better buy two bags of wine, then.'

'He doesn't like people making fun of his accent,' snapped Nicola.

'Exactly. Wouldn't be worth doing so otherwise,' I said, grinning at Mike amiably. His scruffy look and laid-back attitude were deceptive, concealing an intelligent and thoughtful young man with a first-class engineering degree and a temporarily restless spirit. We got on well together and I was pleased to see him again.

It was on Mindil Beach that Nicola and Mike launched the two-pronged attack that would ultimately lead to our breaking down 400 kilometres along a dirt track in the remote Kimberley Ranges in Western Australia.

'We thought we should buy a campervan,' said Mike thoughtfully, tipping some more white wine into my glass. He lifted his own glass and peered through it at the reddening sun, out towards Indonesia. I noted without comment the *we*. If all was not right between Mike and Nicola, it was obvious they were still good friends, hatching plots together. Reconciliations must have taken place that afternoon: as the outsider, all I saw were snippets of their relationship, arranged in odd sequences, from which I had to piece together the entirety of their lives. This was what friendship was like—and travelling too, an imaginative assortments of hints and vignettes fitted together in an attempt to find a story.

'Yes,' my sister was echoing. 'A campervan.' She nodded like a mandarin about to impart ageless wisdom.

'Oh. Where are you going?'

'Well, not just us. The three of us,' Mike hinted.

'Meaning you're coming with us. It's the only way to see the outback, you know. Have to have your own transport,' Nicola elucidated.

'I thought you both said you had hardly any money left—didn't have a brass razoo, as Eddy put it?' There was a sudden silence before enlightenment hit me. 'Ah, you mean *I* should buy a campervan.'

'Yes. Contribute, of course. Pay you back eventually. Three-way venture.'

'Three-way venture,' nodded Nicola solemnly.

'And where are we going?'

'Up to you, of course,' Mike lied grandly, waving his arm out across the beach and knocking over his wine glass. ('You're so clumsy,' said my sister, more with affection than disapproval.) A map of Australia materialised as if by chance from Mike's pocket and was spread out on the sand. 'But we thought Kakadu National Park just to get us started, sort out any initial problems we might have with the van.' He swept his hand over an area south-east of Darwin that looked the size of Switzerland. 'Then on to Western Australia, along the Gibb River Road through the Kimberleys, down the coast to Perth, um . . . across the Nullarbor and eventually to Sydney.' His finger jabbed across the map, hopping great swathes of uninhabited desert, and came to rest east of the Blue Mountains.

'And of course, after resting up in Sydney we could go on south.'

'That would be quite far?' I suggested cautiously. I had once seen a map of Australia superimposed on a map of Europe; Darwin to Perth, as the crow flies, is about the same distance as Oslo to Madrid. At Perth I reckoned we would only be at the halfway post on our journey.

'Well, you know, few thousand kilometres. Well, maybe about ten thousand,' said my sister as if mentioning a Sunday outing. 'We've just hitch-hiked three. And you did enjoy it. Better than the coach. Thanks to me!'

'Mm. And the Nullarbor would be the place with no water and no trees and no anything where the Asians should be sent?' I added, to Mike's mystification.

'Yes. And the sun on the road will rip out your eyeballs and there's no bends for a hundred kilometres so you'll be screaming with boredom, and if we break down they'll find our skeletons decades later,' added Nicola as if forestalling another question.

There was a silence as the sun slipped down into the waters of the Timor Sea. I still had not yet made any concrete plans for journeying through the outback. I had been swept up to Darwin on the tide of my sister's enthusiasm, which it seemed was going to drown any of my own ideas entirely. I did not like to be manoeuvred into things. On the other hand, Mike and Nicola were aiming to travel to much the same areas as I wanted to see anyway. I enjoyed their company and I knew it would be impractical, even foolish, to travel on my own in such remote regions.

The fiery crimson ball of the sun had almost dissolved into the darkening ocean. Watching it disappear in the direction of Africa, I took a quick slug of wine.

'All right,' I said.

And then we drank some more wine, and soon driving thousands of kilometres through Australia's interior didn't seem like such a difficult proposition after all.

Australian men once had a tradition known as the six o'clock swill, which took place as soon as they left work at the end of the day. This tradition had an Australian simplicity: it involved drinking as much beer as possible with a maximum amount of speed. For a brief hour Australian men could indulge in their legendary adolescent liking for alcohol, uncouth behaviour and good laughs with the mates. They had to make careful use of their time, as the pubs closed at six o'clock and after that there was nothing for it but to go home to the wife.

Although the six o'clock swill was now a thing of the past—forty years in the past, in fact—and even Australian men had changed somewhat, many of the continent's pubs, particularly in the outback, had remained in a time warp. Their décor still pointed to the excesses of the famous swill, for a minimalist spirit reigned. There were few decorations and only the cheapest of furniture in case it should all be smashed in a rowdy moment. Customers were encouraged to lean against the wall or bar, as there were few places to sit— one might as well be ready to dash back for a refill—and the walls and floors were either concrete or tiles so they could be hosed down at closing time. Pool tables and televisions were the only concessions, I concluded, to modern times and longer opening hours.

'Might as well sit and drink in a laundrette for all the difference in atmosphere,' as Mike observed succinctly. This, however, did not seem to have stopped him frequenting the pubs of Darwin, especially notorious for their hard drinking and violent clashes.

'You're lucky in Darwin if you're carried out of a pub merely drunk and not wounded,' Mike commented one evening when we wandered into town with the last dying light of the day. Mike seemed happy and my sister eager as we set out to sample the night-life. I was not reassured by his observation, troubled once more by the apparent lack of adventure in my spirit.

'The Nightcliff Hotel has a show,' said Mike. 'Anyone can volunteer to get up and do an act on the stage, protected by wire netting. When the audience has had enough they throw bottles and beer at the performer.'

'I see.'

'And they have wrestling competitions between women covered in various sauces.'

'I think we might possibly give that a miss.'

The pub Mike brought us to was not crowded: it was probably too early. Two men in checked shirts with beer-bellies the size of beach-balls were propped up against the bar swigging from schooners of beer. A man and a woman were playing pool and screaming at each other over the tattered green surface of the table, and an Aboriginal woman in a grubby pink dress sat in one corner fiddling with her split ends. The television was blaring, showing a blonde woman with breasts of improbable size doing a strip-tease. Many men in the outback (and not a few in the cities) spent a good deal of their non-working lives in such places. The Australians drank more beer than anyone else in the world except for the Germans and the Czechs—and the Territorians drank the most of all. The Territory also laid claim to the world's most capacious beer bottle, once two-and-a-quarter litres and now merely two: the Eighty-Ounce Darwin Stubby. ('Record drinking time, sixty-two seconds,' claimed Mike.)

Only among Aboriginal people, it seemed, was alcoholic excess frowned upon in these parts. Aboriginals drank openly in the streets and parks; white Australians found such public behaviour unacceptable unless it took place behind the doors of a pub. Aboriginals were not welcomed in these establish-ments: they could no longer be explicitly denied entry, but dress codes effectively excluded them, at least in the outback.

I learnt that Australians were ashamed and rather afraid of drunken Aboriginals, who were often harassed and even imprisoned for the offence. Not a few Anglo-Saxon Austral-ians, however, seemed proud of their own renowned abilities to down great quantities of beer, and were fairly tolerant of drunken behaviour among their own ranks. Australian men would tell me with pride that Bob Hawke, the former prime minister, was in the *Guinness Book of Records*, having downed two pints of beer in only twelve seconds when a Rhodes Scholar at Oxford. They would often follow this up with long and monotonous tales of their own exploits in the field. It doesn't take a visitor long to learn picturesque Aussie slang for vomiting: having a technicolour yawn, chundering, praying to the porcelain. Australian men use such terms with easy familiarity.

The young man who came banging into the pub after us already had a few beers under his belt. He collected three more tinnies from the bar and, although the pub was almost empty, sullenly sat down uninvited at our table. No one spoke as he lined his three cans up in a neat row in front of him, shifting them with light touches of his fingers until they were placed to his satisfaction. Then he picked one up and opened it, taking a deep swig.

'And where might you be from?' he demanded belligerently. We explained our origins and our business in Australia. He appeared satisfied with the information we had imparted, or maybe just uninterested.

'I'm from Townsville,' he claimed. 'Least, I'm from Brisbane really but I live in Townsville now. Wouldn't live anywhere else.'

'Oh! I've just been there, and—'

'How long did it take?'

'How long did what take?'

'Get here from Townsville.'

'A while. We stopped off at Charters Towers. After that we came direct—three and a half days.'

'Hitching,' Nicola volunteered proudly.

Our new-found drinking partner didn't look impressed. 'I've driven here in two days, started off Wednesday arvo, just arrived,' he said grimly, wiping the beer foam off his lips with the back of his hand. I must have looked doubtful. 'Yeah, just kept on going. Use these pills of course to keep me awake.' He fumbled in his pocket and drew out a box of caffeine pills, popping one out of its silver foil and swallowing it with a dash of beer.

'How many of those have you taken?' asked my sister solicitously.

''Bout twenty. Keep me awake, see?' He turned ravaged pink-rimmed eyes in her direction.

'What did you come to Darwin for?'

'Business,' said the man almost coyly.

'And that is?'

'I'm a shark's fin salesman.'

'You came here to sell shark's fins?'

'Nah, just came here to make local links, you know, for supply. We don't sell many in Australia—too damned expensive. It's all for overseas markets, Hong Kong and Taiwan mostly. Pay a fortune for shark's fins over there, it's considered a delicacy. Good for your virility and that.' He said it not leeringly but rather sadly, as if he doubted the medicinal properties of his own product. Then he brightened up.

'So you're going to travel in the outback? Better watch out for taipans, then.'

Taipans! Taipans were the most feared of Australia's many poisonous snakes, perhaps because they were the most venomous, the fiercest and the longest, averaging two and a half metres but sometimes growing up to four metres in length; or perhaps because they were reputed, unlike other snakes, to chase and repeatedly attack their victims. They were found along the coast of Queensland, in the north of the Northern Territory and in Western Australia, with a particular and fabled liking for sugar-cane.

'What does a taipan look like?' asked Mike.

'Kind of pale brown on the top, right, more yellowish underneath and white around the head. And orange eyes! You can tell when you've met a taipan by the orange eyes.'

'And have you met a taipan?' I encouraged.

'You bet. Didn't I tell you the story of how I was chased by a taipan?' the man exclaimed, snapping open his third can. I did not point out that we had only just met and so this was unlikely.

'I've read that it's a myth that taipans chase you,' said Mike. 'An old wives' tale.'

The shark's fin salesman turned a shade of puce. I felt it was rather undiplomatic to compare a drunken Australian male to an old wife.

'Course it was a fucking taipan!' he yelled. The Aboriginal woman in the corner looked up from her split ends at the noise, boredom in her eyes.

'I was twelve, right, walking out in the bush on my own. Just gum trees and mulga, minding my own business. And suddenly right on the path in front of me I see this taipan.

Longer than me. I knew it was a fucking taipan 'cause of the
orange eye and creamy snout and fucking pale brown colour,
right?' He glared around at us as if daring us to contradict
him again. We stared back at him in fascination.

'It's got fangs the length of your girlfriend's fingernails,
right, mate?' (As Nicola was an incurable nail-biter, this
metaphor was more imaginative than accurate.) 'There's no
way you survive the bite of one of those snakes unless you
get some antivenom within half an hour. I tell you, when
I saw that taipan sitting on the ground in front of me I
thought I was a sure-fire goner.

'So I turns tail and starts running like hell along the path,
and sure as Elizabeth's the Queen of England the fucking
snake came after me! Jesus could that thing move . . . Then I
thought, maybe it would be more difficult for it to follow me
off the path. So I started crashing through the grasses. Slowed
it up a bit right enough, but slowed me up too. Thought my
lungs were going to burst, I was running faster than a possum
up a gum tree.'

The man stopped, draining his last can of beer. He shook
the empty can from side to side mournfully, then peered
wistfully towards the bar.

'My shout,' I said in my best Australian, though it wasn't.

'Too right, mate.'

'So what happened?' I said when I returned to the table
with a fresh supply of beer. Up on the television, to the
accompaniment of raucous music, contestants were now
throwing buckets of water at buxom women clad in little but
clinging T-shirts. The room was now filling up, and a barmaid
was selling tickets in a chook raffle. The salesman waved her
away irritably.

'What happened? Dunno,' he replied lamely. 'I suppose the
snake just gave up. Eventually I realised it wasn't behind me
any more. Lucky, I suppose. Would have been dead otherwise.' I had encountered the same gloomy satisfaction when
Australians talked about Gallipoli, a great disaster in their
history that was commemorated by a national holiday: the
sun-loving, smiling Australians had a preoccupation with
death and a Germanic melancholy that often caught me by
surprise.

'Shit, I hope I never see one of those again.'

The salesman traced a pattern with his finger in the spilt beer on the table. Then he fingered his packet of caffeine pills thoughtfully. He looked as if he were finally going to pass out into a much-needed sleep. Over in the corner a group of men were voting on the best pair of TV breasts. There were only two women in the pub, apart from the barmaids and my sister: the Aboriginal woman and the female pool player, looking as rough as her partner, dribbling ash from her cigarette all over the baize. The door burst open and two more Australian males, outsized as Eighty-Ounce Darwin Stubbies, came staggering in.

The night was still young, by Darwin time, when we left the pub. Later it would become more crowded, more rowdy. Fists might fly, and more: sometimes one could hear police and ambulance sirens wailing loudly through the city like the voices of housewives gone troppo. There were reputations to be upheld in Darwin: another obsession of the Australian male, this constant defence of their own masculinity through beer-swilling, violence, chauvinism and antisocial manners.

It was time to take cover in the war zone.

I knew nothing about cars, never mind campervans, but in Darwin I trailed in the determined wake of Mike and Nicola, looking for a suitable vehicle for outback adventures. We looked at several and found a VW Kombi whose owner was soon going to England for a year. All I knew about his vehicle was that it was blue with a broad red stripe down the side. It was twenty years old but appeared to be in reasonably good condition. Mike poked around in the engine and pronounced it healthy. We brought it to a garage and the mechanic, advising us to change two bald tyres, otherwise agreed.

I had bought a book in a second-hand bookshop in Darwin —*Absalom's Guide to Safe Outback Travel*—and was reading it surreptitiously.

'We haven't got a limited slip differential,' I said to Mike casually on the afternoon we bought the van. He looked at me as if I had sprouted horns. 'Yes, I mean this is only a two-wheel drive, so don't you think a limited slip differential might be a wise idea?' I rolled the words off my tongue with pleasure. I had no idea what I was talking about.

'I'm sure that's not vital,' said Mike idly. I opened up my new book and flicked to page eleven.

'It says here, "If you are going to purchase a vehicle for outback travel, then there is only one that you could possibly consider—a four-wheel drive."'

'But we won't actually be driving off the road,' said Mike. 'I mean, we're not going to go careering through the bush.'

'But they will be *dirt* roads. In the *Kimberleys*.' I was glad to see that Mike was beginning to look harassed. 'And what about a crank-handle? Otherwise automatic cars are dangerous to drive in the outback. That's the opinion of Jack Absalom,' I announced, tapping my book.

'Who the hell's he?' Mike snapped rudely.

'An *Australian*,' I answered, making it clear they were altogether a better breed than Yorkshiremen. 'Who has driven in the outback.'

'Well, yes. That's one thing that's maybe not so good. We would have been better with a gear-shift.'

I said smugly: 'I see.'

The more I thought about it, the more I concluded that this journey was going to be a disaster. Somewhere in the wilderness we were going to realise the folly of not having a limited slip differential. My only satisfaction would be reminding Mike of the fact before we starved under the pitiless sun.

Stars illuminated the heavens and brilliant meteors streaked through the sky on the night Darwin harbour was discovered by the crew of the HMS *Beagle* in September 1839: it seemed an auspicious start. The place was named after the *Beagle*'s former passenger and naturalist, but there were those who were not amused by this recognition of one who had debunked the biblical creation. The tiny settlement was renamed Palmerston, after the respectable British prime minister, but the name never stuck.

It was not until the end of the 1860s that Darwin was considered with any seriousness as a settlement. George

Goyder, a government surveyor, arrived here from South Australia (which then administered the territory) and was so delighted with Darwin's surroundings that he dreamed of a city springing up here to rival gracious Adelaide, with wide and pleasant boulevards and immense parks. A surveying team was astonished to chance upon a group of friendly indigenous people (already well-known for their powers of mimicry and musical talents) who burst into song, rendering 'John Brown's Body' and 'Glory Hallelujah!' to perfection, although none of them spoke a word of English.

Such varied good omens had little basis in reality. Darwin remained unrelievedly provincial, the most remote settlement of any significant size in Australia: an inward-looking town of gossipy neighbours and restless boredom. Geographically stranded, its inhabitants had nowhere to go and not much to see beyond the suburban confines of this tiny city, which nevertheless contained a full half of the population of the vast Northern Territory. Americans or Canadians visiting the country might remain sanguine in the face of Australia's vastness, but to me, coming from a Europe subdivided into crowded nations, it was a source of constant amazement. The nearest towns with comparable populations to Darwin were Mount Isa and Alice Springs, both well over 1000 kilometres distant, and the roads that linked them had not long been surfaced. The nearest Australian capital cities were Perth and Adelaide, 2600 kilometres away as the plane flies; Jakarta was half the distance.

The people in Darwin seemed proud of their isolation. It was quicker to get to Singapore than to Sydney, they would say in a rather bored and abstract way that suggested they had little intention of visiting either place. And yet if the people of Darwin looked anywhere it was towards Asia. After all, the yellow hordes against which Australia supposedly defended itself would invade from the north (Darwin had been bombed during World War II in confirmation of the belief). The Northern Territory did substantial trade with Asian countries, particularly Japan, and geographically was much closer to the Indonesian archipelago than to the populated coastal areas of Australia. Indonesian was taught in more than half the schools of the Northern Territory, and

Darwin retained close links with the government in Jakarta, sometimes warmer than those between Jakarta and Canberra. It was probably the least Anglo-Saxon of all Australian cities, adapted fully to the tropics.

Not only this: the population of Darwin itself, as a flick through the X, Y and Z columns in the telephone directory revealed, was swollen with immigrants—Xanthapolous, Xenikos, Xi, Xiao, Yamaguchi, Yamamoto, Yan, Yao, Yap, Zaatini, Zhang, Zhou, Zimmerman, Zivkov. There was a fair scattering of Eastern Europeans, Germans, Italians and Greeks, and an impressive showing of names from various parts of Asia: Chinese, Japanese, Malaysians, Vietnamese, Indonesians, East Timorese who had fled the violence on their nearby island. Small, lost and provincial, Darwin was yet paradoxically a city with a large ethnic mixture, where one could eat Vietnamese rolls or Sichuan hotpot or Cantonese noodles as easily as Australian meat pies. It was these people who contributed character to the blandness of what would otherwise have been just another outback town.

Here, finally, I would find my Chinese. They had long had connections with this region. It was thought by some that Cheng Ho, the great Chinese explorer-general, had made landfall here. It was firmly established that he had sailed through the Indonesian islands in the early fifteenth century and had discovered Timor, although debate continues on whether he, or other Chinese explorers, added Australia to the list. Certainly, according to Eric Rolls in *Sojourners*, his history of the Chinese in Australia, since around 1000 AD the Chinese had had the technological and seafaring ability to have made it as far as Australia—it has been determined that they reached California long before Columbus ever set foot in the Americas. Anecdotal Aboriginal stories about the yellow-skinned trepang collectors in Arnhem Land lent weight to this possibility.

More concretely, the Chinese had first come to Darwin as labourers on the Overland Telegraph line between Darwin and Adelaide, and later to work on the railway; they hired themselves out for a shilling a day. The first shipload of 200 arrived in 1874 and the local population, outraged by their opium-smoking and insanitary habits (they threw their dirty water back into the well, it was claimed) forced them all to settle on Cavenagh Street, then no more than a name on a government survey map. More Chinese flocked into the new settlement, which formed a rest and recreation stop and supply centre for the Chinese working the Territory's gold mines. Cavenagh Street soon became Darwin's Chinatown, known as Little Canton. The *Picturesque Atlas of Australasia* (1886) described Cavenagh Street thus: 'The buildings are of the flimsiest, and usually consist of a mere framework of poles covered with galvanised iron or bark. Umbrella-like hats, pig-tails, wide sleeves, sandalled feet, bare legs, and indeed the sights, sounds and odours of China abound. At the morning market the fish and vegetable hawkers obtain their supplies, but gardening is the Chinaman's speciality.'

Little Canton was said to have been the most Chinese of all Australia's Chinatowns, cluttered with stores and restaurants, laundries and houses, and crowded with clerks, laundry men with their hot irons steaming on open fires, waiters, and tailors who could stitch up a suit overnight for those who put in at the port. In fact, Darwin was in many respects a Chinese city—letters of outrage were written to the papers complaining about the caterwauling of Chinese opera emanating from the back streets every evening and all day Sunday without cease. The opening of the temple (or joss house) was celebrated by a procession over a mile long, with gongs and drums being beaten for more than three hours, and dancing dragons. The temple had doors of solid teak, decorated with fretwork, which had been imported from Hong Kong at a cost of £1000, attesting to the material success of the Chinese immigrants.

But it seemed my hunt for the Chinese was forever slipping from my grasp. Cavenagh Street had been destroyed by Japanese bombs during World War II; the old joss house had been closed and looted by Australian soldiers, then it too had been blown to smithereens. As if this were not enough, on Christmas Day 1974 a cyclone had flattened the entire town. Where were the Chinese now? Was there no Chinatown?

'No. The Chinese in Darwin are well assimilated,' the woman in the tourist information centre told me with surprising primness. I was impressed by her off-the-cuff knowledge of the Chinese here: she told me about Cavenagh Street, the bombs, and Harry Chan, Australia's first Chinese parliamentarian, who was president of the Northern Territory Legislative Council and Mayor of Darwin in the 1960s ('There's a Henry Chan Avenue not far from here'). 'A high proportion of the Chinese here are Australian-born, a fact clouded by the many other newly arrived immigrants from other parts of Asia,' she pointed out. I was impressed again. And the new immigrants?

'A good many Timorese,' said the woman hesitantly, so that I gathered her knowledge of these reluctant Indonesians was not as good as of the Chinese.

I pressed on with my old theme. 'Didn't some Chinese refugees come here in a fishing boat recently?'

'Yes. But they're in the detention centre.'

'For . . . ?'

'Until the legality of their claim to be political refugees is determined,' said the tourist official with the assurance of a politician. She stirred restlessly.

'So where will I find some Chinese now?'

'Go to Mindil Beach on Thursday evening,' she suggested, sensing she was about to be rid of me. No doubt she thought my question among the more bizarre requests for tourist sights. 'You'll probably find the Chinese there.'

I went back to Mindil Beach on Thursday to find a market had been set up under the palm trees, selling crafts and knick-knacks. A variety of food stalls supplied a startling array of cuisine, from Indonesian black sticky rice to Sichuan chilli prawns, from gado-gado to green Thai curry.

And I found a Chinese, though not one of Darwin's Australian-born settlers. Xiao Li—who now called himself Mark—was a Chinese from Shanghai who had been in Australia only since 1989. Because of the Tiananmen crackdown he had been permitted to stay in the country along with fellow Chinese students. He was delighted when I used my few words of Shanghainese.

'I'm actually from Wuxi in Jiangsu Province,' he admitted when he realised I was familiar with China. 'But nobody knows that place, so I just saying Shanghai, which is near by. Though I think many people don't really know where Shanghai is either!' He seemed more amused than unhappy at this ignorance of Chinese geography.

'I came to study English originally, then Tiananmen happened so I stayed here . . . Permanently? I like to, but now the Australian government is maybe changing its mind. It says now that we all have to go home, that it was only three years they let us stay, which have ended long time before.' He smiled a very Chinese smile: fatalistic but not despairing.

Mark normally lived in Sydney, where he sometimes worked as a cook in a Cantonese restaurant. He had hitched all the way to Darwin, where he had been dithering for weeks, appreciating the tropical heat and the large Asian community. He was thinking of settling here.

'What surprised you most when you first arrived in Australia?' I asked him. Mark seemed puzzled by the question.

'I mean, didn't you find anything strange or unexpected?' I had long been fascinated by immigrants, by their sudden leaving of familiarity and arrival in hostile and unknown places, the frightening psychology of adaptation.

'Not really.' Mark shrugged. 'You know we've got pretty good idea of Western countries looking like from TV and films.' He paused for a moment, contemplating. 'I suppose I was surprised how empty Sydney seemed. I remember going over the streets of city and thinking, *aiya*, where are all the people? It was a Sunday too, so it seemed even more deserted. Not like Shanghai. I was worried, I really thought maybe something terrible happened!

'I wasn't very happy the first six months I spent in Australia, in a room in Stanmore in Sydney. I was very homesick. Sometimes I wanted to kill myself, sometimes I wanted to kill someone else, most of the time I just wanted to sleep. I was very lonely. We Chinese not used to being alone.'

'Didn't you have any neighbours?'

Mark grimaced. 'I had one called David, living across the stairs. He was drunk all time. One day he saw me in the street and asking me for a dollar, he didn't even recognise me. He had a girlfriend who always coming round and laying in front of his door. "Open the fucking door!" she would yell. He would answer: "You bitch! Fucking go away!" This happening until five o'clock in the morning. I was very shocking by their behaviour, that is not our Chinese style. Later I moved in with another Chinese boy, that was much better for me.'

Later I asked him if he thought the Australians racist.

'Not really. Not so much towards the Chinese. Especially when they know I am here reason of Tiananmen. You know the Australian prime minister cried on television because of what happened in China!'

Ah, yes, Bob Hawke's tears and the Chinese. In 1886 the *Bulletin* carried a cartoon entitled 'The Mongolian Octopus: His Grip on Australia'. It showed a caricatured oriental face on the body of an octopus, each leg representing a different vice such as cheap labour, opium, immorality, robbery and gambling at fan-tan. Another drawing in the *Boomerang* (1888) was even more dramatic. It depicted a Chinaman with a knife clenched between his teeth creeping through an open window (the name South Australia above it) towards an unsuspecting beauty lying supine and ravishing on an elegant canopied bed. 'Wake, Australia! Wake!' read the caption. Pictures said so much more than words.

It was because of television pictures that the student demonstrations in China had been called the 'Tiananmen crackdown', although Beijing was far from the only city involved. Still, no pictures was as good as no news. Bob Hawke's weeping on television was a picture too, a memorable one, and the episode was much referred to in Australia when talk turned to the Chinese. Australians were certainly much more sympathetic now than they were in the 1880s. This latest picture, although it involved only one man, suggested a caring and sympathetic Australia far removed from the ugly days of colonial racism.

'Maybe Australians have some respect for Asians because we working hard and we don't making ourselves very noticeable. And they like Chinese food! But I think they are a little frightened of Asians too, because they don't can understand us. Often I was frightened or nervous in Sydney too, after I arrived, by Australians just doing the very ordinary things. So they don't want too many of us to come here.'

If white Australians saw Asians as belonging elsewhere even if they were born in this country, this attitude was almost encouraged by Asian Australians themselves. Of the many I was to meet, not one claimed to be an Australian: they were Vietnamese and Laotian and Cambodian and Chinese, even the ones who couldn't remember what the country of their origin was like. Now Mark told me: 'I'm a Jiangsu-*ren*'—a man from Jiangsu Province. 'I like Australia, and I want to stay here, but I'll always be a Jiangsu-*ren*. I'm glad to work in this country and contribute to it. But I'm still proud to be a Chinese!'

And yet, compared to the Chinese I had known in China, Mark did not seem particularly Chinese to me. A few years in Australia had already bequeathed him an Aussie accent (if not good grammar) and long hair and a laconic, flexible attitude to life. I thought he would have a difficult time assimilating if he was obliged to return to China. No longer a national of just one country, he had become part of a still young nation also trying to forge its own, unique identity. He was a person, like so many on this continent, of neither here nor there; and I could easily understand that.

I did not really know where I came from, either. And here for the first time, on Mindil Beach, I thought: perhaps I could be an Australian too.

I went with Nicola and Mike to see *The Hand that Rocks the Cradle* in a Darwin cinema. It was one of the many psychological thrillers that had become fashionable in Hollywood in recent years: an outwardly normal woman, masquerading as a nanny, was in reality a deranged psychopath determined to destroy the very family she had been employed to look after. The tension mounted, tempered only because I knew that eventually she would come to a sticky and well-deserved end.

The nanny was played by Rebecca de Mornay. She could have been an Australian, with her long blonde hair and pale eyes. As she was pushed further over the edge of her tenuous sanity, one could well have believed she lived in Darwin instead of small-town America. In this city of soaring tropical temperatures and intense humidity, it would not be difficult to be driven to destruction and madness, or at least to confused cultural identities. Was it not madness to think of being Australian when I had only been here a matter of weeks? When we left the air-conditioned comfort of the cinema hall the air hit us like a wave and the tropical insects screeched from the palm trees. It was winter, the cool month. I was glad not to be in Darwin during the wet season, from the end of September to late April, when the monsoons drenched the city in hot rain and people went troppo. It was easy to believe that nannies went insane here as a matter of course.

Darwin was a new place: nearly every building had been constructed after the 1974 cyclone. Like most adolescents Darwin was loud, with a barely repressed aggressiveness and an undeveloped personality. There was nothing unpleasant about the place; its streets and shopping malls were well-kept and clean and rendered exotic by the great bursts of tropical flowers, lemon-scented gums, Norfolk Island hibiscus and palm trees that grew in abundance. But it had little history and, it seemed, no real purpose; its suburban bungalows, so similar that they appeared to have been produced from the same mould, huddled together as if for protection against the vast emptiness of the landscape. Darwin's blandness was relieved only by its underlying violence and the bold, crazy defiance of its existence and its people. Only through its immigrants would Darwin achieve adulthood, but the immigrants too seemed confused and adrift.

In the main street, under an Illawarra flame tree, an old man picked out 'In the Bleak Mid-Winter' on a xylophone glittering under the tropical heat as if it were a challenge. This too seemed like a kind of madness. It was Australian winter, almost, as we drove out of Darwin in our new campervan, the sun already hot over the horizon. Maybe I was the only one mad: I thumbed through my guide to survival, muttering to myself, and let my sister drive us off into the wilderness.

the top end

the top five

My schoolboy's atlas proved an eternal source of fascination to me in my childhood and adolescence: perhaps one of the reasons I travel so restlessly. On maps of the physical world most of Australia was flesh pink or dark pink. *Pre-Cambrian (exposed)* and *Pre-Cambrian (overlaid)* said the key starkly. As a schoolboy I did not clearly understand the meaning of these descriptions, but they sounded far bleaker, more desolate, than the other scientific names used for the shaded areas that coloured Europe. On the world food map Australia was a huge patch of black dots (*Desert or semi-desert*) surrounded by bands of pale green that seemed not much more promising: *Extensive grassland*. On the map of population density the cartographers had given up: Australia was white, a blank seemingly devoid of humans. Conversely when it came to world temperatures the continent was flushed deep fuchsia, even dark red in places, almost off the end of the temperature scale on the key underneath. Only on the minerals maps did Australia seem a hopeful place.

This was the outback, these patches of furious red or helpless white surging across the continent's maps, giving way only around the east and south-west coasts. This was an inescapable part of Australia that sometimes shouted to be noticed, sometimes remained misleadingly quiet in muted browns and sketchy blues that might have been lakes but on closer scrutiny were only seasonal salt lakes or saline mud-flats, lost in a vast expanse of roadless, waterless beige.

I was in the outback now, driving along a red dirt road through Kakadu National Park and through the maps of my vanished school-days. To me Australia had always been the outback, just as I was seeing it, though with the addition of rather more hopping kangaroos. Australia was the country of 'Waltzing Matilda', with its casual use of strange, outback words; of Aboriginal people going walkabout through the heat-swollen desert; of early explorers pitting their feeble human strength against the immensity of the Red Centre; of babies eaten by dingoes under the brooding shadows of Ayers Rock; of incredible, mutant animals with equally bizarre names: platypus, wallaby, echidna, thorn bird. It was a vast, empty continent where one desert melted into another, changing only in their inappropriate, suburban English names: Victoria, Simpson, Gibson.

I was not alone in my view of Australia, for that was the way many Australians themselves saw their own country, the way their literature, painting, traditional songs and popular legends portrayed it until very recently. It was the irony of urban Australia once again, for the people lived in concentrated areas of high population density, clinging to the island's lush coastal zones much as indigenous Australians had done for millennia. The Australian outback had never been a source of adventure, of limitless possibilities like the American West. Unlike American pioneers, early Australians spread westwards only reluctantly, and even today seemed to turn their backs on the vast, haunting interior. Few Australians lived in the outback, which was seen primarily as hostile and lifeless, and few ever travelled far into it. Few Australians were bushrangers, explorers, jackeroos, sheep-shearers or jolly swagmen (whatever they were): the great majority of them worked in offices in large cities. In fact, the outback was closer to the American Dream than the American West: a fantasy expressed more through wishful thinking than reality, without for a moment diminishing its significance.

Away now from the urban confines of Darwin, I was heading once more back into the Never-Never, back into the evocative landscape of dreams and imagination that formed the heart of the continent, and in it I hoped to learn more about the mind of Australia.

It was not surprising that we had passed a minute town called Humpty Doo as we drove south-eastwards: the name meant 'nowhere' in the local Gagadju language. Soon we entered Kakadu National Park, a wilderness area stretching 20 000 square kilometres out towards the Arnhem Land Escarpment. Behind the escarpment lay an Aboriginal reserve closed to tourists: a vast and relatively unknown corner of Australia between the Gulf of Carpentaria and the Arafura Sea. The didjeridu was once played only by the Aboriginal people of Arnhem Land, who belong to more than a dozen different groups. Most of Kakadu itself was owned by the Gagadju and leased back to the National Parks and Wildlife Service. One of the most ancient landscapes in Australia, it was crowded with primitive eucalypts, ancestors of all Australian gums, and with many unique animal species virtually unknown to science.

We were visiting Kakadu in what the Gagadju, with their complex vocabulary for the changing months, call the Wurrgeng season (June and July). Most of the creeks had stopped running and the flood plains of the monsoon season had dried out, fringed by red river gums and ghost gums pale against the yellow grass and eroded brown hills. Flocks of cockatoos, white among the trees, flashed their yellow crests in annoyance as we slowed down to peer out the windows at them; wallabies grazed on the grass by the roadside, twitching their ears suspiciously in our direction.

Kakadu that winter was stunted trees growing out of the sides of cliffs, their long, exposed roots clutching at the crumbling sandstone; billabongs afloat in reflections and white water-lilies; plants with leaves as enormous as decorative Chinese wall-fans, gleaming as if polished; great teetering piles of stone, sandwiched and contorted into odd weathered shapes, layer upon layer of stacked rock. Kakadu was a wilderness of strange trees, with bark peeling in long, crumbling brown strips fragile as dried tobacco leaf, or studded with humps like miniature rhino horns, or pitted with dents, warped as old armour. Grey bark, rough under the fingers and cut through by thin grooves; bark pink as salmon flesh, smooth and cool to the touch and crossed with delicate lines of oozing black sap; bark of trees grey-white, catching the moonlight and standing ghostly in the silent darkness.

Kakadu was heat, and clouds of flies and mosquitoes. (At night it was also surprisingly cold, the air rising off the waters in the early morning like a Scottish mist, the interior of the campervan a tin icebox.) In mid-afternoon the countryside was harsh, exposed brown and washed flat under the relentless glare of the sun, the air shimmering over the hot rocks; but in the most beautiful moments of early morning and late evening the colours and shapes seeped out of the landscape, coaxed by the pale light—ochre and violet and biscuit-brown and yellow and blue, moulded and shadowed into fantastic dimensions. Parrots, encouraged by the cool air, tumbled through the trees in scarlet and gold and white: rosellas and lorikeets, budgerigars and cockatoos, cackling in glee.

Kakadu, indeed the whole of the Northern Territory, was also termite mounds. Some, grey and hard as poured concrete, were shaped like gravestones with jagged tops, their long axis aligned north–south to equalise exposure to sunlight: rows and rows of outsized tombs, abandoned among the long dusty grasses. Other termite mounds were gigantic, towering heaps of red earth shaped like a child's mud-pies; some were over six metres high, weighing several tonnes and housing more than a million worker termites. The mounds were rough under my touch, staining my fingers red, but immensely strong. We were to see thousands of such mounds scattered through the outback, billions of busy termites sealed into their stone fortresses.

'Good tennis court surfaces when ground down,' the slow-driving Richard had informed Nicola and me at Elsey Station. 'Very resistant. Most of the courts on outback cattle stations are made from termite earth.'

Later Richard had said, with a natural human eagerness to impart esoteric information: 'They have thin skins and soft bodies. Termites wouldn't last under the sun, so they travel underground. When they find a bush they surround it by walls made from earth mixed with a special liquid from a gland near their jaws. Under cover they can then make a meal out of the bush at their leisure.'

Other mounds, apparently, are purely for habitation. They have ventilation ducts to allow air to escape upwards, and deep foundations sunk into the moist earth far below the dry surface. Termites collect water and spray it on the inside walls of their mounds to keep them humid, thus enabling them to survive in the harsh Australian climate. I admired the scientific complexity of the termites' nests, but they were works of artistic genius too. In the evenings in Kakadu, these red termite mounds changed colour and glowed, ecclesiastical towers twisted as Gaudi architecture, reflecting the eerie light of Australian sunsets.

He was driving a BMW with Queensland plates: a big insolent car in navy blue with tinted glass and two suits suspended on hangers at the back window. It crunched to a stop on the gravel beside our battered campervan, and a cool wave of air, smelling of leather and metal, rolled out towards me as he opened the door. This was the way the devil would appear, I thought to myself: a sophisticated, twentieth-century devil, springing up in the Australian wilderness through a shimmer of air-conditioning. He was dressed in good trousers ironed to a knife edge, a blue pin-stripe shirt open at the collar, and a tie with the knot slung low around his third button. He wrinkled his nose up in the heat, the gravel crunching under his office shoes like shells crushed on a beach. Shading his eyes, he grimaced over at the three-star hotel floating on an unnatural sea of water-sprinkled emerald-green grass.

'How are yez?' he said breezily in our direction; no devil could have spoken with such a friendly Australian drawl.

Mike was sitting in the doorway of the van, Nicola and I on camp stools, with our lunch spread out before us on a rickety table that we had bought second-hand for a few dollars. Mike was wearing his florid batik trousers and a three-day stubble; my own T-shirt was dusted in red earth kicked up from the dirt roads. It was a measure of Australian equality that the man had spoken to us at all, let alone stopped in our vicinity. We courteously replied that we were quite OK.

'Not staying here, then?' said the man, more as a statement than a question, flicking his thumb over at the hotel.

'No. Just stopped for petrol. And water.'

'And to fill up the gas bottle. Which runs our fridge and cooker,' added Mike, cordially informative.

The man propped a buttock on the gleaming bonnet of his car. 'Travelling, eh? Couldn't do it myself.' He flapped at a fly which had settled momentarily on his cheek. 'Well, I mean, I do it all the time, but not your sort of travelling. I'm a salesman, see? Farm machinery for John Deere. Spend days and days driving around outback stations, staying in motels, always on the go.' He slapped the side of his car affectionately. 'Couldn't do it without the BMW.'

'You're a Queenslander. Aren't you a bit far off your usual run?'

'Yep, no farming in Kakadu anyway. This is a holiday. Or at least that's what the wife calls it. Said Kakadu was *the* place to see in Australia! But I reckon you've got to be a few slices short of a loaf to come to this God-awful place. Sick of the bloody outback, I am, driving through it twenty days in the month and damn-all to see anyway. But my wife insisted, right? So I said, fine, but I'm going to stay in that swanky hotel—not this one, right'—he glanced at its whitewashed tidiness with contempt—'but the famous one in the shape of a crocodile. I told her she could go out and see Kakadu, and I'd stay in my hotel room and watch a video of the place!'

'Mm, not quite the same, though,' I suggested. 'No heat and no flies and no smell of the gum trees.'

'Exactly!'

'I agree there's not that much to see in the outback as such. It's just the atmosphere,' I explained a trifle pompously. 'I find it quite incredible.'

The salesman shrugged as if the outback atmosphere was the last thing that interested him.

'Maybe you'd prefer visiting a city?' Mike suggested.

'Too right. A city in Australia.' Like all natives he gargled with the name, wrenching it apart in the middle and casually discarding the last syllable with a small grunt. 'Can't be bothered with these foreign places. The wife wanted to go to Singapore, you know, shopping. So finally we went last year. Turned up at this hotel, right, all the receptionists were jabbering away in Singapore, or whatever it is they speak there. Didn't understand a word I was saying to them!'

'Jabber' was a word I was to find often used by white Australians in reference to people speaking Chinese. ('All jabbering away in the bus in their own language,' an elderly woman was to say to me in Sydney. 'Why can't they speak English?') No one else in Australia, it seemed, ever jabbered, and I found the choice of the word derogatory; then too, these people who complained showed an astonishing ignorance about what language was being spoken. In my experience, Singaporeans spoke good English, but I was not surprised the receptionists could not understand this salesman, as I was having difficulty with his accent myself.

'Bloody hot, too. Hot as the Earl of Hell's living room. I told my wife she could go and do her damn shopping, I wasn't going to move out of the hotel room for a week!'

I did not say so, but I felt rather sorry for the ever-suffering travel-hungry wife. Her husband struck me as being a wowser: a killjoy, a wet blanket.

'Where's your wife now?' said Nicola.

'Walking around in the bush,' replied the man vaguely. 'If that hotel's got an air-con bar then that's where I'm going. You take care now . . . Enjoy Australia,' he added uncertainly, as if he thought that might be difficult.

And then he crunched off towards civilisation and a cold beer.

Australia has a post-nuclear landscape. This was how the world might look after the Big One. The *Mad Max* series had been filmed here about the world after a nuclear war; Nevil Shute's *On the Beach* showed Australia finally engulfed by poisonous clouds of nuclear fallout that had drifted from somewhere to the north. Even the animals looked like mutant survivors, with huge hind legs and shrivelled front paws, with snouts and spines and poisoned fangs. The toads were bigger than dinner-plates, the jellyfish killers, mammals laid eggs, birds grew bigger than humans and the platypus had the bill of a duck on an otter's body. Trees shed their red or blue bark and plants had stinging hairs that could cause agonising pain. They existed in a landscape reduced to bare essentials: heat and rock under a vast sky, sunsets made spectacular as if by the dust of a holocaust.

At Ubirr, overhanging rocks on a hillside once provided shelter and shade for the indigenous people of Kakadu, and on the protected rock face they had left relics of their passage: a vast series of paintings, sometimes drawn one on top of the other, showing human figures, animals and spirits from the dawn of creation, that period when immortals walked the earth and shaped the land. These paintings, too, could almost have been the remnants of a nuclear blast: shadowy outlines in black and red of skeletal fish and kangaroos left imprinted on the cliff, just as the outlines of humans had been left imprinted on the few remaining walls of Hiroshima and Nagasaki.

The oldest of these paintings—simple outlines in ochre showing mimi spirits and the Tasmanian tiger—were thought to be at least 20 000 years old. Others, in the famous X-ray style of the Arnhem Land people, showed fish and kangaroos displaying their bones and internal organs. One painting showed a European sailing ship, and a figure with his hands in his pockets, smoking a pipe. Beside him were depicted a gun and an axe. These objects were indicative not only of the Europeans' dangerous potential but of their material superiority. At the time these pictures were drawn, the Gagadju had no pottery, no clothes, certainly no money, no written records and only a few disposable tools, weapons and metal implements that they traded from the Indonesian islands to the north. Just as it is difficult to comprehend the spiritual complexity of their culture, so it is hard for us to imagine their relative material simplicity. After the arrival of the First Fleet in Sydney Harbour, for example, one local from the Eora tribe burnt himself attempting to lift a fish from a cooking pot—he had not encountered boiling water before, never having had a container of any sort in which to hold it. (Although one might wonder about the value of boiling water—many of the indigenous peoples of the Pacific and

Australia, used to eating their flavorous foods raw or baked, were bemused by the desire of the English to boil everything to a limp and watery sameness.)

The man with his hands in his pocket depicted on the wall at Ubirr must have been a source of wonderment to the Gagadju, who assumed at first that clothes were an integral part of this strange human (one of Captain Cook's mariners had been ordered to drop his pants to satisfy Eora Aboriginal curiosity, and much embarrassed had demonstrated his manhood to cries of approval). This was so-called contact art, representing the first contact of native Australians with Europeans. The term was sadly innocuous. What the rock art at Ubirr showed was the arrival of Aboriginal doom: a now terribly ironic interpretation of the apparently friendly white man, lazily smoking, standing casually on the edge of a newly discovered continent with his gun and his English sense of superiority.

These rock paintings also testified to their own decline as an art form. Although bark painting had remained popular among Arnhem Land peoples, rock art had virtually disappeared since the arrival of Europeans on the continent. One of the few exceptions was the vast array of paintings at Nourlangie Rock, also in Kakadu. Although this was a site dating back thousands of years, most of the paintings were done in 1964 by Nayombolmi (known to Europeans as Barramundi Charlie), and depicted—perhaps not surprisingly—dangerous spirits, the lightning man, doomed people going to a ceremony.

To me this was Kakadu, indeed the outback: an old, worn-down country that seemed inadvertently to have survived some terrible disaster; and an old, outnumbered race of ancient people swept aside by the changing tides of history— as a Celt I could appreciate that. The vibrant energy of the rock paintings was merely secondary: in my eyes it seemed tempered by a melancholy not originally intended but now evoked by historical hindsight. So too did the landscape (outlined in the same traditional Aboriginal colours of black and red, ochre and white) appear melancholy. The paperbark trees, with their narrow grey leaves and their cream bark crumbling and peeling, seemed struck with a wasting disease;

ghost gums haunted the flood plains, with pale white bark and timber red as blood. Patrick White, Australia's Nobel Prize-winning novelist, once described native Australian trees as 'professional martyrs': no description could be more apt.

After viewing the rock art, Nicola, Mike and I climbed Ubirr Rock, a great mound of tumbled stones on the edge of the escarpment. From the top of the hill there was a magnificent view over Kakadu in the clear light of the dying day. Vast flood plains green as Ireland, fringed by straggling copses of gum trees that outlined the vast extent of the wet season flood waters; scrub-land turning brown, parched of colour; and in the distance the sandstone wall of the Arnhem Land Escarpment, its valleys hiding lush patches of tropical rainforest while its top was crowned by arid bush and grasses.

I sat on the summit and watched the cockatoos wheeling against the cliff face. Nicola and Mike had been scrupulously polite to each other all day, like old friends who had become business rivals caught in the throes of a take-over bid. Their good humour on Darwin's beaches and pubs had grown to annoyance in the confines of the campervan. Now they roamed about with their tripods and lenses, taking photos and studiously avoiding each other. Finally they sat down on separate rocks, staring out over the flood plains.

The approach of evening brought lightning, which lit up huge areas of billowing, jaundiced clouds like Halloween lanterns, and sometimes escaped from behind the clouds to fork silently across the sky, releasing vast quantities of tropical energy. There was no rain at this season, only towering cliffs of fluffy cumulus rising hundreds of metres into the sky. Two sheets of blue—the sky and the flood plains hazy in the evening light—met on the horizon, broken only by the verticals of the solitary gum trees. It could almost have been a Monet painting, but no European view could have matched that tropical light: the blue almost palpable in the air, intense, luminescent, like a distillation of all the colours of blue to give something that was neither blue nor purple nor indigo but some perfect mix. In those moments outback Australia was suffused in dying light, a blue the colour of melancholia; blue like a relationship falling reluctantly apart.

As dark drew in, the few tourists were left to stumble back down these hills of worn-down rock, past the fading patterns of Aboriginal paintings, while the wind sighed through the hidden valleys and parrots shrieked like banshees among the eucalyptus trees.

Aboriginal Australians inhabited both the real outback and the outback of the country's imagination. In reality most Australians looked down on indigenous peoples, despising their alcoholism, poverty, apparent indolence and lack of material advancement, rarely acknowledging as individuals (though the government had done so) that Anglo-Saxons were largely responsible for the condition of Australia's native people. In the landscape of the imagination, however, Aboriginal Australians were admired for their long culture, their creation legends, their rock art and their intimate knowledge of outback survival: they still were the noble savages once so fashionable in England in Georgian times. (Indeed, early sketches of Aboriginal Australians showed them as proud, strong warriors, posed with spears and reminiscent of heroes on Greek friezes; but these were soon replaced, in a startling volte-face, by miserable-looking creatures with tangled hair and scrawny limbs.)

This was another Australian paradox: Aboriginal people were at once feared and admired, despised and yet promoted in advertising as a romantic symbol of this vast nation, materially poor (and therefore clearly uncivilised in this era of rampant materialism) but spiritually advanced—and perhaps in those terms favoured with a secret to life that fascinated urbanites. Australians seemed to see no apparent contradiction in admiring Aboriginal art, having examples of it in their museums and travelling hundreds of kilometres to see it on the sides of cliffs, and yet treating the creators of such art as inferior beings.

Indigenous Australians had been on the continent far longer than anyone else—had been living in Kakadu for possibly 50 000 years—but had only legally become Australian citizens in 1967. Only in 1992 had the High Court rejected the concept of Australia as *terra nullius*, a legal fiction under which the early colonists had asserted that the indigenous people had no claim to the land because they did not cultivate it. Deliberating on the Mabo case, the High Court had found that the Mer people (a group from the Torres Strait Islands) had, in fact, owned their land prior to its annexation by Queensland. This had strengthened the legal position of all Aboriginal Australians. Certainly Aboriginal people now had a political clout far out of proportion to their present numbers. The reasons: white Australian guilt, increasing political agitation among indigenous peoples, and the growing importance of Australia's human rights obligations under international law.

A full quarter of the Northern Territory's population was Aboriginal. There were about 300 living in Kakadu National Park, keeping very much to themselves. Only at the end of our stay, in a remote part of Kakadu little frequented by tourists, did we meet any of Kakadu's traditional landowners. We had driven to a look-out point high above the plain, offering a view down over endless acres of gum trees, to find the vantage point already occupied by five Gagadju. They welcomed us amiably when we climbed out of the van. A man was building up a fire, the woman beside him plucking a bird: the easily recognisable black neck and tail and black-and-white flanks of a magpie goose.

'Stay with us. Bet you haven't tasted magpie goose before,' said the Gagadju man by the fire with casual generosity.

'We're vegetarians,' said Nicola, wrinkling her nose in distaste at the dead bird. The Aboriginals looked baffled at the whims of the white woman but politely made no comment.

'Oh, well. My mate will take you to see the view. It's better round there through the trees a bit.'

Nicola and Mike ambled off with one of the men. I lingered behind, more interested in conversation than in views.

'I'm not a vegetarian,' I said apologetically.

'That's all right then. Have some goose when it's cooked.'

'I don't know if we can stay that long. Have to set up camp before dark.' I regretted my refusal as soon as I had uttered it.

The woman continued plucking at the magpie goose, sending black and white feathers swirling around her ankles.

Now and then she banged the bird's limp body against a rock.

'Make it tender,' she said, seeing me watching her.

'Hard to catch those birds?'

'Easy, especially at this time of year. The flood plains have dried up now and there are only a few remaining areas of water left, so they're crowded with birds, see? Nice and fat too; they've just had a few months of good eating during the Wet.'

The woman threw the bird on to the top of the fire to singe off the remaining feathers, keeping a hold of its head and turning it slowly on the handle of its long neck. I looked out over the tree-covered plains, hazy in the heat.

'Are those all ghost gums?'

'Not those ones. Them over there though,' said the man, swinging his hand round and pointing towards the left. 'Good sap, ghost gums. Keeps away leeches in the wet season. Antiseptic too.'

'Is that so?' I marvelled.

'Yep. Bark's good for colds and all. Boil it up in water and make an infusion,' the woman imparted casually.

'Do you all live in Kakadu?'

'Yes. This is our home.' The man stared out with quiet pride over the long, pale line of the escarpment and the tumble of trees over the valley: thousands of square kilometres of back yard. 'And you?'

'Irish.'

'Irish?' The Gagadju man wondered about the location of Ireland and I enlightened him. Never having lived there myself, I rarely felt perturbed that many of the people I met travelling in various countries had never heard of this chilly island, a mere one-sixteenth the size of the Northern Territory, on the far side of the planet.

The woman by the fire digested my geographical information without comment. There was a silence broken by the sound of sizzling goose feathers.

'You like Kakadu?' one of the men asked.

'Yes,' I said slowly. 'I wasn't sure at first. But it grows on you. It's a very beautiful . . . very powerful landscape.'

The Gagadju man grinned happily. 'You're welcome. You're welcome to stay here and enjoy it.'

'Thank you,' I replied, accepting the privilege.

There were crocodile warning signs by the banks of the rivers and billabongs of Kakadu. I copied one down:

- Seek local or expert advice before swimming, camping, fishing or boating.
- Look out for large crocodiles, especially when children or pets are near the water.
- Large salt-water crocodiles have no fear of humans and will swim towards small boats, so keep clear.
- Don't paddle, clean fish, prepare food or camp at the water's edge. Fill a bucket with water and do your chores at least 50 metres away, but don't return regularly to the same spot at the water's edge.
- Don't lean over the edge of a boat or stand on logs overhanging the water.
- Stand at least a few metres back from the water's edge when fishing.
- Dispose of food scraps, fish offal and other wastes properly and away from your camp site. Don't feed crocodiles.

I found it odd to think that anyone should take it into their head to feed a crocodile, as if it were a deer in a botanical garden. Much to our disappointment we had not seen any of the reptiles in any case, though in our imaginations every river bank was crawling with crocodiles and danger lurked, omnipresent, at every sight of water.

Finally we joined other avid crocodile-spotters and took a boat out on Yellow Waters very early one morning, when the air was cold and crisp and the globe of the sun was only just rising above the horizon, staining the sky and water orange. As the Gagadju man I met had said, the waterways were crowded at this season with birds that had followed the receding floods: rainbow bee-eaters, herons, egrets, eagles,

kites, pelicans, brolgas, parrots of every description, jabiru
(the stork-like birds that have given their name to Jabiru, the
only town in Kakadu), Jesus birds that walk on the water-
lilies with their delicate, widely spread toes, kookaburras,
owls roosting in the shade. Kakadu, with over 260 species, is
a bird-spotter's paradise, and when we finally did see crocodiles, half submerged in the water, eyes gold flecked with
black, they seemed little more than an optional extra, a
momentary *frisson* of excitement among the abundance of
multicoloured waterfowl.

'If you're lost in the outback you can find water by
following birds,' suggested the boat operator. 'Birds such as
finches and pigeons fly fast towards water sources and rather
slowly on the way back home, being replete with water.
Though only seed-eating birds. You wouldn't want to follow
kookaburras or parrots or cockatoos or birds of prey, since
they're insectivores or carnivores and aren't reliable when it
comes to pointing out the location of water.'

How does one tell when a finch is flying quickly and when
it is flying slowly? And how does one follow a fast-flying
bird through the tangled undergrowth and gum trees of the
outback? As information this was interesting enough but
not, I thought, entirely practical. I puzzled over it as we
floated over the limpid water, the reflections of trees crystal-
lised in its depths.

'There's another croc,' said the guide casually, pointing out
a mottled snout lurking under the water-lily pads. He was
virtually the only Australian I had met, I suddenly realised,
who did not warn us about the dangers of the outback.

'Beautiful creatures, crocodiles,' he merely commented.
'Dinosaurs really, over a hundred million years old as a
species. Supremely adapted to their environment. I've always
found it strange that people hate crocs so much, consider
them evil almost. Should admire them, really, just as we
admire other predators—lions, tigers, bears.'

That evening we camped near a creek, a safe fifty metres
from the water as recommended by the warning signs. Mike
had buried his head in the engine, up to his elbows in black
grease. I had settled down on a camp-stool, a bowl of water
on my lap, peeling potatoes for the dinner. Nicola, on the

river side of the campervan, was pegging out clothes on a washing line strung between two trees when suddenly she let out a violent yell that froze my heart.

'Crocodile!' she bawled, and in what seemed like one leap was in through the van door. 'Crocodile, get in!'

I jumped up, slopping water and potatoes at my feet, Nicola's shriek ringing in my ears, and followed Mike into the back of the campervan, slamming the door behind us.

There was a heavy, petrified silence as we all stared at each other, aghast but excited.

'Crocodile!' gulped Nicola. 'Just right there in those bushes.'

'Did you actually see it?'

'Yes. Big shape coming right up this way.'

We sat peering out the windows into the undergrowth for ten minutes, not seeing the slightest movement.

'There it is!' Nicola cried out, pointing into the long grass under the ghost gums. Mike and I gazed at the mottled browns and greens, the ambiguous cross-hatchings of the shadows.

'Don't see anything.' Despite this I was genuinely unnerved at the thought of an unseen four-metre reptile possibly creeping towards us.

'Right there. You can see its eye.'

Neither Mike nor I could see a crocodile, never mind a crocodile's eye, but Nicola was so adamant that we remained in the campervan for another twenty minutes, getting steadily hotter under the metal roof.

'I'm getting out,' announced Mike irritably, wiping the perspiration from his forehead and leaving it decorated with a smear of black grease.

'You'll end up like Beryl.'

'Who the heck's Beryl?'

'A woman eaten by a crocodile on the Daintree River in Queensland,' said Nicola. I related the story to him in more depth, down to the polished fingernails. Mike lapsed into silence and stared out the window. He made no more moves towards the door. We all sat on uncomfortably.

'Well, maybe I didn't actually *see* anything,' admitted Nicola at last. 'But I *heard* it.'

There was a sigh of exasperation. 'Heard what?'

'A rustling.'

'Do crocodiles rustle?' said Mike sarcastically. His irritation now seemed more directed at my sister's near presence than at the situation in which we found ourselves; from their constant carping I was aware that their relationship was deteriorating rapidly.

'There was a rustling.'

'Are you stupid or something?' said Mike. It was one of his stock phrases when he was seriously annoyed.

None of us was quite sure if a crocodile rustled. More time passed before we decided that we would have to get out of the campervan or remain imprisoned for the rest of the day, with our food and most of our equipment scattered outside.

'Send Mike out first,' I said. 'He's so skinny. Crocodiles always go for the smallest victim.' Nicola gave a nervous giggle.

We stood in a huddle by the door, listening. Over in the grasses something did indeed rustle. And in a decorous line, five small birds with the look of partridges came bustling innocently out of the undergrowth.

Heading south-west, we left Kakadu to pick up sealed road again on the Stuart Highway near Pine Creek, a former mining town dating from the gold rush of the last century. It was the discovery of gold by an engineering party sent out to work on the Overland Telegraph line that generated the settlement of the Northern Territory, and particularly the development of the mining industry, which is still a vital part of its economy, contributing a staggering 80 per cent of its gross value of production. Mining here had initially been dominated by the Chinese who flocked in, largely from Singapore, and who numbered 6000 in the Territory by 1888 —six times the number of Europeans then living there. The South Australian government planned to base the development of mining on Chinese labour, but a backlash from white settlers put paid to the plan. Later, legislation was enacted preventing the further entry of the Chinese and banning them from holding mining licences, so that they had to work for the Europeans. There was a sharp decline in the Chinese population and, for a period, in mining production. Anti-Chinese sentiment continued to rise until the turn of the century, when tubs of cyanide were placed out in the streets in Pine Creek and Brock's Creek in the vain hope that the towns' drunks would kill themselves, and the Chinese would either kill each other or the local indigenous people.

'The Chinese normally worked in teams of thirty and would carry two tons of equipment and supplies from Darwin to Pine Creek.' This from George Masters, a local historian. I had an introduction to him from a friend of a friend of my brother, and had buttonholed him in his office in Darwin, pestering him with questions. He had answered patiently, with slow and careful thoughtfulness.

'How long would it take from Darwin to Pine Creek?'

'Oh—between two and three weeks, I imagine. And that with a ration of a bag of rice each. They usually had one white man with a gun to protect them from the Aboriginal tribes, who had become increasingly hostile.'

The heat and the emptiness, the dangerous creatures and aggressive Aboriginal Australians: this was northern Queensland all over again in a different, but equally demanding, setting. I was amazed at the resourcefulness of the Chinese, here at the far ends of the earth.

'Yes,' said George contemplatively. He ran a hand through his hair and shifted in his chair. 'Not all of them survived, of course. The bodies of Chinese prospectors, and Europeans too for that matter, were often found in the bush. But as the Chinese were well known to smuggle gold illegally back to Canton or Singapore, the diggers who found their bodies often cremated them on the spot and panned the ashes. There was one recorded case of three Chinese bodies yielding fifteen ounces of gold.'

'How grotesque!'

'Mm. But of course they must have thought it was worth the hardship and risks, because they got the chance to fossick around Pine Creek. There were always those who struck gold and returned home wealthy men.'

Later, when I had taken pity on him and we had retired to a café: 'They mostly did go home, the Chinese?'

'Yes. That particularly characterised the Chinese immigrants—they were always temporary, though "temporary" sometimes meant twenty years.'

'But conditions and various laws made it difficult for them to stay.'

'Increasingly, yes. But even in the early days the majority returned voluntarily to China. There were always exceptions —there are numbers of third- and fourth-generation Chinese in Australia—but it wasn't really until the 1970s that Asians started coming here as permanent settlers in large numbers.'

'Is that why they seem so overlooked in the history of Australia?'

'Perhaps one of the reasons. Though I wouldn't say over-looked, especially not in the mining industry. Perhaps just underestimated and under-recognised.'

Now, ironically, the Northern Territory's economy de-pended on Japan, which bought much of its minerals. There was also once again a higher proportion of Asian immigrants here than in any other Australian State. Mining in the Northern Territory was booming once again, but production in Pine Creek peaked at the turn of the century and had long ago ceased. The town hardly deserved the description any more: just a stop on the Stuart Highway, an inconsequential backwater scattered with abandoned but solid-looking stone buildings left over from its days of glory. It was a dry and forgotten place, with streets of dust and wooden houses, giving it the look of a film set for some budget Western. If one had to stop here at all, there seemed little enough to do but drink, as Eddy had done when Nicola and I had passed through with him on our way up to Darwin. Now we followed his memory back into the pub, hung with metal street signs and stuffed animals, and drank to the successful conclusion of our first dirt-road journey.

Later I wandered around, fossicking for the remains of Chinese camps: stone sleeping platforms which offered pro-tection from flooding in the wet season, the crumbling walls of old dams, the shafts of the industriously dug mines. Old nails had been found here, handmade by Chinese miners, as well as the occasional tool; but it was a melancholy search, in the dust and the heat, and offered no hint of the human struggles of these early immigrants.

It was a smooth ride back down as far as Katherine. This area had been first explored by Europeans—more exactly by one of early Australia's famous figures, Ludwig Leichhardt—in 1844. Katherine had only received its name later, after the daughter of a wealthy South Australian who had financed some of the journeys of another well-known explorer, John McDouall Stuart.

Little more than a stopping-post on the Stuart Highway and a supply centre for outlying cattle stations and Aboriginal reserves, Katherine was nevertheless renowned for its gorges, which lay some kilometres distant from the town. This series of gorges had been cut by the permanent waters of the Katherine River; flood waters in the gorge during the wet season could rise an astounding eighteen metres. It was another area of beauty lost in the immensity of an often monotonous outback: a meandering river haunted by fresh-water crocodiles, heated scrub-land alive with dancing white butterflies, great crumbling cliffs of red rock. There was a deep silence after the day-trippers had gone, the pale gum trees, the ancient, eroded cliffs cracking under a hot sun. Held up by a delayed bank transfer, we camped for days by the river, photographing blue-winged kookaburras ('Not the kind that laugh,' Nicola told me with authority when I commented on their silence), bower-birds and the wallabies that crept out of the bush in the evening, grazing under the shadows of the rocks.

From Katherine one either went north to Darwin, south towards Alice Springs or west to Kununurra: the three narrow strips of tarmac met unheralded in this dusty town of garages and supermarkets. Back in the town, on the watered green strip dividing the main street, Aboriginal men were still squatting placidly, waving away flies and gazing into the middle distance as they had been when Nicola and I had hitched through weeks ago.

From here on, much of our route would be distant from major habitation, shops or garages. The next sizeable town we would pass through was Broome on the far-off Western Australian coast; on our way there we were intending to traverse the Kimberleys, a remote region of scattered cattle stations, few of which lay directly on the route that we would follow. In Katherine, having finally wrested money from the bank, Nicola and I raided the supermarket, stocking up on tins and packets of pasta and rice. Mike roamed the garages, buying tools; I made a check-list from my outback survival book.

'Wire cutters?' I asked Mike.

'No.'

'Spanners?'

'Yes, got a set of those.'

'Fan belt?'

'Yes. And engine oil and brake fluid,' added Mike, flinging two metal containers into the back of the van.

'Hacksaw blade?'

'No.'

'Hammer and chisel?'

'No,' muttered Mike, rattling a few pieces of metal together as if adding something to the tool box. I was not fooled.

'Set of feeler gauges? Vulcanising clamp? Radiator hoses? Set of distributor points?' I demanded, firing out the alien words with relish.

'No. No. No,' replied Mike, looking hassled again.

'And a shovel,' I concluded.

'Shovel? What's the use of a shovel?'

'Dig our own graves,' I prophesied laconically. 'After we've broken down in the middle of nowhere without a proper tool kit.'

'Are you stupid or something?'

We rattled out of Katherine early on the morning of my birthday, weighed down with baked beans and sacks of rice and gallons of water.

'"Be careful not to overload your vehicle,"' I quoted pessimistically, reading once more out of *Absalom's Guide to Safe Outback Travel* as we trundled slowly westwards. '"If you hit a gutter in an outback road and the car is overloaded, you stand a good chance of breaking springs and blowing tyres."'

'Shut up, you old moan,' said Mike agreeably.

Nicola pressed down on the accelerator and the ancient VW surged forward in a burst of speed, ninety kilometres an hour flat out towards Western Australia.

gibb river road

If there were marvellous landscapes hidden in the outback wilderness, there were also, in between, vast areas of relentless emptiness. We could drive for hours and hours, even an entire day, and see little more than a couple of road-houses rising up through the shimmering heat, ugly oases of corrugated iron and neon lighting. After hours of driving on a straight strip of tarmac, blinding in the heat, we would look forward to these road-houses with an absurd interest: but they consisted of little more than a couple of petrol pumps, a small shop stocked with cold drinks and stale Cadbury's chocolate bars, a sad-looking camp-site under half-a-dozen sparse eucalyptus trees. They were not places designed for lingering, and after a few minutes we would drive on in disappointment.

We were to experience thousands of kilometres of such uncompromising monotony before reaching Sydney, none more daunting than on that first day when we headed out from Katherine in such high adventure. Both the road and the countryside were flat, flat and featureless as far as the eye (squinting against the glare) could see; so flat one might almost have seen the earth's curve but for the shimmering hot air that dragged the horizon in close. Few trees, no hills, no houses, no animals, no electricity cables, no fences, rare signposts, only the odd straggling line of telephone poles staked out across the middle of nowhere, heading towards some distant station: a landscape plucked clean of all that was familiar, leaving an emptiness that gaped open as a wound. It was an intimidating flatness, a vast sky that pressed down all day until the long-awaited cool of evening, when the hot air was finally flung up in vast sparks of red sunset and the twilight beaten into flakes of fire.

Flat and silent, not a sound but the drone of our own motor, and when we finally stopped by the roadside for the night a silence so palpable it almost became a sound in its own right. True, there was a defiant chirping of cicadas and other insects, miniature musicians struggling against the emptiness that surrounded them: but after a while one realised how thin and fragile a music it was, against the ever-continuing yawning sound of silence. I couldn't remember which composer it was who said the important part of his music was the spaces between the notes, but it was certain that in the outback the quiet was a symphony in itself, evocative of various moods: sometimes peaceful, sometimes mysterious, often threatening.

On my birthday, that first day out of Katherine, the sunset was particularly fierce, setting the horizon aglow with uninhibited displays of red and purple. Tired from a day's driving, demoralised by the emptiness, we sat by the campervan drinking vodka and orange, produced by Mike and Nicola for the occasion in memory of my birthday the previous year, which the three of us had also spent together, in China. There, for want of any alternative, I had been obliged to make up the orange from a bottle of Chinese drinking powder. Now we had fresh orange, chilled in our fridge; smug with the decadence of it all, here in the middle of nowhere, we toasted away the dying day. The endless expanse of the sky, which had been almost white during the heat of the day, turned an immense blue, suffusing the landscape in an eerie glow that was almost physical. Then the sky started turning yellow on the horizon, burning into orange like an edge of paper held to flames, finally exploding into a great fiery display of scarlet, red, rust and finally purple and mauve as the last light slipped down behind the hills. Then, as if the sunset had been shattered into glittering white sparks, the stars emerged, splashing the heavens with extravagant swathes of crystal light.

Most of the vodka had vanished and the sky had darkened, reluctantly giving up the last streaks of colour, when we heard a van approaching us, its wheels crunching over the gravel at the road's edge. We had retired inside our own van by then, draping the windows and door with mosquito nets. We heard footsteps approaching and a rap on the side of our vehicle.

'Anyone there?'

We decanted ourselves from the van to be confronted by an elderly couple. Like many Australians of a certain age the man was wearing shorts and knee-length white socks, giving him the air of an overgrown schoolboy. His wife had pure white hair, cropped stylishly short, and a pair of immense horn-rimmed glasses that magnified her eyes and suggested permanent amazement.

'Hope you don't mind if we share your space,' the man said cordially.

Actually I did mind: I felt that in the immensity of the outback there was little necessity for anyone to camp up our rear bumper. But I did not say so. I gazed at the couple benignly through a haze of vodka.

'It's just that we were camping a little further back,' said the woman. 'But then we saw a car full of Aborigines passing by. What with them being all drunk, we felt a little unsafe. We started worrying about it, about what might happen if they came back the same way, because they must have seen us . . .'

I rolled my eyes at Nicola and at the bottle of vodka sitting on the table inside the campervan.

'It's not that we have anything against the Abos,' said her husband disingenuously. 'But they get violent when they're drunk. Can't hold their drink. Real two-pot screamers.'

This description was so delightful I wanted to write it down in my notebook immediately, but the woman was still wittering on about Aboriginal Australians. 'Layabouts, up to no good,' she was saying firmly. 'So now in case they find us at least we're five.'

Mike was making reassuring noises. I stared at the retirees silently. Five white people in the outback, surrounded by hostile tribes of natives. I giggled inwardly. I had no reason to believe we would be attacked, nor that these people passing in a car would even be the least bit interested in finding us.

I simply wondered, with curiosity, where roistering people might be going along this road at this time of night.

'The Aboriginals of Far North Queensland used to hang the Chinese from trees by their pigtails,' I said tipsily, 'before they—' But a sharp dig in the ribs from Nicola and I fell silent. The woman ('Call me Sarah') harangued us at length on the low nature of indigenous people: their laziness, alcoholism, the way they took advantage of social security (bludging, she called it), the disgrace of having Aboriginal reserves where ordinary Australians (in their very own country!) were not allowed without permission. Her attitude was not unusual, but I thought it sad. Aboriginal Australians had the worst housing conditions, literacy rates, unemployment levels and education of any ethnic group on the continent. They also had the worst health care, infant mortality rates and adult life expectancy of any people in the whole of the developed world. Two hundred years of European settlement in Australia had done little, if anything, for these ancient people (in fact their sometimes ruthless eradication, especially in Tasmania, gave the lie to the comfortable myth that British colonialism was generally benign), and I thought the woman's opinions showed a lack of understanding of the history of her own country, though I knew there was little point in saying so.

'I've got a shotgun,' said her husband ('And I'm Martin'). He heaved it out of his van and waved it about in front of him as if it were a Zulu knobkerrie.

'Not that I'd use it, mind you. But just in case.'

Sarah and Martin had sold their house and put their furniture in storage. Like those other retirees, Richard and Mary, they were intending to travel for a year in order to see something of their own vast country. They had driven up from Melbourne, through the Red Centre, and had also been to Kakadu National Park. Now they were heading towards the Western Australian coast.

'We'll stick to the surfaced road, round by Halls Creek and Fitzroy Crossing. Steer clear of the Kimberleys. Don't think our van would make it along the Gibb River Road.'

I looked at their spanking new Toyota campervan with its windscreen shield and kangaroo bar and two spare tyres and metal drums of extra petrol, and then back at our own twenty-year-old bus. I was sure they had a tool kit replete with vulcanising clamps, radiator hoses and even a shovel.

'We're doing the Gibb River Road. We'd like to see the Kimberleys,' said Mike confidently. The couple looked at us fondly, smiling. They did not offer any comment: I knew they thought us irresponsible and possibly of unsound mind.

It suddenly dawned on me that all these wandering retired couples were not, after all, really leaving home. Their spirit of adventure was to be admired, but after all they carried their homes with them: spacious new campers or caravans replete with televisions, microwave ovens, photos of their children. In Europe one could barely travel 300 kilometres without meeting a new language, new culture, new food. In Australia you could be 3000 kilometres from Melbourne, and although the landscape was different the country remained fundamentally the same. The people still spoke English, you could still go to Woolworth's and McDonald's, you could still buy Heinz baked beans and Vegemite and Arnott's biscuits, the TV channels had only slight regional variations—all the familiar frames of reference were intact. The only thing they didn't have much of in Melbourne was Aboriginal people: and this couple were afraid of the Aboriginals, the unknown element outside their experience.

'Pommies, are you?' we were asked later on.

'A curious word, Pommy,' I commented, without answering the question.

Martin ventured: 'It is said that when the early convicts arrived in Sydney, their faces were red with sunburn so they looked like pomegranates. Hence Poms.'

I had heard this before, but I was not taken by the explanation. I did not think pomegranates were a fruit that sprang easily to the minds of Englishmen. Apples or tomatoes seemed like a more obvious choice.

'Then they would have been called Toms!' exclaimed Mike.

'Actually, that is another theory,' said Martin cordially, 'though not from tomatoes. Some people think Pommy is a corruption of Tommy, the slang word for British soldiers.'

Later on, the remaining vodka hidden away in the cupboard, we looked at the night sky together: a vast display of stars and moonlight that dusted the gum trees with silver shadows and added glamour and intimacy to a landscape so often harsh and exposed during the day.

'The Southern Cross.' Sarah pointed to where it hung in the sky like a benediction.

'Yes.' The Southern Cross was always disappointing, small and rather insignificant amid the extraordinary Australian blaze of alien stars and constellations. I could see Orion lying on its side, sprawled out of alignment.

'There's a satellite,' said her husband, pointing his finger up into the night sky.

'Couldn't be,' I said doubtfully. I had not realised one could see satellites. 'Must be a plane.'

'Be fairly off course if it was. Too high, too fast. And plane lights wink. It's a satellite all right. You can see plenty of them. There's another one.'

Once you knew what you were looking for, they were easy to see. We watched the tiny dots of light skimming across the blackness like wandering stars lost against the Milky Way. I could almost forgive having my birthday celebrations interrupted: I had never seen satellites before. I peered upwards until my neck ached, marvelling. It might be a spy satellite, I mused, and peering down with its infrared sights it would detect upturned, wondering faces, pinpoints of humanity stranded in the middle of a great expanse of nothingness.

Next day the flatness continued and the heat built up, flowing through the windows of our van like great blasts from an open oven. This semi-arid land, often used for grazing, was prone to drought—in the past century Australia had suffered no less than seven major national droughts, as well as innumerable others affecting particular areas—and even now the land appeared parched and cracked. After we decided to stop for lunch we drove on for nearly another hour, searching for trees by the roadside substantial enough to offer us a modicum of protection from the sun. Like the jolly swagman in 'Waltzing Matilda', we would have preferred a coolabah tree, which had spreading branches and provided good shade.

Luckless, we finally halted under two straggling eucalypts that threw a reluctant pattern of inadequate shadow, delicate against the noonday sun. A dilapidated barbed-wire fence meandered through the grass and bushes; on the other side, in the distance under another tree, a lone cow stood motionless, head sunk in torpor, solitary representative of Australia's great herds. They rounded up cattle by helicopter in these parts, the thousands of animals lost, like this one, in the immensity of the outback.

For the purposes of pest control, fruit and vegetables would be confiscated on the Western Australian border, which we would cross later that day. We boiled the last of our remaining potatoes, the gas ring adding to the heat inside the van. We sat fanning ourselves, perspiration trickling down our backs, eyes screwed up even behind sun-glasses against the white glare of the sun. Suddenly, shimmering along through the oily air rising off the tarmac, a woman appeared on a bicycle. She was wearing a wide canvas hat with a flap down the nape of her neck, a pink T-shirt and tight black cycling shorts. Wisps of wet hair hung down across her cheeks. On the back of her bicycle, hanging down each side, were heavy panniers (one emblazoned with the Stars and Stripes) and two enormous water bottles.

The three of us stared at her in amazement as she approached out of the wilderness, shimmering along in the heat almost as if floating above the road surface. The thought passed through my head that we should call out to her, offer her lunch or maybe just some water to refill her bottles, but so great was my surprise at her appearance that I was dumbstruck. She pedalled past us, looking neither left nor right, ignoring our presence. Silently we watched her vanish along the road, to be swallowed up once more by the dancing heat.

After lunch we overtook the brave cyclist ('Do you want some water?' 'No.') and drove on. We crossed the State border, surrendering our potato peelings to a Ministry of Agriculture official and turning our watches back by ninety minutes. We drove on and on without seeing a single house or building.

Some time later, towards evening, we entered the small town of Kununurra, gateway to the Kimberleys.

The expansive grasslands of the Kimberley region had long made the north-west corner of Australia an area of great agricultural potential. Pastoralists began settling there more than a hundred years ago, droving their herds of cattle vast distances to markets far to the south. Real development, however, was only spurred during the 1960s with the completion of the long-dreamed-of Ord River dam, supplying year-round irrigation. Sunflowers, bananas, soy beans, corn, melons and peanuts were now all grown around Kununurra, the town established to service the Ord Irrigation Project.

Kununurra was a small town of only 4000 people, with a school and hospital, supermarkets, banks, two camping grounds, a hotel. Employees of the spectacularly rich Argyle diamond mines, lost in the outback some distance away, came here for the entertainment. Just as in Mount Isa, you could water-ski near by: Lake Argyle, formed by the dam, had made water recreation popular in Kununurra, which was uncomfortably close to Wyndham, one of the hottest towns in all Australia. Promotional material claimed Lake Argyle to be the largest man-made body of water in the southern hemisphere, nine times larger in volume than Sydney Harbour. The comparison was all that lent glamour to the region, too remote for the expensive Ord project ever to have been viable. Kununurra and its farms were but a small oasis in the great remoteness of Australia's north, pinned between the Kimberley Ranges and the Great Sandy Desert, and entirely cut off from populated regions thousands of kilometres away to the south.

What Kununurra did have was a tourist office where one could check up on the state of the unsurfaced Gibb River Road, which cut through the Kimberleys for nearly 700 kilometres before meeting up again with the surfaced highway that meandered in a great loop to the south, between the Kimberley Plateau and the desert.

'The road surface is fine at the moment,' the woman in the tourist office assured us. She had a face burnt dark in the sun, paler around the eyes where sun-glasses had protected her skin. 'In fact it has just been graded, so it might be rather corrugated, but otherwise it's dry and passable. Of course the road conditions can change very quickly. You do of course have a four-wheel drive?'

'Ah. No.'

When she heard this the tourist official began thrusting leaflets at us, offering us scenic flights over the Bungle Bungles and the Ord River valley, as if she didn't really believe we would be foolish enough to abandon the highway.

'Is there anywhere we can get petrol on the Gibb River Road?'

The woman pursed her lips. 'It's *possible*,' she said, as if speculating on the arrival of manna in the wilderness. 'Some of the stations out there might have some, but they won't necessarily want to sell it. It depends on when they had their last delivery.' Her tone of voice gave us reason to imagine this event may have been decades ago.

Mike and Nicola and I looked at each other in consternation. Not having a roof-rack, we could not take extra petrol; carrying it in the interior was impractical from the point of view of space, smell and safety.

'You'd need to carry enough fuel to take you seven hundred kilometres on unsurfaced road,' suggested the woman. 'Until you get to Fitzroy Crossing or Derby.'

We peered at the large-scale map of the Kimberleys pinned to the wall, tracing the Gibb River Road across river-beds and through worn-down mountain ranges. Then we wandered around the limited racks of tourist brochures. I plucked out a paper on the Kimberleys. *Carry sufficient water and food to last 3 to 4 days longer than anticipated*, the information hinted unnervingly.

As an afterthought the woman cautioned as we were leaving: 'Look out for wildlife and stock when driving! Most of the roads in the Kimberleys are unfenced.'

There were close to a hundred pastoral leases in the Kimberleys and a total of 600 000 head of cattle: the Gibb River Road had been constructed to transport beef to ports at Derby and Wyndham. Other parts of this area larger than the United Kingdom were nature reserves, or were so remote that they had not been visited since the indigenous peoples of the region abandoned them over sixty years earlier to live on European missions and settlements. Even the cattle stations, for the most part, did not lie directly on the Gibb River Road, but were merely linked to it by narrow, rutted tracks that wound away and disappeared into remote valleys.

The roads might have been unfenced, and there might have been more than half a million cattle somewhere; but we were only to see a dozen cows along the entire 700-kilometre length of the Kimberley track.

We pulled out of Kununurra the next morning, Mike at the wheel, with mixed feelings of reckless excitement and apprehension. We had decided to risk obtaining petrol somewhere; other inhabitants of Kununurra had appeared more sanguine about the prospect than the tourist official. Our petrol tank was full to near overflow, our water canisters bulging, the fridge stuffed with the last fresh food we would be able to buy until we reached Broome on the still-distant west coast.

El Questro was the first station along the Gibb River Road, and although it was not far we intended stopping there for the night. Mike turned off the main road towards the homestead, driving along a precarious and rutted red dirt track for some twenty kilometres. Finally he jolted to a halt, confronted by a river, on the other side of which the track re-emerged and vanished into the trees.

'We'll need to test the depth before we drive across it,' I said. Nicola and Mike looked at me expectantly.

'Oh, all right.' I jumped out of the van and began to pick my way across the rocks. The water was not deep, but the river-bed was a jumbled mass of stones and boulders, entirely unsuitable for our elderly campervan. I stood in the middle of the river uncertainly.

'Are there any crocodiles in the Kimberleys?' Nicola asked coolly from inside the van.

'Yes, according to the leaflets in the Kununurra tourist office.' But I had not thought about them until now. Freshwater crocodiles, I remembered reading, are actually rather common in the Kimberleys, though they are supposedly harmless to humans. There are salt-water crocodiles too in some areas. *Salties*, the Australians call them, making them sound like charming pets. In 1987 in Prince Regent Nature Reserve in the north Kimberleys an American tourist had been attacked and killed by a saltie.

'Ah,' said my sister in acknowledgement when I told her this as I waded on across to the far side of the river.

'I can see the homestead from here,' I called back. 'So I might as well walk. Don't think the van could cope with the river-bed, although the water's pretty shallow.' We would overnight elsewhere on the far-spread station, and had no real reason to cross the river: we only wanted to reach the homestead to apply for camping permission.

'I'll come with you,' answered Nicola. She waded across the stream with indecent haste, stumbling in her anxiety to avoid prospective crocodiles.

We walked along the track towards the buildings in the distance. It was very quiet. There were several paddocked fields but no animals to be seen. Australian outback farms— or stations—were all fairly similar: a homestead, quarters for the hands (the manager, jackeroos, mechanics, a cook, a housekeeper, a governess, depending on the station's size), a garage and machine shop. On a sheep station there would be shearing sheds and shearers' quarters too.

El Questro's buildings, sitting in a sea of dust, were completely silent. We stood awkwardly, waiting for someone to appear. Finally a woman emerged from one of the buildings and approached us: an English university student who had been working on El Questro for three months. Yes, we could camp on station property, she said in response to our query. For a price.

'El Questro's trying to develop its tourist potential,' she added, as if in explanation at the charge.

I stared back at her, at the dusty, dilapidated wooden buildings in the background, at an old Ford with no wheels sitting rusting out in the yard.

'Tourist potential?'

'Well, you're here, aren't you?' The student sounded defensive. I replied that I was, but that apart from our camping fee I would hardly be spending much by way of tourist dollars.

'They're building a hotel and conference centre,' vouched the English girl sullenly. 'There's the hot springs. Horse-riding. Relaxation. Barramundi fishing. Station life.' She said it lifelessly, standing in the debilitating heat surrounded by a silent background of deserted buildings.

'They'd need to build a road. There's a river just back there a little bit,' I observed sarcastically.

'We expect the clients to come in by helicopter,' the English girl said complacently. 'The luxury market.' Her gaze passed over our dusty clothes, and her tongue flicked out like a disapproving lizard spotting a poor relation.

My sister and I fell silent. I could not imagine why anyone would want to have a business conference here in the middle of nowhere. With a mental shrug I handed over a few dollars and the girl logged our names into a big black notebook. Despite the isolation of the place, she seemed uninterested in any more conversation. I felt her inhospitable eyes on our backs as we turned and tramped off down the long dusty track.

'She must be pulling our legs,' said Nicola uncertainly after a while.

We waded back across the river.

The Gibb River Road was made of gravel, clay-pans, loose sand: it took us four unhurried days to drive more than 600 kilometres over pot-holes and fissures and crumbling road edges, around unexpected rocks and through pools of muddy water. Sometimes the road was a great red ribbon of thin, soft dust over a hard-packed surface of natural earth. Because of the dust it was difficult to see the corrugations left by the grading machine that had so recently passed this way. When the van hit them, there was a tremendous rattling: every surface in the vehicle started shuddering, and our saucepans and books were flung off the shelves on to the floor. It was impossible to drive with any speed, and often the corrugations seemed perfectly distanced to cause a maximum amount of vibration. At other times the road was a grey strip of rubble, made up of stones and pebbles that pinged and rattled on the van's under-surface and threatened imminent punctures; and sometimes, infrequently, it was pale sand, causing the wheels to spin and the van to slew violently from side to side.

It was a rugged terrain. We drove across river-beds, dry but for a few remaining pools of water, blue fragments among heaps of stone, and through the eroded hills, purple and rust-red, with gigantic scree slopes topped by sheer cliffs. From the tourist point of view, apart from the novelty of the experience, interest was provided by the many gorges hidden among the valleys. Emma Gorge, near the turn-off to El Questro homestead, was narrow and humid, sheltering tropical vegetation that hid gigantic, tumbled boulders. White butterflies flew among the palms, falling back as the gorge narrowed and became damper. The valley ended in sheer walls—surely an impressive waterfall during the wet season —and a deep pool, black and bitterly cold from lack of sunlight: an almost menacing place, where water trickled eerily but invisibly down a rock face hung with green-black lengths of moss and weed.

Deeper into the Kimberleys, Barnett River, Manning and Galvan's gorges were less intimidating. Indeed they were beautiful places, tight valley ends of plunging rock cupping deep waterholes kept fresh with trickles of moisture that expanded into roaring waterfalls during the Wet. Such lost places were crocodile-free, providing perfect spots for swimming, the cool pools afloat in water-lilies, white with purple edges. Trees, some growing out of the stained rock faces, cast reflections into the still waters. Only the flies disturbed the peace, buzzing in disordered formations around our heads. Only briefly, at Manning Gorge, did we meet any people; on the road we passed but a handful of cars travelling in the opposite direction. The drivers gave us signals of outback acknowledgement, fingers raised off the steering-wheel in salute.

These gorges, with their refreshing water and shaded confines crowded with lush vegetation, offered a well-earned respite from the otherwise unrelieved heat and aridity of the dirt track. Back on the main road we returned to ruts and dust and heat and stones. The van spewed up great clouds of fine red earth that swirled through the open windows, settling on every surface like hundred-year dust in a fairy tale, staining clothes and turning our hair into wire. On the infrequent occasions when another car drove by, we would be momentarily blinded by a great swirl of red powdered earth, while stones kicked up by the wheels ricocheted off the metalwork of our van. Not long after we started down the Gibb River Road one of the supports for our kangaroo bar, its elderly metal troubled by the vibrations, snapped in

half. We carried the heavy metal frame in the back of our
van, heaving it out every time we made a stop: it was a long
way to the nearest repair garage.

Ruts and dust and heat and stones; dry mountains purple
against a harsh sky; grass yellow and brittle as old parchment:

> Here is no water but only rock
> Rock and no water and the sandy road
> The road winding above among the mountains
> Which are mountains of rock without water

It was strange how T. S. Eliot—who as far as I knew had
never been to Australia—inadvertently described the Australian outback so accurately. The Kimberleys were not a Waste
Land, but they had a haunted quality. The bruise-coloured,
eroded mountains smouldered in the sun, and the dried-up
rivers were like wounds dug out of the landscape, devoid of
sustenance.

On the third afternoon, 400 kilometres into the Kimberleys, we turned off the Gibb River Road down a long,
winding track, and camped at Adcock Gorge.

There was another vehicle—a Nissan four-wheel drive—
standing where the track finally petered out, but its passengers
were nowhere to be seen. We parked our van a discreet
distance away, under two baobab trees. These trees, found
only in the Northern Territory and the Kimberleys, have
bulbous, swollen trunks of elephant grey, able to store great
quantities of moisture in order to survive the dry season.
(There is a famous hollow baobab near Derby, fourteen
metres in circumference and thought to be a thousand years
old, formerly used as a temporary jail by the local police.)

After visiting the gorge we returned to the van to prepare
dinner. Mike had decided on baked potatoes, and I volunteered to collect firewood. I wandered about under the
baobab trees, through the long yellow grass, picking up sticks
and pieces of bark that had dried to brittle fragility in the
heat. I came across a circle of stones, charred black, in the
middle of which had been placed a careful bundle of kindling
and three lengths of thick log. Delighted with these leftovers

from someone else's camp-fire, I picked up some of the stones and transferred them to our own site. Then I began tearing the wood apart into manageable lengths.

'I wouldn't do that if I were you.'

I looked up to see a man standing there—presumably the owner of the four-wheel drive and certainly an Australian, with lean rugged looks and a deep tan. He was wearing shorts, big hiking boots with thick woollen socks and a soft leather hat to ward off the sun. A Paul Hogan type, with skin the colour and texture of wood, the deep wrinkles around his eyes betraying long years of outback living, squinting against the harsh sun. (Paul Hogan embodies the characteristics of the outback male fortuitously: Crocodile Dundee was formerly a rigger on Sydney Harbour Bridge.)

'You must be a few sangers short of a picnic to do that.'

'Sorry?'

'A few sangers short of a picnic.'

I crouched among the sticks and stared up at the man in perplexity.

'Sangers. Sandwiches. A few sandwiches short of a picnic.'

I wondered whether I was being particularly obtuse or whether he was as mad as a March hare.

'Daft,' elucidated the man. 'You must be daft turning over those logs and ripping off the bark with your bare hands.'

'Are they yours?' I did not much like people materialising from the wilderness announcing I was daft.

'Nah. It's just that you ought to be careful fossicking for firewood. Snakes and spiders like to hide in places just like that. Poisonous ones. If you ever turn over a stone in the outback, tilt it towards you first, so that spiders escape out in the other direction.

This seemed like good advice to me, though I was not going to admit as much.

'And don't rip off bark with your bare hands and just lift up logs like that. A log could be concealing a mulga snake or a death adder.'

What an ugly name, I thought—death adder. I stood up and edged away from the pile of wood.

'Redbacks like living under bark or in tree stumps,' added the man in the hiking boots relentlessly. He bared his white teeth in what might have been a smile and took off his hat to swat at the flies that were clustered around his face.

Everyone in Australia had heard of redbacks. Cases involving the poisonous bites of these widespread and common spiders outnumbered all the marine stinger and snake emergencies put together.

'There's an antivenom, of course, not that we're near enough to a hospital here,' observed Hiking Boots coolly.

'What are the symptoms of redback bites, then?'

'Agony, mate! Reddening and swelling of the skin, sweating, intense pain, abdominal pain, vomiting, migraine, muscle failure, high blood pressure, accelerated heartbeat.'

I tittered nervously. 'Is that all?' I no longer knew whether to believe these Australian stories of the fatal outback. I had been collecting firewood for weeks and had seen neither snake nor spider. At the same time I was sensible enough to realise this did not necessarily mean I never would.

Hiking Boots grinned suddenly, a big wide Australian grin that signified a sudden acceptance of this crazy Irishman hunting blithely through mounds of spider-infested wood.

'Yeah. That's all.' We chatted amiably about our itineraries, about the condition of the roads, our vehicles. I mentioned El Questro Station, which had looked so dusty and forlorn, and to my surprise the Australian laughed.

'It's funny you should see it like that. It's getting quite up-market these days, actually. There's a hotel on the station somewhere costing hundreds of dollars a night, with spa, tennis courts, swimming pool, what have you.'

'Hm. I can't say that was what we saw.'

'Well, it's a big place. A million acres or thereabouts. And flying people in by helicopter wouldn't surprise me—I'm sure they use helicopters already, for rounding up cattle.'

'I can't believe how many flies there are here,' I finally announced irritably, changing the subject and flapping at the hosts of insects that were hovering around my head. I could see dozens of them clustered on the Australian's legs and the back of his shirt.

I had been told there was a world fly-swatting championship in Australia every year, at a place called Eaglehawk in

Victoria. Competitors had to swat as many flies as possible, with a standard-issue fly swat and a measured section of table. Australians were proud of their flies. Like a fisherman's catch, they were always bigger and better and more abundant somewhere else.

Now Hiking Boots said: 'Nah, not many here. Seen worse than this! Seen clouds of them in some places, so you can't even open your mouth to speak, otherwise they'd be down the back of your throat choking you.'

I digested this delightful information in silence.

'This is the winter! Some places during the summer heat the flies can be so thick on the back of your shirt you can't tell what colour it is.'

I wrinkled up my nose in disgust. The flies here were bad enough: Nicola and I had spent most of the afternoon cringing under great swathes of mosquito netting.

'Seen locusts too in South Australia,' reflected the man. 'Plagues of them. They just arrive like a huge dust-cloud, and suddenly it's all dark and there are millions of the creatures whirling all around you.'

You could never beat an Australian. There was always a Never-Never Land, somewhere else, where something was bigger or better or more dangerous or more difficult. No hardship was enough to intimidate the great Australian male: crocodiles, pythons, melomys, crazed kangaroos on the road, reef sharks, vast distances, Darwin pubs, locusts. The Australian insistence on the unpredictability and dangers of the outback was beginning to puzzle me, for surely most people passed through it unscathed.

Australians, afflicted by the famous cultural cringe, had once been apologetic, embarrassed that things weren't quite the same as England. They had since lost their apologetic manner, but not yet all their feelings of inferiority. Now I saw that this was covered up, no longer in apology but in boastfulness. If Australians thought they could not compete socially or intellectually with America or Europe, they at least had man-eating crocodiles and swarms of flies and the largest man-made lake in the southern hemisphere. The myth and size of the outback and its romanticised hardships gave

Australians both a cultural identity and the means to paste over their inferiority complex by demonstrating their manliness in the art of survival.

Maybe, too, there was some collective memory of the time when Australia was first settled and explored by Europeans, when the hardships were real and immediate. I wondered what lingering memories from the time of the convicts might lurk in the minds of urban Australians.

'After the locusts have passed by there's not a blade of grass nor a single leaf left,' Hiking Boots was saying. 'The trees just stick up like old fish bones, picked clean.'

Our conversation exhausted, the Australian strode off towards his car, swishing through the long brown grasses purposefully, as if about to seek out and strangle a crocodile with his bare hands.

It was with no sense of foreboding that I watched him drive off, back towards the road, leaving us completely alone on the end of a precarious track, camped unsuspecting under the baobab trees.

Adcock Gorge, curved as an amphitheatre, would have made a horseshoe waterfall of impressive height during the wet season. Now its deep pool was smooth as glass, unbroken by the slightest ripple, and the cliffs dry as the pyramids of Egypt. With river-carved footholds and great steps of rock it was a relatively easy clamber to the top. We had scaled the gorge walls to sit on the lip of the waterfall. The river at our backs was nothing but stone and rock, cutting through the vegetation straight and almost as flat as a Roman road, parched of all moisture. Cockatoos, disturbed, had wheeled indignantly along the cliff face, their white wings catching the sunlight as they swooped around the stunted bushes that grew miraculously from its fissures. I had launched small pebbles into the air, watched them spinning as if in slow motion, suspended momentarily in the void before falling into the water-filled canyon far below.

There must have been subterranean water entering the gorge from somewhere; the pool was clear and fresh enough for Nicola and me to swim in the next day. In the early

morning the water was bitterly cold, the gorge in deep
shadow, only the pale trunks of the gum trees standing out
against the shaded confines of the cliffs. After the swim and
breakfast we piled our belongings into the back of our van.
It was still very early when we prepared to depart once more,
wanting to make some headway in the cool of the morning.
Nicola took the driver's seat.

The engine of the campervan made a noise like a elephant
with a bone stuck in its trunk and fell silent.

My sister tried again, and again, with the same dismal
results. Mike and I, in our uneasiness, shouted at her insult-
ingly and bundled her out of the driver's seat. Neither of us
made the slightest impression on the recalcitrant motor. It
rasped painfully in a death-rattle and then expired completely.

Nicola and I looked at Mike expectantly. Of the three of us,
he was the only one who knew anything about car engines.

'Well. If a motor doesn't start it's probably because there's
no spark to fire it, or no fuel is getting through.'

'Couldn't have put it better myself,' I said admiringly.

An hour later we were still parked under the baobab trees,
with the interior of the engine spread out on the ground
around Mike, a Rubik's puzzle of grotesque dimensions. Mike
poked and prodded through the bits, muttering to himself
like a mad scientist attempting to concoct an atomic bomb.
Flies hovered over his bent back, coaxed out by the sun,
which had been steadily climbing and had now risen far
enough to become entangled in the branches of the baobab
trees.

It is a fancy of mine, sometimes, to calculate how long it
might take me, from some foreign spot, to get home to
Geneva, the city in which I grew up and where my parents
still live. I often find these calculations obscurely reassuring,
but in Adcock Gorge I discovered I was probably further
away from Geneva than I had ever been in my life. Even
radio broadcasts couldn't be picked up in this part of the
world. If our car didn't start, it was roughly a two-hour walk
along the secondary track to the Gibb River Road. From
there, if I hitched a lift, it would be about half a day's drive
or more to Fitzroy Crossing, which I reckoned was the nearest
town with an airstrip. Were there direct links from there to

Perth? I doubted it. I would have to fly to Broome or Port Hedland. From there it would be several hours flight to Perth; days by road. From Perth it was twenty-four hours flying time to Europe. Add a derisory fifteen minutes from Geneva airport to my house, just for the record. I couldn't imagine being there within the next three days. I was more isolated than I had ever been in my life.

As if reading my thoughts, Nicola said: 'It's a two-hour walk to the road.'

'Nicola!' said Mike. He always drew out the last syllable when he was annoyed: *Nicol-ugh* . . . The implication that we had no faith in his ability to restore the engine to power had obviously irritated him. He batted at a wandering fly. 'You're supposed to stay with your vehicle if you break down in the outback.'

'That's right,' I ventured. 'Wait for someone to come along.'

'Come along! This isn't the Champs Elysées on a Sat—'

'At least you'll have food and water and shelter if you wait.'

'No one's likely to come along here within the next few days. At least if we walked out to the road someone might pass by.'

'You're going to walk—'

'No, just open my umbrella and flap off over the gum trees.'

'—walk two hours in the blazing sun?' said Mike.

'I could carry water.'

'Right. I can see you staggering along under ten kilos of water.'

'Not ten kilos,' corrected Nicola sullenly.

'It's a four-hour trek to—'

'Two hours.'

'Yeah, well you'll have to walk back again when no one arrives to pick you up.'

Mike banged and tinkered among the pieces he had wrenched from the van's backside. I freely admitted to myself that I was ignorant of mechanics, and I wanted to sit down somewhere under a baobab tree and read my book. Instead I stood around guiltily, poking distastefully at oily fragments of metal to foster the illusion I was doing something useful.

'And we're not the only ones in the Kimberleys,' resumed Nicola about an hour later. 'There was that man yesterday afternoon in his four-wheel drive. He was even down here.'

'We'll he's not bloody down here now. He's off swatting flies in some other lost hole.'

'Hole! Who was the one wanted to come to the Kimberleys anyway?' yelled Nicola.

'I didn't,' I interjected smugly. Self-righteously, I remembered how I had been cajoled into the trip under the influence of cheap Australian wine on a beach in Darwin. 'I told you the tool kit was hopelessly inadequate and we wouldn't have enough petrol.' We had actually managed to tank up at Mt Barnett, buying petrol out of a rusty drum at the station shop, but I did not feel it necessary to mention this.

'We haven't run out of petrol. Are you stupid or something?' Mike banged down his spanner and began hauling the battery out of the van's intestines.

'We could have done!' said Nicola with triumphant cunning.

'Oh, well, if we're going to compile an encyclopaedia about what we *could* have done . . .'

'Well,' I interrupted, seeing the futility of arguing and how this irrelevant squabble could easily deteriorate into all-out war. 'Mike will try and get us going again. Whatever happens we're waiting here for someone else to come along. We've got enough food and water to last us quite a few days on rations.'

We all fell silent, mentally evaluating our stores, counting up the remaining bags of pasta and rice and tins of pineapple. The sun heaved itself free of the baobab branches and climbed heavenward, gathering heat.

Eventually in the late morning, to our great surprise and relief, we heard the sound of a car, and a Range Rover appeared along the track that led down towards the gorge. It stopped not far from us, and two people emerged: another retired couple. By this time Mike had reassembled the engine and was trying to start the motor. When the couple heard the dismal groans and coughs of our barely resuscitated van they approached us in concern.

'Trouble with the engine?'

'Yes.'

'Need any help?'

'I think we're all right for the moment,' claimed Mike loudly, daring us to contradict him. 'Nearly got it. But if you're here a while, maybe you could check with us again before you leave.'

There is a certain necessary solidarity among outback travellers: the couple did not need any persuading. They might be a few hours, they explained, as they wished to visit the gorge and have lunch. After that they would, of course, offer any help we might need.

'Pretty old van, isn't it?'

'1976.'

The woman sucked her teeth in disapproval. I could see her eying the truncated kangaroo bar, which was lying discarded in the grass like a heap of scrap metal.

'Quite rusted,' added her husband, bending down and peering in under the wheels. Australians, I thought, had a nice word for someone as nosy as that: stickybeak. Meanwhile the woman was looking through the open sliding door at the side, casting a despairing glance over the interior.

'Fairly wrecked-up engine. You must be stupid as galahs travelling in the Kimberleys in this thing.'

Stupid as galahs! Now that I thought about it, those pink and grey parrots, though beautiful, did seem a bit witless—not that I liked being reminded of my stupidity by the second person in two days.

Australians, I was discovering, were plain speakers. They called a spade a spade, and travelling foreigners with a 1976 campervan stupid galahs, but mostly their honesty robbed their outspokenness of any insult. Now I agreed with the couple: 'Yeah. A few sangers short of a picnic.'

They laughed at the Australianism. Nicola and Mike eyed me in bewilderment. I smirked to myself. Being broken down in the middle of nowhere at least had its momentary triumphs.

To our great satisfaction Mike got our engine running before the retired couple returned from the gorge. It moaned and protested before settling into a steady hum that seemed to satisfy him, and we started hurling our belongings into the back, afraid it would cut out again. We trundled off down the narrow, rutted track to join the main road once more.

'Well,' Mike commented cheerfully, his good humour restored. 'So we don't have to draw lots to see who gets eaten first after all.'

And the three of us laughed immoderately, almost hysterically, cackling like the rose-chested galahs in the paperbark trees, as the van sped along, kicking up dust and heading towards civilisation.

the empty lands seven

The van hauled its way up through the King Leopold Ranges, between purple hills under a hot sky. Eventually we came to a petrol station, the first we had seen since Kununurra. We tanked up once more, the engine restarting without fault. Soon afterwards we turned south, leaving the Gibb River Road but staying on an unsurfaced track that would lead us back to the main highway near Fitzroy Crossing.

About 350 million years ago this corner of Australia through which we were now travelling had been under the sea. A barrier reef a thousand kilometres long and nearly two kilometres wide had surrounded the area where the Kimberleys now stand. At Windjana and Geikie gorges, much more substantial than any we had yet seen in the Kimberleys, the river had exposed the reef and many of its Devonian fossils by carving cliffs out of the soft limestone. Despite our lengthy delay we made it to Windjana Gorge well before nightfall: a quiet and atmospheric place, haunted by giant fruit bats and freshwater crocodiles. With the evening sun low in the sky, the limestone cliffs, deeply indented and eroded into Gothic fantasies, glowed honey-coloured in the light.

This area had not always been so peaceful. In the 1890s, at Lillimilura police station near the gorge, a Panuba Aboriginal and former police tracker named Jandamarra had killed the local constable, stolen guns and released fourteen Panuba prisoners from the police cells. It has long been a misconception that Aboriginal Australians never resisted European settlement but passively let themselves be marginalised and ill-treated—thus reinforcing the assumption that they were less than human. Recent looks at Australian history have shown that this is far from the truth, as demonstrated in the events surrounding Jandamarra's escape. In 1894 Jandamarra and his band of escapees attacked a group of five Europeans who were bringing cattle northwards into the Kimberleys with the intent of setting up a station on tribal land. In retaliation, police and white settlers indiscriminately slaughtered the Panuba families living in camps around Fitzroy Crossing. Jandamarra managed to evade the police for more than three years and became one of the great figures of Aboriginal rebellion before he was finally cornered and killed at Tunnel Creek on April Fool's Day 1897.

Tunnel Creek was an eerie place, a great cavern where the river had tunnelled through an entire hillside. More easily accessible from the highway than other parts of the Kimberleys, it attracted a trickle of tourists, who ventured cautiously down the unsurfaced road to visit it. The cavern was of immense proportions, tumbled with boulders the size of cottages, with pools of deep black water, silent during the winter, which cast shifting, flickering reflections of dull light on the cavern roof. Deep in the bowels of the earth, Tunnel Creek made me shiver: it was a place of powerful natural forces and violent human history. Outside, around the confines of the rough car-park, the few tourists who made it to this remote corner of Australia rambled among the spinifex bushes and paperbarks, or sat and ate their picnic lunches. They basked in the heat like lizards, mostly silent, as if subdued by the cold menace of the caves.

This whole corner of the Kimberleys seemed haunted, one way or another. Further on at Geikie Gorge, according to Aboriginal tradition, a blind tribal elder on walkabout had drowned during the time of the creation. The Panuba say that the elder can still be heard today in the quiet moments before dusk, sighing and sneezing before sinking under the water for the last time. In the hush of the evening the water does indeed gurgle mysteriously, and one can hear the soft splashes of the plentiful crocodiles, moving down from their sandbanks into the river.

That night, camped in the wilderness between Fitzroy Crossing and Geikie Gorge, we were awakened by sounds outside our campervan: a vague scuffling and rustling and what even sounded like people whispering to each other. The three of us lay rigid, straining our ears. I could feel the nape of my neck prickle.

'They're trying to get into the van,' hissed Nicola under her breath. Was it imagination, or could I hear a tapping of Gollum-like fingers at the vehicle's metalwork?

In those long moments of darkest night the sheer size of the outback, its isolation, seemed not only haunting but threatening. We were three people, fundamentally ignorant of this harsh terrain, camped in the middle of nowhere with only a thin sheet of metal between us and the menace of an unknown landscape that was empty for kilometres but at the same time full of dangers, real or imagined. Perhaps these noises were Aboriginal folk, passing by in the night; and suddenly I could understand the white Australians' fear of these people who, with such a superior knowledge of survival, could hold you in their power. Or perhaps these noises were merely wandering animals—but what animals?—or the wind sighing through the eucalyptus trees.

'Could have been a madman with a chain-saw,' Nicola commented the next morning. 'We couldn't have done anything. There wouldn't even have been any point in screaming, because nobody would have heard us.'

I thought: whatever noise we heard, it wasn't a chain-saw. But I wasn't reassured. Sometimes the outback was so empty it gave my imagination free rein, and anything could happen: it was a landscape that inspired hallucination. During the day I rested my eyes on the vastness—devoid of any human signs and symbols, exposed beneath the blank and pitiless gaze of the sun—and could both see and feel its grandeur and its hostility in the heat and silence and barren rocks. At night, with a vast weight of darkness pressing down, the emptiness was greater and my imagination expanded to fill the void. If the stars sometimes added an intimacy and glamour to a silvered landscape, sometimes too those immense interstellar spaces seemed remote and cold and inimical.

There were times, as in the witching hours between Fitzroy Crossing and Geikie Gorge, when the outback night was like an immense Cyclops eye, staring down open and unblinking and intimidating, exposing one's soul to the terror of the unknown.

There wasn't much to Fitzroy Crossing when we drove into it the next morning: even the solitary supermarket was devoid of fresh food, and the BP station, in the process of being upgraded, was torn apart as if hit by a cyclone. Aboriginal children in torn dresses and ragged shorts wandered the pot-holed streets of the town with a slow indolence born of boredom, watching us as we drove past.

'This place is about as lively as a stoned koala,' the attendant at a petrol station explained when we stopped to fill up once again. He raised his baseball cap and wiped the perspiration off his forehead with his arm. 'You've come to see Geikie Gorge, I suppose.'

'Seen it,' I said. 'We're heading off towards Broome this morning.'

The attendant grunted in acknowledgement but without interest: customers here could hardly have been going any-where else, except back in the direction of Kununurra. South of Fitzroy Crossing there was only the Great Sandy Desert, succeeded by the Gibson and Victoria deserts: nothing until one arrived at the distant Southern Ocean.

'Seen the crossing?'

We had seen it, the place where the original road plunged down steeply, forded the Fitzroy River and then shot up the opposite bank like a roller-coaster. The crossing was dry at this time of year; the ford, devoid of water, not much different from ordinary road. We had driven across it and back again anyway. There hadn't seemed much else to do.

'Been here long?' I asked the attendant. I could not imagine anyone actually belonging here; it was a place one surely came to from elsewhere.

'About a year. Came up with the wife from Perth. Thought we'd try something different. We own the franchise, right.

And then we run the take-away and the store. Good money in it. Nothing to spend it on either, so it's nearly all savings!'

'Must be a change from Perth, though.'

The man shrugged. He banged the end of the petrol pump back into its holder and wiped his hands on an oily cloth. 'Save money. We'll probably stick it out five years or so.'

His wife was in the take-away, manoeuvring wire baskets of chips into boiling oil, her hair damp. In her late twenties, maybe; friendly enough. She answered our questions with cordial indifference: it was something she did every day with travellers who passed through. I wondered whether she counted the days to the end of her five-year sentence, checking them off a calendar every night, satisfied at the growing spread of crosses marking the graves of days ended, but simultaneously despairing at the days remaining. Maybe life in Fitzroy Crossing was not as bad as that; perhaps the woman even liked the place.

Unlike the attendant, his wife did not bother asking us where we were going: she knew already. But she asked us where we were from.

'Ireland,' I said, airily including Mike in the description.

The woman lifted the chips out of the oil and shook them, drops of hot liquid falling with a sizzle, and clipped the basket on to a metal fixture on the wall.

'A green country,' she said.

We drove off into the blinding heat, across a dried-up river-bed with rocks brown as fossils. I knew I would always remember the woman at the petrol station, making chips in a roadside take-away at the desert's edge. I would remember the way she talked of green as if it were a colour she had never encountered, the colour of paradise on the other side of a very distant fence.

It was another long haul from Fitzroy Crossing to the coast at Broome: more leagues of monotonous countryside burnt brown in the heat. It was an apocalyptic landscape that we were to encounter over and over again in Western Australia. The seventh seal had already been opened here; the first angel had sounded the trumpet, after which the third part of trees and all green grass had been burnt up. We came upon broad, flat plains studded with trees left barely standing after bushfires: stark, jagged hands of burnt wood clawing at the hot sky. Vast expanses of cracked earth, here on the edge of the Great Sandy Desert, held nothing but a few withering stalks of vegetation growing up between the broken skeletons of cattle and sheep:

> What are the roots that clutch, what branches grow
> Out of this stony rubbish? Son of man,
> You cannot say, or guess, for you know only
> A heap of broken images, where the sun beats,
> And the dead tree gives no shelter, the cricket no relief,
> And the dry stone no sound of water.

It was back to the wastelands, to a landscape, like poetry, stripped bare of all but essentials.

There was death and destruction and fire, and even plagues of locusts, in Australia. In the outback one could either become a religious fanatic, speaking of Revelation, or a confirmed non-believer, swamped by feelings of menace and futility in a post-modernist landscape deserted by God, presided over only by the shadows of indignant desert birds. Perhaps, I thought, this was why Australians talked so frequently of imminent misfortune or death at the hands of their apocalyptic creatures, full of vengeful poison and destruction. With little sign of any life, only the bones of eroded mountains sticking up through the decaying flesh of parched earth, with twisted trees and stunted bushes, with the silence of twenty centuries of stony sleep, the end of the world felt very near in the remote bush.

'Forty shades of green,' I had said of Ireland to the woman in Fitzroy Crossing. 'So they say.'

'Forty shades . . .'

The woman's voice had not quite been a question, not quite wondering: just a suspension of belief, the way I in my turn could hardly imagine an Eskimo vocabulary comprising forty words for snow. Snow was snow; green was green. In Fitzroy Crossing green was only the dusty, mottled colour verging on grey that one saw on the slender leaves of gum trees.

'I always picture Ireland when I hear "The Lord's My Shepherd" in church,' the woman had ventured finally and unexpectedly. 'In pastures green, you know the bit. He leadeth me the quiet waters by.'

And she had laughed, a little bit apologetically but mostly longingly, and had pushed a strand of hair, wet with perspiration, back off her forehead.

That afternoon we reached the western coast at Broome. Popular legend has it that Captain Cook was the first European to discover Australia, but in fact many others had made it as far as the Great South Land before the visit of the *Endeavour*. Willem Jansz, a Dutchman, landed on Cape York as early as 1606, and his fellow countryman, Abel Tasman, discovered Van Diemen's Land (now Tasmania) and New Zealand in 1642. Many other Dutch sailors on their journeys from Holland to the Dutch colonies in Indonesia—especially when they were blown off course by the Roaring Forties— also landed on, or saw, the western limit of Australia that we had now reached.

Englishmen too visited these waters long before Captain Cook. The privateer William Dampier sailed up the coast of Western Australia in 1688 and again in 1699. Perhaps not surprisingly, he gave such adverse descriptions of what was then known as New Holland that the British government remained for long uninterested in the region. The west coast was not settled until many years after the arrival of the First Fleet in Sydney; and only when Matthew Flinders circumnavigated the continent in 1801–03 was it even firmly established that New Holland and the Australian east coast were part of the same land mass.

William Dampier was the first European known to have visited what is now Broome, landing in the area during his 1699 journey and naming the bay on which it stands 'Roebuck' after his ship. It was not until very much after the visit of the *Roebuck*, however, that Broome was settled and its development boosted by the discovery of shell pearl in its waters, attracting large numbers of pearl fishers from East Asia and the Pacific islands. By 1910 Broome had a population of 5000—the vast majority of which was engaged in the pearling business—and was the foremost producer of pearl, contributing three-quarters of the world's supply. The pearl was mostly used in button-making, and the industry had started to crumble in 1914 when the fabrication of cheaper, synthetic buttons destroyed the lucrative pearl market. Now, though only a shadow of its former glory, the town still supplied cultured pearls; Broome's South Sea pearls were reputed to be the best in the world.

Broome has a graveyard full of worn-down sandstone tombs covered in Chinese and Japanese ideograms acknowledging the many immigrants who lost their lives diving for pearl. In August there are numerous festivals here: the Japanese Shinju Matsuri and Bon festivals, the Chinese feast of Hung Ting, and the Malaysian Merdeka are all celebrated in this remote place. There are even multilingual street signs and the remnants of a Chinatown, now just a street in the shopping area sporting modern food outlets: Wing's, Weng Ho's, Chin's.

In one of Broome's restaurants worked Ni Ming. He was friendly, but after we had been chatting for a while he looked troubled when I said I was a writer interested in the Asian history of Broome and its modern-day descendants.

'You will write about me?' he said anxiously.

'Perhaps.'

Ni Ming glanced nervously around him. 'No, no, no,' he said. 'Everybody here knows me and I will attract trouble.'

'Attract trouble?'

'Not everyone here is so keen on the Asian community,' said Ni Ming. 'They will read what I say in your book and be angry.'

'I doubt there will be a rush on my book, if there ever is one, in Broome,' I said.

'It's not convenient.' Ni Ming, in his broad Australian accent, still had a very oriental turn of phrase.

'I won't write your name,' I said. 'I'll call you Ni Ming.' It was Chinese for 'anonymous', though I did not know if the young man spoke Chinese.

'No name, no restaurant, no country of origin. Just an Asian in Broome,' said Ni Ming insistently.

'All right.' I thought his anxiety overdone.

Reassured, Ni Ming sat down opposite me and huddled close, as if he were a CIA mole about to impart industrial secrets.

'I hate it here,' he whispered, the words coming out in what was almost a hiss. 'Even though I was born in Broome.' He tinkered with the fork on the table in front of him. 'And everybody hates me!'

'Isn't that exaggerating?' Ni Ming seemed a personable enough young man, intelligent and soft-spoken, with a great lock of black hair that fell down over his eyes.

'They don't like me because I'm Asian and because I've been to university. I was *born* here, but I'm still an *Asian* Australian. Have you heard anyone being called a European Australian?' he said angrily.

I replied that I hadn't.

'We're all just "Asians" here, yeah? I mean, we're all just lumped together like we all have the same cultural and social background. That's not right.'

No, it wasn't right. 'Asian' immigrants in Australia were affluent Hong Kong businessmen, penniless refugees from Vietnam and East Timor, Malaysian Buddhists, third-generation Chinese.

'In Broome the Chinese don't have much to do with the Japanese,' Ni Ming said to me later. He had taken me out in his car to see the Asian cemetery, dotted with the gravestones of those killed in typhoons and diving accidents. 'Though of course most of us were born here anyway. And now a few Vietnamese have come, they stick to themselves.' Even the Chinese community in Australia, I thought to myself, was scarcely cohesive, divided into different dialects and social backgrounds: the Hong Kong Chinese despised the mainland Mandarin-speakers, the people from northern China sneered at the folks from Shanghai, the central Chinese were considered stupid.

'So the Asians are just as bad as the white Australians, then. Just as clannish and exclusive.'

'I suppose,' Ni Ming admitted grudgingly. 'But the white Australians around here hate everyone: the Asians, the Aboriginals, even their own women.'

'The women?'

'There's the Roebuck Bay Hotel,' said Ni Ming, scowling, kicking at the dirt with his foot. 'They have wet T-shirt competitions. I mean, if they can't even respect their own women, how can they respect the Asians?'

Ni Ming still had that Chinese sense of delicacy and dislike of public spectacle; and he rarely went to the pub. Did this mean he was not, indeed, a dinky-di Aussie?

'Not by *their* definition,' said Ni Ming. 'I don't care. I hate their crudeness, the vulgarity, their small-town talk. In a couple of years I'm going back to Perth. That's where I went to uni.'

As if reassured by my silence, Ni Ming propped himself against one of the headstones, under the shade of a tree, and leaned towards me, whispering so I almost had to strain to hear.

'And they hate me because I'm gay,' he said. 'Though nobody knows in Broome.' He looked at me, almost terrified, a flush spreading across his cheeks, waiting to see how I would react.

I merely said equably: 'How can they hate you if they don't know?' And to myself I thought: How can one show sympathy to a stranger without appearing intrusive or insincere? One can't; and the traveller merely picks up and journeys on, leaving sentiment behind.

'They would hate me if they did. You try being gay and Asian in small-town Australia.' And when I was leaving Ni Ming said: 'You'll remember not to write my name, won't you? Just say that I'm an Asian in Broome.' And he smiled sadly, and waved at me out of the car window as he drove away.

Its colourful history and tourism had prevented Broome from sinking entirely into the small-town torpor that Ni Ming so feared. In modern times Broome was best known for Cable Beach, which stretched for kilometre after golden kilometre along the coastline and attracted tourists escaping from the southern winter. It was there that we headed, having raided the supermarket for fresh food and otherwise quickly exhausted the town's attractions. There were numerous cars parked along the beach itself, and Mike drove down towards them with eager confidence.

'Practising for the Paris–Dakar?' I asked sarcastically as our wheels kicked up a spray of sand.

Moments later our campervan was trapped. The wheels spun furiously, whining like enraged hornets, when Mike pressed down on the accelerator. With a sudden sideways lurch we found ourselves bogged axle-deep in soft sand.

We clambered out of the van and surveyed the calamity in silence. We dug sand away from the wheels and Mike and I pushed from behind while Nicola stepped on the accelerator: to no avail.

'This is a nudist beach,' Nicola announced after a while, with seeming irrelevance. She had her eyes fixed on a point behind me in hypnotised astonishment. Then she added as an afterthought: 'Or are you supposed to call them naturalists these days?'

I turned around. A man in his fifties was coming up the beach towards us, stark naked, his body burned a deep, consistent brown. He had an enormous beer-belly under which his genitals (as my sister was to describe the scene later) hung in reckless abandon. As far as I was concerned he was nude and a nudist, though now too close for me to be able to inform my sister of my conclusion.

'Name's Tony,' the nudist said amiably.

'Brian.'

'Mike.'

'Nicola.'

'Spot of trouble?'

'You see our van's—'

'Well we were just—'

'—and I thought it was a bit rash but—'

'—stuck in the sand.'

After this babbled interchange there was a short silence.

'You'll never push it out,' said Tony to us equably, scratching at his ribs buried somewhere between rolls of flesh. So assured did he seem among us that I suddenly felt irrationally guilty wearing clothes. For want of anywhere else to look I gazed mournfully at the sunken campervan.

'I'll try and pull you out with my jeep.'

The man moved away across the sand. Compared to his impressive paunch his buttocks seemed sunken and shrivelled, dry and wrinkled as lizard skin. I could just make out his wife lying in the distance like a beached seal in the sun, a book propped up on her breasts.

Tony drove his four-wheel drive down towards us, and we hitched it up to the front of our van by means of a rope.

With a shudder the van lurched upwards, tyres screaming, and then settled even more purposefully back into its hole, buried in the sand up to its rear bumper.

The noise attracted another nudist of roughly similar age, another impressive set of genitalia, another amazed look from my sister.

'Name's Tony,' said Tony again, as if we had gathered for cocktails at an office party.

'John.'

'Brian.'

'Mike.'

'Nicola.'

'In a bit of difficulty?'

'Well you see we were just—'

'—get it out with the jeep—'

'—up to its bumper now—'

'—stuck in the sand,' I concluded loudly in mortification.

The two naked men stood by our van conferring on our problem.

'We need a shovel,' Nudist Two said eventually. I looked across at Mike triumphantly but he did not see my glance. 'And a kangaroo jack.'

We had neither of these tools; John fetched his own from his car. We jacked the back of the van up as high as possible, digging out sand from under the back wheels and laying down lengths of wooden board. Helped by the pull of the jeep, our van was finally free. The kangaroo jack leapt forward, gouging a great zigzag scar through the metalwork.

'Stick to the firm sand. Either down there by the sea or up here near the dunes.' Tony—Nudist One, as I thought of him—pointed and we could now see clearly the hard-packed sand, its darker colour contrasting with the paler, uneven surface in which we had become bogged. We thanked both men profusely.

'And by the way, we're Irish,' Nicola said. 'The Poms have a bad enough name in Australia without you thinking we're Poms as well. We're just daft Irish.'

Tony held back his head and laughed out loud.

'I like it,' he said. 'You may not know how to drive on a beach, but you've got a sense of humour!'

We drove off along the hard sand, soon leaving the congregation of people behind. Big breakers rolled in towards Cable Beach from the Indian Ocean, ideal for body-surfing. Nicola and I tested the waves for hours. Daunted, not a strong swimmer, Mike lurked in the shallows. Nicola called out to him, then with a shrug fell silent. She watched him with annoyed contempt as he paddled; but later, in a brief display of affection and harmony, they went for a walk, holding hands. Their fluctuating emotions bewildered me, but no doubt bewildered them too: they had been together for a long time. For the past year, travelling together, they had been with each other twenty-four hours a day: it took a very understanding and patient relationship to survive that.

We stayed on the beach that night, watching the sun setting over the ocean in a perfect globe of red. A string of camels carrying tourists ambled along by the shore's edge, their humps silhouetted against the orange sky.

We were rocked to sleep by the sound of waves.

Lulled by its perfection and resting after the long days spent driving since leaving Darwin, we remained three days on Cable Beach. On the third afternoon a young shore ranger, with Australian affability, moved us on.

'It's illegal to overnight within twenty kilometres of a campsite in Western Australia,' he told us, his white teeth flashing out of his suntan like semaphore. 'We don't mind it for a couple of nights, but you can't stay here for ever.' With a smile and a wave he got back into his patrol jeep and drove off.

My sister looked after the car as it receded down the beach.

'Now it's a pity *he* had his clothes on,' she observed with a smirk.

'*Nicol-ugh* . . .' said Mike, heaving our belongings into the back of the van. Inexplicably, their few days of harmony seemed to have snapped as suddenly as a guitar-string. They loaded up the van in uneasy discord.

As we headed down the highway, Nicola tapped her fingers irritably on the dashboard, as if sending out distress signals in her own private Morse code.

There is nothing between Broome and Port Hedland, the
next town hundreds of kilometres to the south, except baobab
trees and termite mounds and flat, dry earth. There is also a
road-house aptly named Sandfire. It is famous for its pub,
festooned with hundreds of shirt sleeves which hang from the
ceiling like the pennants of medieval knights in a banqueting
hall. To become a member of the Sandfire Sleazy Sleeveless
Shirt Club you have to contribute a minimum of two dollars
to the Royal Flying Doctor Service and then hack off your
left sleeve, leaving it too as a donation. As a fund-raising
exercise it seemed an innocent enough idea, if bizarre.

Port Hedland was hot and ugly. During the 1930s the
town was already exporting pearl, wool, minerals and live-
stock to other parts of Australia. The discovery of iron ore in
the 1960s, however, put Port Hedland on the map. It became
the biggest tonnage port in Australia, capable of holding the
enormous ships that came from Japan to reap the abundance
of mineral products. It was a dreary town, smelling of rust
and metal, overshadowed by great white hills of salt and the
vast hulks of ships that loomed along the ends of the town's
streets as if tossed up by a violent storm.

The woman in the Port Hedland tourist office was friendly
but almost despairing.

'South Hedland boasts an Olympic-size swimming pool,'
she said without much hope. Behind her a tourist poster, more
boldly and less truthfully, called the area a winter paradise.

The tourist official didn't seem sure what else we might be
able to do in Port Hedland. The sparse racks of brochures
advertised the Hamersley Range, where much of the iron ore
came from—a 'majestic and intriguing natural wonder' of
gorges. They were 300 kilometres to the south, said the
tourist official, trying to make the distance sound negligible,
so that her town might bask in some of the glory.

At last she said reluctantly: 'Actually Wittenoom is the
local tourist centre for the Hamersleys.'

She gave us a photocopied map of the north-west, on which
Wittenoom had been marked by a huge black dot which
made it look like a booming metropolis. *Make Wittenoom
your winter get-away soon*, said the tourist blurb with
inelegant rhyme.

'Are there any Chinese here?' I ventured, but Nicola took me by the arm and dragged me out of the office.

'I find this Chinese business getting a bit obsessive,' she said. 'Why not accept that you're in Australia now, not China?' She hustled me back to the campervan, muttering to herself.

Port Hedland, though larger than most, was not much different from other outback towns. They were nearly all stifling and isolated places in which it must have required great good humour to survive. They were well-kept enough, tidy and clean and often planted with flowering shrubs. Their main streets, once laid out wide enough to turn a team of bullocks, now provided spacious vistas and ample parking; but nothing could conceal the fact that the tarmac ended in red dust and the vista was a flat outback peppered with termite mounds and straggling trees.

Anthony Trollope, visiting Australia in 1872, wrote: 'There is a raw newness in these congregations of houses . . . an apparent mixture of pretension and failure which is indeed indispensable in towns founded with hopes of future greatness, but which creates a feeling of melancholy sadness in the mind of a stranger'. It was still an apt description of these outback towns, settled with an eye to becoming a future Sydney or Perth but overcome by their own remoteness and insignificance, lapsed into rough clusters of garages and bars and take-aways that made them seem all the more transient and insubstantial.

In a garage close to the tourist office, where we stopped to get our kangaroo bar soldered back on to the front of our van, the mechanic wondered what we were doing in Port Hedland.

'Nothing. Just came to get this fixed. We've been lugging it around in the back of the bus since the Gibb River Road.'

The mechanic replied: 'Not much else to come here for. It'll be ready in an hour. Stay and watch if you like: it's all the entertainment you'll find in Port Hedland.' And he laughed.

'At least you can joke about it.'

He grinned. 'Too right. Have to—I'd end up mad as a meat-axe otherwise.'

We left Port Hedland on an ugly road, past rusting railway sidings and scrap metal and salt hills glittering in the sun. We ignored the Great Northern Highway, which turned southwards towards Wittenoom. Although we were heading for the Hamersley Range's majestic and intriguing natural wonders, we had decided to go the long way. We continued westwards, driving past Whim Creek before turning off south on an unsurfaced road: our survival in the Kimberleys (if not our escapade on Cable Beach) had given us confidence.

The dirt road here was smooth and corrugation-free; we made good time. The landscape seemed greener now, and to our surprise we came upon a river, flowing away through the eucalyptus trees. We stopped for the night by its banks, the hills of Millstream-Chichester National Park purple in the distance.

'We shouldn't really be camped under these trees,' I said reflectively after we had eaten, leaning back in my chair and staring up through the branches.

'Why not?'

'Well, according to all these survival books I've been reading, if a sudden wind blew up in the night it could easily cause one of those hefty branches to snap off. They must be quite dry and brittle.'

'It doesn't seem likely that there's going to be a storm. The air's not even moving at the moment,' said Mike.

'Yes, but that's not the only danger. If there's a cool change during the night the branches could snap off just the same. Apparently the temperature change makes the wood cool and contract and then *crack!* the whole lot just breaks off and comes crashing down on your head.'

'On *your* head, you mean. You're the one sleeping in the pop-up roof,' said Nicola with sisterly unconcern. 'Haven't you learned anything cheerful about the outback?'

Overhead the branches of the gums shivered. Little corellas —white parrots with blue eye-patches—strutted about in one of the trees, peering down at us with heads cocked sideways. They shuffled their feet and sometimes they hung upside-down, looking impishly towards us to see if we were watching. It was a peaceful place, where the outback was not menacing at all but curiously soothing, asking only to be understood. The ancient rocks glowed in the evening light, and the surroundings seemed full of benevolent Dreamtime spirits.

If the branches of the gum trees were going to snap off and wreak damage on an innocent underneath, I decided, it wasn't going to happen tonight.

The next morning, soon after we entered the confines of Millstream-Chichester National Park, we saw red kangaroos. I was delighted: they were the first kangaroos I had seen in Australia—at least the first not flattened by the roadside. This was hardly surprising. Although we might have seen eastern greys in the Queensland outback, red kangaroos were not found in the far north of Australia and we were only now entering their territory.

Kangaroos (more precisely, a variety of wallaby) had first been described by a European in 1770 in Captain Cook's journal:

> Saturday 14 July: Mr. Gore being out in the Country shott one of the Animals before spoke of . . . The head neck and shoulders of this Animal was very small in proportion to the other parts; the tail was nearly as long as the body, thick next the rump and tapering towards the end; the fore legs were 3 Inch long and the hind 22, its progression is by hopping or jumping 7 or 8 feet at each hop upon its hind legs only . . . The skin is cover'd with a short hairy fur of a dark Mouse or Grey Colour. Excepting the head and ears which I thought was something like a Hare's, it bears no sort of resemblance to any European Animal I ever saw.

Perhaps Australians today saw nothing unusual in these creatures, but I marvelled at their strangeness as much as Captain Cook. They had a shuffling clumsiness as they grazed on the tough grass, hobbling forwards slowly and, it seemed, painfully, as if suffering from crippling arthritis. When our van approached, their ungainliness was replaced by a power-ful grace, and they bounded away on their enormous hind legs like giant articulated toys with the spring mechanisms suddenly released.

Seeing my first kangaroos reminded me of a conversation I had had in Darwin about Aboriginal languages. Having gone to the local library to look up the rules about former immigration policy, and particularly the dictation test, I had fallen into conversation with a librarian. ('I'm Mrs Jasper. How may I help you?') A confident and knowledgeable woman in her late forties with a stern look and forbidding hairstyle scraped back tightly into a bun, Mrs Jasper had a pair of spectacular multicoloured spectacles on a gold chain that contrasted with her otherwise conservative appearance. After I had satisfied my interest in Asian immigration, our conversation had wandered to Aboriginal languages.

'Each Aboriginal group has its own language, and although some are closely related, others are as different as English and ... oh, I don't know. Greek,' I was told. Mrs Jasper's glasses had caught the light and dazzled me with a blaze of colour.

'How many languages are there?'

'Oh, I'd guess a hundred, though about half of those are now only spoken by a very limited number of people. So many of the Aboriginal languages are dying out. At the time the Europeans arrived in Australia there might have been some two hundred languages. Of course, the common misconception is that these so-called primitive natives have only very basic forms of communication. In fact, quite apart from their extraordinary telepathic abilities, Aboriginal Australians have spoken languages that are grammatically complex and often have enormous vocabularies ...

'The Aboriginal word known to many of the world's languages is kangaroo, of course. Only Aboriginal groups in North Queensland, where Captain Cook first spotted a kangaroo, call it by that name; around Sydney it was known as a *patagarang*, so we might just as easily have been calling it that today.' Heaving Captain Cook's journals off the shelf, the librarian had thumbed through it and shown me the entry where he had described the creature.

'There's a standard joke about the naming of the kangaroo,' Mrs Jasper said after I had finished reading. 'Whether it's true or not I don't know. When Cook asked the local Aboriginals the name of the strange creature he saw hopping in the bush, one of them replied "Kangaroo!" What the poor native, confronted by the gabbling white man, was actually replying was "I don't understand you!" or "I don't know what the hell you're saying!" Of course poor old Cook, the silly Pom, assumed his question had been answered, and we've been calling it the kangaroo ever since.'

'At least the name has a certain ring to it,' I replied. 'The Chinese call it a *da daishu*, literally a big bag-rat, which is not nearly as flattering!' I grinned broadly, as I had always thought the Chinese term hilarious. Cracks appeared in Mrs Jasper's stern exterior, and then her glasses winked at me in red and blue and she laughed too.

'You know,' said Mrs Jasper, 'that there are mentions in very early historical texts of kangaroos or "jumping hares" being sighted in various parts of China?'

'In *China*?'

'Yes. It's one of those things often put forward as evidence that the Chinese "discovered" Australia long before the Europeans, though of course various other explanations have also been suggested.'

'But how would kangaroos have actually ended up in China?'

'Well, apparently the Chinese explorers weren't averse to bringing native species home. I read that one Chinese admiral actually brought back a whole menagerie from East Africa and Madagascar, including a giraffe, zebras and ostriches, and had them paraded through the streets of his home town.'

'Astonishing!'

'Yes. After all, the journey back in those days would have taken close to a year, yet obviously they managed to keep the creatures alive and well on a ship for all that time. Certainly they might have done the same with kangaroos. Or big bag-rats.' To my further astonishment the elegant Mrs Jasper snorted in amusement.

Now, here in Millstream Park, I felt like laughing again, because the kangaroos hopping near the van seemed absurdly comical. They were like animals fashioned from God's left-overs: rabbits' ears, as Cook had noted, the square jaw of a horse, something of the cow in their placid eyes and endless chewing, a rough bark like a dog, hind legs outsized as a frog's, and fox-red fur—bits and pieces of other animals and other designs roughly joined together to produce an unconvincing creature that nevertheless sparked admiration and, in its ugliness, ended up bizarrely beautiful. Was this why it had been chosen as a national symbol? Where other countries have chosen beasts of great strength or dignity—lions, unicorns, eagles—only the emu and the kangaroo figured on Australia's coat-of-arms. It had always struck me as a peculiar choice. The emu is a flighty and somewhat hysterical creature that flees at the first sign of trouble like a large featherduster on legs; the kangaroo is an odd, hybrid animal with little by way of grandeur.

Kangaroos have been elevated in status by Australians, but in reality, whenever I saw them in the bush, I thought of them, affectionately, as rather silly animals. To use an Australian expression imparted to me by Mrs Jasper, you had to have kangaroos loose in your top paddock—be crazy, daft, or maybe just plain eccentric—to turn an I-don't-understand-you, a roo, a big bag-rat, into a symbol of national pride.

There were strange trees in Millstream-Chichester, stranger even than most Australian trees. They grew up tall and thin and straggling, and their leaves hung down in great, long hanks almost grey in colour, like an old hermit's beard, or as if a haystack had been blown into the branches and was now hanging down disarrayed in long wisps. The ground underneath was ankle-deep in fallen leaves, dry as straw, that cushioned every step. It was very silent. I would have been unsurprised to see a goblin emerging from between the trees.

We had been walking for a couple of hours along a small track when suddenly we were confronted by a sign:

> Anyone for tennis? Only joking. Mum reckons it's too hot. The court was Bill Cleland's idea you know. He was a state champion tennis player and worked here as a jackeroo. It's made from termite mounds. Bill says if it's properly looked after, it's the perfect combination, speed wise, between grass and hard courts.

Nicola, Mike and I stopped in front of the sign and read it in astonished silence. More than astonished: uneasy. What was this sign doing here, apparently in the middle of nowhere among the odd, bearded trees—and what did it mean? Having appeared so unexpectedly, and in such strange surrounding, it seemed surreal, almost sinister. There was certainly no tennis court to be seen.

We walked on a short distance. The trees opened out and we came upon a small stream and another sign:

> Hang on, we better call out first, see if anyone is in there.
> Grandfather Irvine built the first bath-house but Dad has
> done it up real good. His pride and joy is the big ochre slabs
> he's laid in the creek for a floor.

Once again there was no bath-house, nor anything else, to be seen: only the sign of silver-coloured metal stuck in the ground.

Not much further on, the mystery was finally solved. We stumbled upon Millstream Homestead, centre of a former sheep station and now the headquarters of the national park. The homestead had been preserved and converted into a small museum, and was occupied by a woman who sat behind an enormous table covered in leaflets.

'I was wondering what those signs were,' I asked her.

'That's our walk,' replied the woman.

'Oh?'

'From the point of view of a young boy. It's as if he's talking to you, giving you a guided tour of the station.'

'The one we saw was talking about a tennis court, but I didn't actually *see* a tennis court,' I said, with the uncomfortable feeling that somehow I was being deliberately obtuse.

'No. There isn't one now. But it's where it used to be in the days when this was a sheep farm.'

I felt like saying, to make it clear: So there's an imaginary boy taking us on an imaginary tour and showing us an imaginary tennis court. Instead the woman said: 'The boy lived here briefly in the thirties when his parents ran the station. Have a look through there.' She pointed through a door into one of the other rooms.

The room contained some mundane biographical information and a picture of the homestead painted in 1932 by Doug

Gordon, aged twelve. It showed the house surrounded by neat fences, the native camp with two frizzy-haired Aboriginal men, the shearers' quarters in the bottom left-hand corner, and two spots marked *Stuart found two queer birds here* and *Dad shot an eagle-hawk here*. If there was a Chinese cook on this station, he was not shown. In the middle of the picture was a large grey animal that looked like an elephant or even a behemoth (it was the same size as the homestead). DOG, said a laconic and thoughtful label underneath in earnest child's script.

Outside, not far from the house, there was a permanent waterhole fed by the stream which we had already crossed. Doug Gordon and the rest of his family had, by all accounts, greatly enjoyed this refreshing natural swimming pool, way back before the Second World War. Now the surrounding bush had been burnt fairly recently, and the tree trunks stood up black and charred, topped by untouched palm fronds. It was hot and still, and a smell of ash still hung in the air. Against the burnt landscape the waterhole was beautiful and green, covered in water-lilies that had opened in great star-bursts of pure white petals, fragile as Belleek pottery.

Bushfires were an ever-present danger during the dry season, when the outback was a tinder-box of drying grasses, long and abundant after the rains. *We like our lizards frilled not grilled*, an imaginative fire-warning sign had commented on the road south of Darwin, alluding to the giant ruffed lizards of the Northern Territory. But controlled fires were fairly common: they had long been used as a method of environmental control by Aboriginal Australians, and park managers and pastoralists had also realised the value of deliberately lighting fires in order to reduce the amounts of dry grass, which would otherwise build up to dangerous levels through the long dry season. I was certain that the charred areas so close to Millstream Homestead were the result of controlled burning. Such fires lit early in the season were carefully monitored, limited in area and of low intensity, often dying out overnight and causing little damage to permanent growth and trees: hence the dull green fronds still sticking up jauntily, like oversized feathers on an Indian headdress, from the tops of the soot-black palm trunks.

It was nevertheless a daunting sight when, on the road away from the homestead, we rounded a bend and were confronted by a bushfire. The flames leapt greedily in the dry undergrowth, an immense wall of heat in yellow and orange like the backdrop to some hellish pantomime. The trunks and branches of singed trees stood out against the violent colours in black, like skeletal drawings, tossing in the great wind of heated air. The noise was immense, a huge yawning roar loud as a factory furnace. Towering plumes of grey smoke spiralled high into the sky, circled by birds of prey waiting for victims fleeing from the heat.

Mike brought the campervan to an abrupt halt, and we stared at the fiery cataclysm moving towards us, towering high to the left of the dirt road but only flickering in low, dull red on the other side, beginning to lick at the bushes and lower tree trunks. I made an indeterminate noise through my teeth, awed by the sight.

'We're not going to have time to turn,' said Mike, gazing out over the steering-wheel as if hypnotised, while the fire roared towards us, preceded by dried grass already sparking and glowing in anticipation. Sparks were jumping from tree to tree, igniting the leaves in great explosions of white flame.

'I read somewhere that the flames from a bushfire pass by in about four minutes,' I observed. 'Apparently there's not much chance of the petrol tank exploding in that time.'

'Not *much* chance!'

'So meanwhile we just sit here and hope for the best?'

'You're supposed to wind all your windows up and sit with a blanket over your head,' I said hesitantly. The advice sounded more comical than serious. 'But that's in a real bushfire. This is probably just a small, controlled one. I mean it's not actually burning on the road, and it's fairly low on the right—'

'Maybe we should reverse—'

'Oh, drive on!'

And drive on we did, through a brief tunnel of flame, with the stench of charred wood filling the campervan, while hawks circled overhead, drifting without effort on rising columns of air.

On our second day in the park we lunched early, gazing over a broad expanse of low, rounded hills banded into distinct layers of colour. Below us the valley bottom was minutely chequered in red and green, clumps of spinifex alternating with patches of hard, dry earth. In the distance, washed out blue against the horizon, were other hills, flat-topped as children's sandcastles.

When travelling I always notice similarities in landscapes. There is something reassuring in finding that an exotic destination reminds me of home, or of some other distant country I have already visited. It makes things more familiar, more easily acceptable, more comforting. I can say to myself, *The world is a small place after all.*

The Australian outback was virtually the first place I had been to that reminded me of nowhere. Its landscape was completely alien and without reassurance. There was nothing there that I knew, no familiar plants or animals or colours or contours. The rivers were dry beds of dust, blowing in the harsh wind; the mountains ground down to low, worn-out humps of rock; the valleys great savage slices of red cut deep into the plains. Even the colours were all wrong: the trees white with blue leaves or black as burnt corpses, the rocks red and purple, the grass yellow, the earth orange—stark, uncompromising colours that stood out boldly, like great blocks and slashes on a modern painting, at once attractive and disturbing. The unique relationship of the indigenous people with their environment, framed by creation legends and supported by thousands of years of practical experience in finding sustenance in the wilderness, meant little to my European mind. To me the outback was a hostile place, a place of heat and dryness and intense, suffocating silence; a place of possible suffering and hardship where it seemed no one came, or had come, since the making of the world.

Squinting out over the valley, crunching up my eyes against the glare of the noontime sun, I was distracted from the view by a couple of magpies, pecking hopefully around in the stones near our feet with an eye to fallen sandwich crumbs. They were big Australian magpies, actually butcher-birds, with black breasts and white patches on the back and wings and under the tail. Hopping up and down like moon-walkers, they glared at us in annoyance, clicking their grey beaks.

'They can attack you,' said my sister grumpily, kicking a leg out in their direction. The magpies fluttered up uncertainly, then resumed their desultory search for food.

'Don't you start. We have everyone we speak to telling us about how we're going to get bitten, stung, poisoned, mauled or clawed to death by the local fauna,' I said; not that I was immune from repeating such warnings.

'Well, they can. They're the most aggressive birds known. They peck your eyes out and claw your scalp in the breeding season,' Nicola said.

I eyed the birds beside us suspiciously.

'Is it the nesting season now?'

'How should I know?' my sister replied crossly, scowling.

'Presumably the breeding season is in September, in the spring,' Mike ventured.

The magpies, as if embarrassed by our conversation, hopped off to a discreet distance. For the remainder of our lunch I stood there nervously, gulping my sandwiches hurriedly and waiting for an attack. Much later I received corroboration on the subject in the *Sydney Morning Herald*:

> It's magpie attack season again, and upturned ice-cream cartons as helmets are coming into their own. It's become a war at Crestwood Primary at Baulkham Hills, where one particularly aggressive magpie became a health hazard. It dive-bombed one girl, who fell down some steps and broke her front teeth trying to get away, and several children suffered gashes from its beak.

Eventually, according to the article, the unfortunate magpie had to be shot by wildlife authorities.

The Millstream magpies, docile at least temporarily, caused us no trouble. When we set off on a walk they followed us inquisitively for a while, alternately rock-hopping and fluttering behind us. Finally, as if with a mental shrug of their shoulders, they flew off down the hillside and vanished.

We were following what had once been a camel trail, an old trade route that meandered through the north-west. It was named the Afghan Track after the many camel-drivers who had worked in Australia during the nineteenth century— though most had come not from Afghanistan but from India.

It was one of the many fascinating minor stories of the settlement of Australia. About 10 000 camels had been imported into Australia from the 1840s, and had played a significant role in some of the early explorations of the interior, as well as in early settlement, the building of railways, and in supplying materials for isolated mining and sheep-farming communities. After the turn of the century, when the development of roads and railways made them unnecessary, many of the camels—technically dromedaries—had simply been turned loose. As a result, Australia was now the only country in the world with a significant population of free-ranging camels, numbering in the tens of thousands.

The Afghan Track, now much overgrown, was not an easy walk in the heat of the day. There were no trees to provide shade in this part of Millstream, only low-lying saltbush and blue-bush and dwarf eucalyptus, well-adapted to surviving in the dry climate. It was the kind of vegetation common in much of the continent's interior, the plants supplying just about enough food to support a limited cattle population on outback stations. (That the cattle population was not limited enough and the true desert was advancing was one of the great polemical topics in Australia.) Spinifex was abundant, growing in great independent clumps of needle-like leaves. Biologically interesting, providing shelter for all manner of small mammals and reptiles, the spinifex leaves were also extremely sharp. Walking through clumps of spinifex, sometimes waist-high, was not pleasant. It had a suitable name, the final syllable harsh as shards of glass, and we picked our way along carefully.

Millstream National Park had a landscape more alien than any I had yet seen in Australia, but if the strangeness seemed hostile it was also awe-inspiring. The outback was rarely frightening in the sense of evoking terror; a certain apprehensiveness sometimes, but mostly the kind of uplifting fear resulting from feelings of reverence and respect. In the way that religious fanatics feared God, so one could fear the awesome and impressive outback. Now I was beginning to see that its uniqueness, its hostility, its silence, its vastness did not always grind down unbearably. The outback, for these same reasons, could be spiritually uplifting. If civilised man could feel intimidated by the finality of the landscape, I thought, there was nevertheless an element of this vastness that was fascinating to our restless and expansive spirits.

At that moment I tripped and fell into a clump of spinifex, which cunningly pierced every soft part of my anatomy. Nicola and Mike shrieked with glee, and suddenly the outback didn't seem so fascinating after all.

west eight

west coast

We headed south once more, following a winding ribbon of dust towards the Hamersley Range. Beyond Millstream's park boundaries the landscape became flatter and there was little to see apart from an iron ore train bound for Port Hedland, hauling past us for many long minutes. Some of the trains of this railway (the longest private stretch of track in the world) were more than three kilometres long—three hundred wagons and six locomotives.

Just before Wittenoom we returned to surfaced road. Despite its prominence on the map we had been given in the Port Hedland tourist office, Wittenoom was a minute place, a motley collection of houses, garages and caravan parks, with an airstrip cut out of the bush on its outskirts. The 'Wittenoom Business Guide' pasted on a notice-board at the entrance to the village listed six accommodations with uncomfortable-sounding names (Wittenoom Bungarra Bivouac, Nomad Heights), two tour offices, a tourist shop, Ashburton Shire Council Office, and Wittenoom Traders, which comprised a garage, a general store and a post office all under the one roof. We stopped outside the latter with relief: our petrol tank was once again close to empty.

'Emma Chisit?' I said to the owner when he had filled up our tank. I chuckled to myself inwardly; I got great pleasure out of using the phrase.

'Thirty-three dollars, mate,' said the garage-owner without batting an eyelid.

Once, on a visit to a Sydney bookshop, the English author Monica Dickens had inscribed a book 'To Emma Chisit', before discovering that the customer was uninterested in the signing session and merely wanted to know the book's cost. Reported in the *Sydney Morning Herald*, the anecdote encouraged sackfuls of other correspondence and eventually a series of articles about what became known as Strine—a corruption itself of the word 'Australian'. There was soon a Strine Association, which went so far as to translate Shakespearian comedies, and a dictionary was produced containing such classic Aussie phrases as *laze and gem* ('ladies and gentlemen') and *keen ebb tide* ('a keen appetite').

Now the garage-owner said what sounded like: 'Weir yez gewing?'

As in many parts of the outback, where there was only one road, it was more a friendly overture than a serious question, and our answer, that we were heading into the Hamersleys to see the gorges, could hardly have surprised him.

'Poms, are you?'

'Irish,' I corrected him. 'And by the way, do you know where that word comes from?'

'Pom? Yeah. From P-O-H-M. Prisoner of His Majesty. Convicts, right? Get it?'

I told him I did get it, and I had to admit to myself that I was quite taken by this etymological proposal; it seemed more reasonable than the pomegranate explanation. Other Australians were later to suggest another abbreviation along the same lines, P-O-M-E, for Prisoner of Mother England.

'Of course,' said the garage-owner unexpectedly, veering off on another tack, 'there were far more convicts sent to America than were ever sent to Australia. Not many people know that.'

True: large numbers of English prisoners were sent to farm the plantations in Virginia and elsewhere. The American War of Independence obliged the British to reconsider their options for disposal of their undesirables, and they turned their attention towards the possibility of packing them off to the newly discovered and satisfyingly distant Botany Bay. But America had never been purely or even mainly a penal settlement, and so it escaped the taint of the convict system that had burdened the Australian consciousness for so long.

'People didn't often call them convicts then, and I don't suppose they called them Poms—or POHMs—at that time either. They were referred to as Government men.'

A pretty little Georgian euphemism, I thought to myself, as we took our leave of Wittenoom and encamped in the shadows of the Hamersley Range.

Australia is an old, old landscape, battered and bruised, its immense alpine chains worn down to smooth, slight humps, its soils infertile, desiccated and eroded by millennia of alternate wet and dry seasons and the merciless heat of the sun. The Methuselah surface of this giant continent is dried up and wizened, its bony rocks brittle and splintered, its freshness and vitality lost to unimaginable geological time spans. Mostly the eroded vistas seem to slumber, sunk in the quiet introspection of old age, the silence interrupted only by the gossip of insects at night and the scolding of gaudy incongruous parrots by day. Even the trees are ancient, twisted into tormented bonsai arrangements by heat and wind, their arthritic joints gnarled and stained, their leaves grey as the face of a dying man. They shed their bark like flaking skin, jealously guarding their leaves, and sometimes they creak and groan with an unbearable melancholy, as if lost in unhappy dreams.

The Pre-Cambrian rock of the Hamersley was 2000 million years old, far surpassing the young Cainozoic mountain ranges of Europe, Asia and America, which were no more than 65 million years old. The landscape of much of Western Australia was formed of inactive, stable blocks of rock in ancient, complex arrangements that indicated their convoluted geological history. The exposed rocks lay bare, and on the faces of the Hamersley gorges mineral impurities had been twisted through metamorphosis into great swirling bands of red and purple, orange and white, punctuated by the odd blue streak of asbestos. In Wittenoom Gorge an old asbestos mine and its associated settlement lay abandoned under the shadows of the overhanging rock, as if the population had been wiped out by a plague.

Oxer Lookout offered a view over four gorges that met at this point, immense walls of rock converging in a bewildering tangle. Knox Gorge, one of them was called; the puritanical Scots name seemed out of place in this flamboyant, almost mystical landscape. The Hamersley Range was red, the same orange-red as termite mounds in the Northern Territory, the same orange-red that has made Ayers Rock a photographer's delight; and in the evening the red seemed to seep out of the flesh of the earth and shimmer upwards, setting the sky on fire until it glowed with tongues of flame, and the rock grew darker, its colour rusting into black. In the sky the sunset glowed eerily before it too vanished, and the rock and the sky were one.

'Think about it, mate—why should we have your fucking Union Jack on the corner of our Australian flag?'

I had escaped from Nicola and Mike and was sitting in a pub in Carnarvon nursing a tall beer, perched on a high stool at the bar beside a person called Justin. Justin, barefoot and wearing a pair of skimpy blue shorts and a singlet, might have looked more at home on the beach, but to judge from the familiar way he treated the bartender and quaffed his drinks he was obviously no stranger to pub life. In his mid-twenties, he already had Australian crinkles around his eyes from the sun.

'Not exactly *my* flag,' I said, just to annoy him. 'I'm Irish.'

This response seemed to throw Justin into temporary confusion. He called the woman behind the bar over and ordered himself and me a drink, as if to atone for his mistake. But then, gathering strength from another throatful of beer, he seemed determined to pursue his line of thought.

'Well anyway—why should we have the fucking Union Jack?'

'A historical footnote?' I hazarded. 'Aren't flags supposed to convey information or something?'

'Historical footnote! Historical fucking footnote!' he repeated, as if determined to work what I was fast coming to recognise as his favourite word into the sentence. 'That's the whole point! Australians have spent so much time feeling ashamed of their historical past—their convict past—and for what? It wasn't the Australians that organised the fucking convict system. We should be proud of what we've made out of the mess the fucking British left behind them! We've come a long way in two hundred years.'

'Yes, I do see that. Perhaps the Union Jack isn't saying you're proud of it, it's just saying it happened.'

'I mean, this is the fucking 1990s! The Australian Constitution is actually a colonial relic, this country's an autocracy run by the Governor-General who represents our head of state, wandering around Buckingham Palace with a tiara stuck in her permed hair!'

I began to pay Justin more attention now. In the middle of his indignation and colourful language some interesting gems of intelligent, if hardly original, observation were emerging.

'I wouldn't say Australia was exactly run by Queen Elizabeth,' I said placatingly. 'As if it were some sheep station.'

'Yeah, but look. Our parliament and prime minister aren't even mentioned in the Constitution, but there's plenty about the fucking Governor-General. He's head of the armed forces, signs legislation into law, chooses the government and—'

'Chooses the government? Pardon me for thinking people voted in Australia.'

'An autocracy! Like in Britain! Ultimately someone has to be invited by the Queen—or Governor-General—to become prime minister.'

'All right, but in reality—'

'Sir John fucking Kerr did actually dismiss the elected government under Gough Whitlam in 1975,' Justin reminded me. 'And it was only in 1986 that the Australia Act ended the fucking British government's right to amend the Australian Constitution! A bunch of old deadheads sitting around in Westminster deciding what's happening in Australia!'

'Well I'm not supporting the fucking British government!' I shouted. Justin's turns of phrase were catching. Then I said more calmly: 'What you say is true in theory. But on the other hand, Australia is still one of the most advanced social democracies in the world, in my opinion.'

'Huh.'

'Why don't you change the Constitution and get rid of the Governor and the Queen?'

'Well! I'd bloody like to, mate! But it's not that easy, is it? Amendments to the Australian Constitution are hardly ever approved; and why not?'

'Because nobody really wants to amend it?'

Justin bashed his fist down on the table top, making me jump. 'Nobody wants to! It's because the proposals have to be put to both houses and then to a fucking referendum. They have to have a majority of votes in a majority of States, and a majority of votes overall. Fucking impossible!'

'Oh,' I said uncertainly, trying to work this out.

Justin, thinking my hesitation was disbelief and wanting to show me he knew what he was talking about, added: 'Section One-Two-Eight of the Constitution.'

'I suppose eventually the republican cause may gather enough support to succeed,' I suggested.

'Yeah. We used to think Britain could protect us, but that went down the fucking drain kicking and screaming with the fall of Singapore in the war. We all used to have relatives in England, but then immigrants started arriving from southern Europe and Asia, so who has a fucking English granny these days? We had lots of trade and investment with the Mother Country, but they went and dumped us in favour of the European Community. So what's left? Loyalty? Sentiment? But they're not worth a hot drink on a summer beach to young Australians.'

I was impressed by this swift analysis. Personally I was in total agreement that ties between Australia and Britain were now little more than an anachronism and that Australians had little need for an irrelevant foreign royal family.

'Some Australians would like to see a republic by the year 2000, wouldn't they?' I said.

'Yeah. Maybe not by then. But we'll be a republic one day. Maybe we'll get rid of the fucking Union Jack too.'

'Ah, yes.' Argument over this surfaced sporadically in Australian newspapers. Apart from the presence of the Union Jack, the other complaint about the present flag was that it was too easily confused with the flag of New Zealand. Now I asked Justin: 'And what would the new flag be like?'

'Green and yellow, I think, since they're the unofficial Australian colours already.'

'And perhaps with the Stars and Stripes in the corner instead of the Union Jack,' I added provocatively.

I thought Justin was going to erupt. At the last moment he realised I was egging him on and with good grace he laughed.

'I mean, there aren't many ties with Britain now, but lots of Australians have been busy in recent decades cuddling up to America, haven't they?' I said. Justin grinned a rueful grin.

'And that's another whole kettle of fucking fish,' he said.

We had found the sea once more at Carnarvon, known as a centre for banana and avocado growing, otherwise just another remote, outback town perched on the crumbling western edge of Australia. Southwards the highway was flat and the coastline ragged and dangerous, tumbled with great, flat shelves of rock battered by the Indian Ocean, the waves a surly swell that sometimes exploded in blow-holes that flung up spouts of salt water, the shock rolling like cannon fire across the bleached scrub-land.

Shark Bay, enclosed in generous arms of land, was tamer, the calm, scintillating water as blue as a kookaburra's wings. The first European to discover Shark Bay was Dirk Hartog, captain of a Dutch trading frigate, the *Eendracht*, who sailed into this natural harbour on 25 October 1616; one of the bay's islands was named after him. On an earlier voyage Hartog had unwittingly entered the history books by becoming the first white man known to have set foot in Australia. If others—the Portuguese, perhaps—had been there before him, they did not realise the significance of their landfall, and no written records survived to tell of their exploits.

Shark Bay is home to stromatolites, promoted in tourist brochures as 'living rocks'. These are formed by secretions of lime which create tablets and columns, grey and rocklike in appearance, but spongy to the touch. They have been created by blue-green algae, or cyanophytes, among the most ancient of life forms. The first organisms to contain chlorophyll, which makes it possible for them to photosynthesise using water, they were responsible millions of years ago for the build-up of oxygen levels in the earth's atmosphere, thus enabling other life forms to develop. Cyanophytes flourish in Shark Bay's Hamelin Pool, and wading among the weird living rocks, at the edge of a crumbling coastline almost devoid of vegetation, was like seeing the world as it was in the dawn of its creation.

If these were extraordinary, more astonishing still was Shell Beach, where shells lay ten metres deep on a hundred-kilometre stretch, sometimes packed so densely they had been cut out as blocks and used in local building construction. We walked along the sea-shore, picking out whorls of pure white, fragile chips of pink and pieces of black stone worn onyx-smooth by the waves. Nicola and Mike put their heads together and peered at each other's findings before taking photos of the shells with their close-up lens.

Stromatolites and shells were the least of the area's attractions. While Shark Bay was a name straight off a buccaneer's chart, hinting of danger and adventure, the coast here was renowned not for predatory fish but for dolphins. The beach at Monkey Mia was the only place in the world to be frequented by wild dolphins that regularly came close to the beach to feed. (The curious name Monkey Mia, it was surmised, might have been a derogatory term derived from the numerous Chinese and Japanese who once lived here, attracted by Shark Bay's pearl shell.) Monkey Mia was that recurring phenomenon, a place renowned for its unsullied nature that had become a tourist attraction. Rows of caravans were encamped among the sand dunes, and there was a car park and visitors' centre where a careful display informed tourists of the life cycle and habits of the bottlenose dolphins they were about to see. But few people bothered to amble around the displays and watch the video—they were all out wading near the beach and waiting for the dolphins themselves to arrive. One didn't have to know their Latin name (*Tursiops truncatus*) or about their pregnancies (eleven months long, about eight in a lifetime) to enjoy the spectacle.

There was an air of anticipation and subdued excitement among the gathered crowd. Children splashed around and harped at their parents ('But *where* are the dolphins? When are they coming?'), there were several false sightings, and Mike fiddled with his camera lens and aperture settings. Finally, almost unnoticed, there they were, and the circus began. Their fins approached through the water ('A shark, mummy,' yelled one of the children, and burst into tears), more onlookers entered the sea, and a ranger in gumboots issued a stream of instructions. If you have to stroke them, do so along their sides: don't touch their blow-holes or fins, and please, restrain your children from trying to insert objects into their blow-holes. 'Why?' he was asked. 'Someone once rammed a bottle top in and the dolphin asphyxiated,' was the answer. Be careful, it was impressed upon us, these are wild animals and might bite—but it hardly seemed likely. The dolphins swam up to us, circling our legs and allowing themselves to be poked and prodded while camera flashes popped. The ranger distributed buckets of fish, one of which Nicola grabbed, and she began distributing food to the eager dolphins, which snickered and cheeped in appreciation.

The rangers were anxious to inform us that the dolphins did not rely on these handouts—feeding times were varied and on some days they were not fed at all; the fish distributed would only account for a third of their entire intake. Maybe so, but the dolphins were intelligent enough to know where they would get an easy meal. They were wild, but might as well have been in Sea World for all the difference it made to the onlookers. The children loved it, and so did my sister, but I thought it was absurd.

There was not much fun in this subjection of wild creatures to the interests of tourist entertainment, even if they were free to turn flippers and head off back into the open ocean. I suddenly found it all very sad, and left the visitors to their wading and watching, and sat on a bench, where I was harassed by a malevolent pelican.

The dawn at Shark Bay was grey and damp, and as we headed south we realised for the first time that it was winter in Australia. That afternoon it rained, a thin and mediocre drizzle: the first rain since the day Nicola and I had been stranded in Prairie. We drove with our windows up, divested

ourselves of our sun-glasses and wide-brimmed hats, remarked on the absence of dust.

Outside the window the landscape was still flat and
featureless. In my adolescence I had had a recurring nightmare in which I was being chased across such a grey plain by
sword-wielding warriors on horseback. As we drove southwards it came back to mind, although I had neither dreamt it
nor remembered it for years. The frightening thing about the
dream was not only that I knew the horsemen intended to cut
off my head, but that they were garbed in black, with black
hoods and shadowy faces, lacking all personality. (I had been
much taken by *The Lord of the Rings*, and no doubt my
pursuers, I now realise, resembled Tolkien's Pale Riders.) In
my dream I was completely helpless. Although I was running,
running, the plain was so flat and empty that it offered no
opportunities for hiding or taking evasive action. There was
nothing I could do but run, run in the knowledge that I
could not possibly outrun galloping horses for long.

I always woke up, gasping and sweating, with the sound
of hoofs at my heels. It was the same plain now, smooth and
grey and empty and stony, stretching on and on to nowhere.

Geraldton: another unremarkable outback town. Nicola
and Mike sloped off on their own and I wandered into the
coach station—coach and railway stations always seemed to
me indicative of the character of a town. I sat on a bench
and watched people walking about, and then I was approached by a woman in her thirties, with short dirty blonde
hair tied back in a purple ribbon.

'I've got a bladder problem,' she announced in a loud
voice. There was a silence, and then the woman sat down on
the bench beside me. She had the slightly vacant eyes and air
of almost angelic indestructibility of the mentally disturbed.

'Yeah, had it all my life,' she bawled. I did not answer, but
gazed at the opposite side of the station hall, embarrassed
but at the same time secretly delighted by the odd public
outburst. A young teenager with a freckled face and a duffel
bag plonked himself down unwittingly beside the woman.

'What bus are you waiting for?' the woman demanded
loudly.

'The 16:30 to Mullewa.'

'Where's that, then?'

'Out east of here.'

'What you going there for?'

'Stay with my grandparents.'

'Where did you say Port Mullewa is?'

'Not Port. Just Mullewa.'

'How long's the bus take?'

'Dunno,' said the boy sullenly. There was another silence. A coach drew in, heading for Perth.

'That your bus?'

The boy hesitated. 'Yes.' He grasped his bag and scuttled off into the safety of the coach terminal. The woman sank into a meditative silence, plucking at her lap with her long fingers. Eventually a man sat down on the end of the bench: blue slacks, a scruffy blue jacket. He opened his copy of the local paper.

'Where are you going?' the woman shouted. I turned away to grin at the renewed onslaught. She was a writer's delight, asking questions I frequently wanted to ask but rarely did: how I longed to descend on some unsuspecting local, interrogating them with aggressive questions about their life!

'Just Perth,' the man replied.

'What are you going there for?'

'Meet a mate.' The words were almost a mumble.

'What did you say?'

'Meet a mate,' said the man reluctantly but more clearly.

'Oh, your mate lives there, does he?'

'In a home,' the man muttered in confused embarrassment, eyes flicking desperately over the columns of his newspaper.

'A home? What kind of a home?'

'Boys' home.' A short silence. The man rustled his newspaper in agitation.

'What's he done, then?' shouted the woman. 'Why's he in a boys' home?' Silence. I waited anxiously for the answer. 'Been stealing, has he?' the woman yelled.

'Stole a car.'

'How long's he been there?'

The man mumbled an answer, which I did not catch: it sounded as if it might be three years.

'Do they ever let him out?'

'Yeah.'

'What do they let him out for?'

'To go to . . . to go . . . to go to court.'

'How old is he?'

'Seventeen.'

'Why you going to visit him?'

'He's my mate,' said the man with dignity.

'Your mate, is he?' sneered the woman. And then, with precipitous loss of interest, she picked herself up off the bench and ambled away into the coach station. I looked at the man out of the corners of my eyes. He had disappeared behind his newspaper. I wanted to yell at him some more, force out some more details—how could I call this woman mad, when she shouted about things we all wanted to know? I sat silently, cursing the dictates of society.

This was Geraldton to me: a bus station strewn with empty Coke cans, a sullen teenager bound for his grandparents' home, a young man faithfully visiting his friend in detention, a mad woman curious about her fellow humans.

Out of sight I could hear the mad woman shouting at someone else, asking them where they were going. And then I met up with Nicola and Mike again, and we drove away. I took my own madness with me, my obsessive hunt for Chinese, my uncertain future, and headed towards Perth. The monotonous flat scrub-land stretched, characterless, as far as the horizon, as far as a dark man on horseback might gallop.

Western Australia was only reluctantly settled, and then partly because the British were worried about growing French interference in the area. It was not until 1826 that a brig set sail from Sydney, under the command of Major Edmund Lockyer, with intent to colonise the west. In addition to its regular crew, the HMS *Amity* carried twenty-three convicts, eighteen soldiers, two army and four naval officers, a surgeon and a storekeeper. They reached King George Sound in Western Australia on Christmas Day. Men went ashore from the brig the following morning with six months supplies and founded Western Australia's first white settlement. (Or its first official one: another reason for establishing a military base here was to control the escaped convicts and itinerant whalers who had already encamped on these shores.) Today Albany, now a thriving town on King George Sound, boasted a replica of the *Amity*—a small two-masted brig, not much roomier than one of the small, suburban bungalows scattered around the town itself. It seemed a fitting testimony, in an early history that was often brutal or shoddy, to the great courage of many of the Australian settlers.

The original settlement at Albany managed to last only five years. Meanwhile, in 1827 Captain James Stirling of the HMS *Success* had been sent to explore the Swan River, and had returned to London keen to establish a colony on the west coast. An advance party was sent to the Swan River under Captain Fremantle of the HMS *Challenger*, who claimed the western third of the continent for Britain in May 1829. A month later the official party arrived under Stirling's command, and the colony was proclaimed on 17 June 1829; Western Australia thus became the first colony to have the word 'Australia' as part of its official name.

Fremantle's name was given to Western Australia's chief port, now a suburb of Perth containing many fine Victorian buildings: the Town Hall, the Esplanade Hotel, the court house and jail, Samson House. The Round House supplied evidence that the arrival of the British was more an invasion than a settlement: used to house Aboriginal prisoners, it was one of the very earliest buildings in Western Australia, dating from 1831.

For years the early settlements struggled along, barely existing at subsistence level and often relying on food supplies sent from the east coast. The abolition of convict transportation (the last convict ship bound from England to Australia arrived in Fremantle in 1868) did little to help the situation, as it took away the settlers' supply of free labour. The development of Western Australia received a boost only with the discovery of gold during the 1890s and the subsequent development of agriculture. It was not until the 1960s, however, that the region really made strides with the discovery of immense mineral wealth, particularly in the Hamersley Range.

The mining bonanza had made Perth the fastest-growing city in Australia, a self-confident but slightly reckless boom town. Many of the great Australian entrepreneurs of the 1980s —Alan Bond, Robert Holmes à Court, Laurie Connell—came from the west. Fringed by beaches, receiving more sun than any other Australian city, superbly sited on the Swan River, Perth was a beautiful city. It was a city glittering with sky-scrapers and office blocks in steel and glass where, reputedly, fortunes and corruption were planned. The heat shimmered off the roofs of cars; it flashed from skyscraper to skyscraper like a secret signal, and was repulsed only by the tinted windows and air-conditioning of shopping malls and offices— reptilian windows, blank and staring and pitiless, looking down on the glittering waters of the Swan River. Perth scintillated, it coruscated. Perth merited such extravagant words, for Perth was an extravagant place: the most remote city in the world, a monument to big business and power, an unabashed celebration of piracy and shady dealings and devious business conducted under a thin veneer of British respectability.

Perth was the lawlessness of the Wild West somehow made genteel. Historic buildings had English names—the Deanery, the Cloisters, His Majesty's Theatre—and English architec-ture, like the Victorian Gothic Government House and Old Perth Boys' School and the Georgian-style courthouse, not to mention a mock-Tudor lane surmounted by a clock where St George and the dragon battled as the chimes rang the hours. Outside the city centre there were suburbs with streets of English houses with their English gardens and sticks of pruned rose bushes, and there were carefully tended bowling greens where retirees played this most English of games.

But the Englishness was now being somewhat diluted by an increasing influx of immigrants from South-East Asia. Singaporeans and Malaysians had already invested heavily in the city and were now being followed by rich Indonesians. The Hyatt Regency and Princes Plaza hotels, as well as many of the downtown office blocks, were owned by Asian compa-nies. Wealthy immigrants bought houses in the posh suburbs of Booragoon, Nedlands, Peppermint Grove or Claremont: huge million-dollar mansions nestled behind jacaranda trees.

These new arrivals knew all about Perth's attractions: its cleanliness, its insignificant crime rate, its health-care system, its lack of pollution and uncongested roads, its golf courses and, of course, its relatively short distance from Jakarta and Singapore—only about four hours by plane.

Perth was a marvellous place, a booming frontier town trying to become respectable, a place where life was easy and the beaches glorious, resolutely Anglo-Saxon but with a growing Asian population. It was a mixture, it seemed, of everything I liked and appreciated. Perth had fine museums, an efficient post restante, and good chocolate cake too. I hated it.

There comes a moment when one realises that all travel is entirely subjective. There is no intrinsic interest or beauty or value or enjoyment in any building or landscape: all depends on one's perceptions. I realised now how much of Australia had been tempered not only by my own character, but also by my own fluctuating emotions. I had appreciated Kakadu, but perhaps Nicola, sitting silently with her back to Mike on top of Ubirr Rock, had found it sad. Now in Perth, having received unhappy news at the post restante from China—a letter signalling the end of a relationship, the end of many plans—I had no choice but to hate the city. If Aunt Augusta in Graham Greene's *Travels with my Aunt* was right, and travel is merely an accumulation of memories, then I have no happy memories of Perth, and so it is a city of no appeal. When I think back now, I find it sad that a city so beautiful and so new and so vibrant should be a place to which I will never care to return.

I felt despondent and depressed, more aimless than ever, and after the vast openness of the outback the skyscrapers and busy streets made me uneasy. I groused at Mike and was impatient with my sister and glanced around glumly at the city with ill-concealed indifference. The people and the cars tired me out after months in the emptiness and solitude of the outback, and in the Chinese faces in the street I saw only reflections of another life. Only in Fremantle did I appreciate my surroundings, walking by the promenade in a strong wind, the rain splattering at my face. I watched the yachts tugging at their moorings, falling back into the water with hard slaps, while overhead the gulls turned and twisted in the turbulent air currents. The clouds were black on the horizon for almost the first time since I had arrived in Australia. It was beautiful weather. I battled along the promenade, the wind stinging my eyes into tears, while inside I wept too for a happy past and a bitter-sweet love and an uncertain future.

Martin Anderson was standing in the rain attempting to busk for money by moonwalking and performing other robot-like dance steps. Since the rain was now coming down steadily and the wind was rising, this seemed like a quixotic effort. And, as I had nothing else to do and had always been curious about buskers, I invited him for a coffee: a distraction from other thoughts.

'You've got to enjoy it,' he said, smiling ruefully, when I told him I thought busking in a high wind on Fremantle harbour seemed like a waste of time. 'Anyway, when I started this morning the weather wasn't too bad. Might as well pack up now, though.'

'You mustn't earn much in the winter.'

He shrugged. 'Poor weather doesn't necessarily mean poor earnings, though certainly if it's actually raining it's hardly worth the effort.'

'You don't *sound* as if you enjoy it.'

'It has its ups and downs. Sometimes I just can't seem to find the right spot, or it's a bad day, or no one seems interested. Sometimes you get abused by the public, by irate shopkeepers who imagine you're putting customers off coming into their shops, by mad dogs, barracking drunks. The kind of day you know you're only doing it for the money and all you want to do is go home . . .'

'So what about the ups?' I laughed.

'I'm my own boss, I work when I like. And I get a buzz out of the positive comments I sometimes get from the crowd. The fact that I'm entertaining people. Especially kids, though unfortunately kids rarely give any money.'

'Who does?'

'Women and Japanese tourists!'

Since Martin was everyone's idea of the good-looking Australian surfer, with a healthy tan and shoulder-length blond hair, I was not surprised.

'Yeah. I dance in nothing but shorts in the summer. I always earn more on the days I bare my chest.' He grinned.

'People think busking is easy, but it isn't. It's not like theatre. There you've got a more-or-less captive audience who have already paid their money and are therefore unlikely to actually walk out unless it's really bad. With busking it's just the opposite. People haven't paid anything, and will walk away in a moment as soon as their attention is distracted. You've got to keep them entertained and hope they'll cough up.'

'Most people mustn't. I know I rarely do.'

'You'd be surprised. Nearly everyone who actually stops will throw something in the tin, even if it's only a ten-cent piece. I must average about fifteen or twenty dollars an hour on a good day.'

'That could be a lot of money in the summer.'

'Oh, yes. Tax-free too!'

A reasonable living, if an uncertain one, I thought as I twiddled my coffee cup. I admired buskers: their lack of embarrassment, their initiative, their endless optimism. Perhaps this was why there were so many buskers in Australia, for sometimes these characteristics seemed very Australian. Then too, weren't the characteristics of the donors Australian as well—the understated sympathy, the casual generosity, even the quiet amusement?

I did not say all this to Martin: to have done so would have seemed ridiculous. I wanted to find meanings in everything, to find Australia in a Fremantle café through the medium of a teenage busker who might in some peculiar way transmit an understanding of this other world.

Absurd, I told myself. And I went on my way, into the rain and Chinese faces, and the world I was thinking of, suddenly, was not Australia at all.

We had temporarily abandoned the campervan in Perth and were enjoying the civilising effects of more solid accommodation, which included the dubious delights of a television. I had always thought television a useful medium for gaining a quick insight into the culture and pleasures of a foreign country. In any case, it continued to rain and there seemed little else to do but watch TV.

A great deal of local Perth television (as in other major cities, I was to find) was a mixture of inane American soap-operas and corny British situation comedies. Evidently Australia still looked to these countries for cultural standards, or at least entertainment—a need I found perverse, though admittedly there was not much capital in the industry for producing local shows. Popular current-affairs programmes were more gossipy than journalistic, and the quality of the news was appalling. The public channels—ABC and more particularly SBS—were the exceptions, but I was frequently informed that 'no one watches SBS'. I could understand why. On one evening it offered the following selection: *Say Aah* (a comedy series from the Netherlands); *Welcome to Canada* (a movie about the arrival of a boatload of illegal Tamil immigrants in that country); *Swiss Cheese* (a story of a woman who screams at her husband about his affairs); *La Dent* (a black-and-white film about a man who tries to rid himself of a toothache); and *Uranus*, which consisted of shots of a squid with an ironic voice-over. But SBS was Australia's 'multicultural channel', and although few people watched it many seemed to get satisfaction from the fact that it existed.

Advertising is always indicative of the symbols and stereotypes of the nation, and I soon became interested in the advertisements produced by Mojo, a company founded by Alan Morris and Allan Johnston, which was among the first to produce TV advertising with a local atmosphere and Australian accents and vocabulary, as opposed to the British and American voices that I was told had characterised Australian television prior to the 1970s. (Australianisms had now penetrated even current-affairs programmes; the well-known presenter Ray Martin often used 'mate' and other idioms, although he had been much criticised for this by more highbrow journalists.) It was Mojo that introduced Paul Hogan to the unsuspecting public, and Aussie words like 'bonzer' and 'mate' punctuated the ads with an idiom familiar to the ordinary person in the street. One of Paul Hogan's better-known roles was throwing shrimps on a barbie for a Mojo advertisement for the Australian Tourist Commission. Their 'Wonders Down Under' campaign for the United States market in 1984 had made Australia the number one destination Americans wished to visit. The advertisement highlighted Australia's sun, beach and barbecue culture. (These days, tourist ads focused on adventure sports for the American market and cultural events for the Europeans.)

Such advertising gave a new prominence to the Australian language and life-style and was part of the evolving image of an Australian national identity that grew stronger in the 1970s and 1980s. Australian idioms had entered advertising (the jingle for a Speedo advertisement went: 'The way it fits the body almost should be banned, that's why it's heading for the coast like a Bondi tram') and advertising jingles had become part of the idiom too: 'How do you feel?—I feel like a Tooheys or two'. Mojo advertising in the 1990s appealed directly to an Australian patriotism and national pride that would have been almost alien concepts a few decades earlier. Qantas's highly successful advertising campaign relied on a feel-good song: 'No matter how far or how wide I roam, I still call Australia home.'

The Qantas advertisement showed splendid shots of the outback, and the outback certainly featured prominently in the Never-Never of the advertising world. I became particularly interested in the Ampol petrol company's advertisements, with their use of familiar outback images and rural stereotypes that encouraged the viewer to feel patriotism and the desire to be part of it all—although the target audience was comfortable, middle-class and resolutely urban. It was a marvellous advertising campaign, appealing to the emotions, highlighting the sentimental appeal of the outback against all logic, punctuated by laughter in the self-deprecating kind of way in which Australians specialised, and showing the face of Australia—namely young and white and blonde. There were no Chinese in this advertisement, no station cooks or market gardeners. Minorities were rarely seen on Australian television.

I jotted down the scenes from one Ampol advertisement. They showed a homestead and metal windmill with blowing dust; a young woman (laughing) battling through a flood with her suitcase; a boy sitting in front of a horse in the dust, proudly holding up two lizards he has just caught; a camper-van bowling along a dirt road kicking up a cloud of dust; a man on a motorbike with a cattle-dog in front of him and a blonde woman behind him; a young freckled boy in an Akubra; two men chatting outside a general store in the middle of nowhere; a weather-beaten man brushing flies off his face; and a final shot of a homestead complete with veranda and windmill against a romantic sunset. Over it all came the appealing jingle:

> Whispering wind I can hear you call,
> I've got to get out and be part of it all,
> I'll only stand tall with my back to the wall,
> I'm as Australian as Ampol.
> Don't look too far in search of gold,
> You'll often find it's right under your nose,
> It shines from the smile that just says hello,
> I'm as Australian as Ampol.
> There's flies in the heat and long muddy roads,
> If it isn't too hot it's bound to be cold,
> That's why I like it I can only suppose,
> 'Cause I'm as Australian as Ampol.

With the exception of Aboriginal Australians (too controversial, perhaps), just about every traditional image of the outback was referred to in this advertisement, whether in images or words. This was the Australia I had experienced, this was Australia's Australia, it was even the world's Australia—but it certainly was not the 'real' Australia. I was in the 'real' Australia now, watching a TV in the middle of a city. Yet I could sense the fascination of the Never-Never. This was a superbly crafted advertisement. I was not Australian, but even I could feel the sentimental pull, the pride in the battler, the achievement of survival, all the while laughing in the face of the odds. Who wouldn't want to get out and be part of it all? Australians were great. Australia was great. And Ampol was certainly the best petrol I had ever used.

plains and mountains

Things were not going well with Nicola and Mike. They bickered in the rain, and in the evenings, when we played cards, they fought over the score and scowled and muttered. Behind each other's backs they talked to me about their plans and ideas, and it was obvious now that neither included the other in these futures. But they still sometimes held hands and wore each other's clothes, neither knowing how to let go and maybe, despite everything, not wanting to.

'Mike just wants a ride back to Sydney,' observed my sister in a moment of enlightenment. 'After Sydney there will be nothing.'

What could I say? Mike was her first serious boyfriend and only she could learn to find her way among the rapids of emotions that whirled and swirled around the ends of relationships. I could not really focus on her problems, to be honest, too preoccupied with my own affairs in this unfamiliar and rain-splattered city. I had come to Australia to think, but now I seemed more adrift than ever, no closer to any decision about what to do with myself, even where to live.

We bundled our belongings together once more, and set off towards the Nullarbor Plain with the east coast in our distant sights. Travelling from Perth to Sydney was the equivalent of traipsing across all Europe: about the same distance as Lisbon to Istanbul, and the Nullarbor would have been most of Spain and France laid waste. 'The fault of all Australian scenery is its monotony,' wrote Anthony Trollope with careless generalisation in 1873. On the Nullarbor at least this was true, for there was little enough to see on this vast and featureless stretch. At Balladonia there were clay salt pans; at Caiguna a petrol station, and at Eucla the sorry remains of an old telegraph repeater station and some sand dunes; only when the road skirted the Great Australian Bight did the scenery abandon itself to impressive cliffs and blue surf dotted with the distant figures of playing dolphins.

The longest stretch of straight road in Australia was here: 145 kilometres like a ruler through the middle of nowhere, and at night we camped on its edge while road trains thundered past in a cloud of diesel exhaust. Crows, it is said, fly backwards on the Nullarbor to keep the dust out of their eyes, but there were not even any crows to be seen, only a solitary bird of prey that kept lonely vigil in the sky over Madura.

The region's legends were greater than its scenic interest, and I kept myself occupied by reading about Edward John Eyre, the early explorer after whom the road across here was named. Born in Yorkshire in 1815, he had emigrated to Australia when he was just seventeen. He was to become the first European to travel from Adelaide to Albany across the Nullarbor Plain, setting out in 1841 on the six-month journey. He had been accompanied by John Baxter and three Aboriginal people, and the tale of his journey was a true adventure— horrific as well as heroic. Overcome by exhaustion and the harshness of the terrain, they were obliged to abandon most of their supplies, their coats, their guns and the greater part of their tools. Two of their pack horses finally dropped with thirst and weakness—they ate what flesh they could, then left the ravaged corpses to the birds. Halfway into the journey two of the Aboriginal men shot Baxter dead and ran off with most of the food supplies and the two remaining guns. (Eyre apparently felt no rancour at the two men who had shot Baxter and almost caused his death, for he later wrote of the British settlers and Aboriginal Australians: 'It is a lamentable thing to think that the progress and prosperity of one race should conduce to the downfall of another.')

Eyre and Wylie, the third Aboriginal, plodded on, wrapped in blankets against the night's chill, unnerved at being constantly followed by their two murderous companions, licking dew that had collected on their rags and nearly dying of hunger. They ate half a kangaroo and then, still starving, ate a whole penguin, skin and all, which they had caught on a beach. Finally, half dead, they were spotted by a French whaler, the *Mississippi*, the captain of which offered to take them to Albany. Eyre refused, staying on board but the few days needed to recuperate sufficiently to continue the journey. More hardship: a camp fire destroyed most of the provisions given to them from the *Mississippi*, and on the last leg of their journey they were confronted by fierce rainstorms.

Nothing was achieved, nothing discovered except that the route was impractical for the movement of stock, but Eyre's journey became a great classic of Australian exploration. Later he was to become a highly unpopular Lieutenant-Governor of New Zealand and then Governor of Jamaica. Here, in retaliation for a rebellion, he had 600 people hanged, hundreds more flogged, called in the army and burned down houses, earning the dubious nickname 'Hangman Eyre'. He was never offered another colonial post and retired in obscurity to Devon, where he died in 1901. Queen Victoria died the same year, and it seemed to me that Eyre had personified the heights and depths of the Victorian colonial ideals of her reign. It was appropriate to read about him here on the Nullarbor, where courage had triumphed: another example of bravery and adventure transcending the frequently vicious story of Australian settlement.

We stopped at Port Augusta to reprovision, then headed into the Flinders Ranges, where we encountered rain. We sat huddled in our campervan playing countdown whist before driving on through the surrounding countryside. This was a sad place. At Kanyaka stood the forlorn remains of farms and shearing sheds, cottages and stone bridges built by hopeful settlers but abandoned to ruin and futility; lush now under the relentless rain, this was marginal land unsuited to grazing. Seventy families had once lived here, finally departing in the 1870s after a series of droughts, and all that they had left behind in the graveyard were bones and forlorn epitaphs to their foolish bravery. Quorn, once a major railway entrepôt, was now a minor town; Bruce and Hammond had been abandoned altogether, and at Bangor the ruins of a hotel stood staring blindly across a road that now carried travellers through without pause.

We gave up and drove on as if fleeing some dreadful cataclysm, skipping over the border into New South Wales along evening roads teeming with rabbits and wallabies, finally stopping in Broken Hill. The discovery of lead, silver and zinc deposits here in the 1880s saw the start of Australia's industrial and mining economy and a drift away from a long reliance on pastoralism. The town was pleasant enough, belying the high rates of alcoholism, sexual assault and domestic violence that had given it an infamous reputation. The post office, in the late Victorian architecture typical of outback towns, had wide green-roofed verandas and a squat clock tower in red brick. There was an old Roman Catholic cathedral too, a grand and ornate trades hall, a stock exchange, a town hall in the Italianate style, and an iron mosque built for the many 'Afghans' who once worked the camel trains. Curiously, despite its isolation and unsavoury reputation, Broken Hill was home to several well-known painters and had more than a dozen art galleries. In Pro Hart's gallery hung paintings by Monet, Rembrandt, Picasso, Dali and Australian artists. It seemed odd to come across them here— but no odder, after all, than a Japanese cemetery in Broome, a shark's fin salesman in Darwin. Oddity was what tourists noticed, but there was much in Broken Hill that appeared perfectly normal.

Not far from Broken Hill, Silverton was a ghost town once dependent on the mining of silver chloride. More artists lived here, and the place, particularly its pub, had often been used as a film set: the *Mad Max* series, *Razorback*, *A Town Like Alice*, *Badge of Honour*. Television commercials were filmed here too: wild teenagers on snowboards parachuting from aeroplanes and surfing down against the red earth of the outback, just as I had first seen it on my arrival, in search of Coca-Cola (or was it Reeboks?), the harshness of the outback still providing glamour to urban Australians. Part of the success of the movie *Priscilla, Queen of the Desert* relied on this very incongruity: gay, urban sophistication against a background of redneck roughness and intimidating outback. It was amusing in *Priscilla*, but this was the way of all Australia. We camped overlooking the vast plains outside the village, a waterless expanse of grey, stunted trees and orange desert that glowed in the early evening light, lending the scene a strange, false aura of intimacy and cosiness.

At its height in the 1880s Silverton had numbered 3000 people, though many of its buildings had been only semi-permanent, the miners often living in tents or makeshift shacks. We wandered around the small settlement, with its red dust and broad streets and scattering of buildings (a Methodist church and a schoolhouse still stood, as did the Municipal Chambers, abandoned the very year of its completion), and it did indeed seem more like a movie set than a real place, the façades brightly painted and evocative of another era, the backs of the same buildings dilapidated, their yards filled with junk metal and piles of bottles. I thought I recognised the general store that featured in the Ampol advertisement, though I couldn't be sure.

'You might say I'm a camel-catcher,' said the camel-catcher in the famous pub, used in scenes from many films. I had been flicking through the scrapbook, which recorded the visits of production teams and camera crews and actors. The camel-catcher looked just like a character in one of the films. He pushed his Akubra back from his brow and wiped his forehead. Tendrils of dirty blond hair hung down over his ears and deep lines were etched around his eyes.

'And why would anyone want to catch a camel?'

'Good money in it, mate. Ship them abroad. A camel sells for between a thousand and three thousand dollars. Once they get to Arabia, of course, a really good racing camel could eventually change hands at over a million bucks. They're considered as highly as racehorses.'

'Too bad camel racing isn't all the rage in Australia, then.'

'Yeah, well. There are some camel races here, though, like the Alice Springs Camel Cup. They play pocomela up around there too.'

'Pocomela?'

'Polo on camels,' said the camel-catcher.

'We saw some camels up on Cable Beach at Broome,' Nicola ventured.

'Yeah, there's some up there. Camels for tourism are big business now, especially in the Northern Territory. Worth millions of dollars a year. That woman, what's-her-name Davidson, made camel treks all the rage.'

Robyn Davidson had made a quite extraordinary 3000-kilometre journey by camel from Alice Springs across the desert to the west coast of Australia and written about it in *Tracks*. It seemed a far cry from the gentle rides the tourists had taken at sunset along the length of Cable Beach.

'It was mostly the Afghans who drove camels here in the last century. Afghans rode behind the hump on a so-called Indian saddle. Not like the Arabs, right? You been to Arabia?'

'No.'

'Seen *Lawrence of Arabia*?'

'A long time ago. But I can't say I remember how he rode a camel.'

'The Arabs ride between the hump and the neck. Different, right?'

'Hm. I suppose the hump does get in the way. Not as convenient as a horse.'

'Yeah. Horse's a smoother ride, too, right, because they move two diagonal legs at the same time, whereas the camel moves both legs on the same side simultaneously. That's why it kind of rolls. Flaubert wrote that it lurched like a turkey. Makes you seasick if you're not used to it.'

If the incongruity of this weather-beaten Australian camel-catcher quoting Flaubert struck me, I had travelled too much and met too many exotic people to be surprised by it. Instead I merely said: 'How would you catch a wild camel, anyway?'

'From the back of an open jeep, mate. You could use a knotted rope on the end of a long pole and snare its neck. But I prefer bulldogging myself.'

'You use dogs?'

'Nah. It means jumping off the jeep on to the running camel's neck or hump. Knock it off balance, right, and bring it to the ground.'

I was impressed by this, but not as impressed as I was later, when I discovered young male camels could weigh a tonne and run at more than fifty kilometres an hour.

'Once it's on the ground it's tethered and blindfolded, and becomes relatively docile. Training it takes a couple of months, but I don't do that myself.'

'You just hurl yourself at them and wrestle them to the ground?' said Nicola.

The camel-catcher smiled, no offence taken. 'It's a skilled job,' he said amiably, before seeing us on our way.

Later, as we drove back to Broken Hill, camels crossed the road in front of our campervan. Nicola leapt out and ran after them with her camera, but they had already disappeared into the surrounding scrub.

Mike had been silent all day. He sat on in the van, tapping his fingers against the steering-wheel, waiting for Nicola in annoyance. When she climbed back into the passenger seat we sped off in a cloud of dust that hung behind us, hostile against the blue sky.

My brother Simon was pleased to see us when we arrived at the Parkes Radio Telescope, but he looked aghast at our ragged appearance. I was wearing the only sweatshirt I had with me, which I had been wearing since before our arrival in Perth: it was dusty and frayed at the cuffs. Mike was still wearing his weird batik pants, and Nicola's hair had grown out of control like a European weed in the outback, sprouting vigorously. We hadn't had showers since Western Australia, and we had been driving all day on a long and dusty road from Broken Hill.

My brother was an astronomer who worked for the Commonwealth Scientific and Industrial Research Organisation. Although based in Sydney, he frequently spent time at Parkes and occasionally at other Australian telescopes in order to collect data for his projects. After we were showered and changed and were looking half respectable we walked out to the telescope.

'The dish is about to go back up,' said my brother. 'Let's have a ride.'

The telescope's dish was tipped so that it almost touched the ground at one point of its circumference, and we stepped on to it. Minutes later we were grinding slowly upwards as the dish lifted back into its working position, pointing up towards the heavens.

'Parabolic, sixty-four metres in diameter, made of perforated aluminium panels,' said Simon over the whine of the mechanism that moved it. 'Opened in 1961, designed by the same consulting firm who designed the Sydney Harbour Bridge. And Barnes Wallace was on the team too—the engineer who created the dam-buster bombs.'

When the dish had stopped tilting we climbed further, up into the aerial cabin of the focus box some sixty metres above the ground. Said Simon: 'Radio waves are focused here on to a receiver shaped like a horn after they bounce on to the dish. There are two amplifiers kept at two hundred and sixty-nine degrees below zero by liquid helium. From the amplifiers the signal is sent down one of the supporting legs in insulated wires to the control room.' But I wasn't really listening, gazing out instead at the surrounding countryside, rolling fields of farmland scattered with houses and cows— the first fertile-looking land I had seen since South Australia —and at the clouds, which were blushing into pink and mauve as the sun dipped down towards the horizon.

'Of course, when the place was built, the site was chosen because it was free from radio interference,' muttered my brother. 'Which is no longer the case.'

'You mean people can interfere with this thing?'

My brother scowled. 'Why not? I remember at Jodrell Bank some woman on a nearby hill bought a new microwave and totally disrupted all the signals we were receiving. We thought we were about to have an alien landing! We had to get a massive lead shield placed around it to absorb the microwaves.'

'I'm sure that delighted her.'

'Someone has to push back the frontiers of science,' Simon replied with a smirk, poking me in the ribs.

'So what interferes here?'

'Mobile phones, which are banned on the actual site. The airport radar at Parkes. Anytime anyone mows their lawn, the lawn mower causes constant disruption of data. Car and tractor ignitions—when you turn on the engine it emits a blast of radio waves. And Russian spy satellites passing overhead.'

Later he said: 'In the old focus cabin, water sometimes got into the receiver, since the whole thing wasn't very water-proof. Whenever it rained I had to climb up to the focus cabin about once an hour with a hair drier and dry the receiver off. I used to go in my slippers, up the ladder in the dark and the rain. Everyone thought I was mad.'

I thought so too, though it didn't seem appropriate to say so. Nor were interference and rain the only problems to be encountered at Parkes. Galahs chewed the cables that came down from the focus cabin into the control room, and there was a galah alarm that could be sounded to chase them off.

'At Narrabri a cockatoo once chewed through a cable and put the whole antenna out of work,' said Simon. 'And one night someone left the lights on, which attracted insects and then frogs. The frogs got electrocuted on the power points and shut down the entire power supply—we had to use a back-up generator.'

At Parkes another problem was bogong moths. A laser beam kept the telescope locked into position, but the red light of the beam attracted the big moths, which flew through it and thus knocked the dish out of alignment with the segment of the sky the astronomers wished to study.

'We have to clamber up with a can of insect repellent and try and get rid of them . . . Not that it does much good.'

I smirked to myself. Australia was a world leader in astronomical research, and the radio telescope at Parkes was one of the world's most important, a multi-million-dollar instrument of advanced engineering attached to a roomful of computers and attendant scientists that analysed its data. Nevertheless, when it rained my brother had to clamber around its superstructure in his bedroom slippers, with a fly spray and hair drier, in order to prevent it from malfunction-ing. I was delighted: the frailty of technology against the forces of nature, and the ultimate puniness of human beings, seemed a salutary lesson in this modern world. I was no technophobe, but society's total reliance on technological advance I found worrying. People panicked when their electricity went off, put their lives on hold when their cars were under repair, didn't know what to do without a television—I found this amusing, but it was frightening too.

We clambered down through a hatch in the dish and descended the supporting tower by a series of ladders and low doors that reminded me of a submarine—not that I had ever been in a submarine. Down in the control room the frontiers of the universe were being mulled over by banks of electronic gadgetry that winked and blinked like the control panels on the starship *Enterprise*. Computers controlled the telescope's movement, recorded incoming radio signals, stored data. ('I don't know what Simon does,' Nicola muttered to me. 'I mean, the computers do everything.')

'Interferometry here. And that's the correlator, used for spectral line work and so on,' Simon was saying, flapping a hand at another machine, as large as a wardrobe, with more flashing lights.

'What's spectral line work and so on?'

'Well, you know. It's for people who want to look at spectral lines, such as the OH lines—you know what they are, hydroxyl molecules.' His faith in my knowledge and comprehension was gratifying, if astonishing, so I said nothing.

'And what's that?' said Nicola, pointing.

'A coffee machine.'

Now in the control room a Canadian, doing her doctorate in astronomy at Princeton, was scribbling on a piece of paper, while a visitor from an institute in Bologna was playing Minesweeper on a TV monitor. There was a Chinese here too, called Jin, participating in a China–Australia collaboration to set up pulsar stations in China. But he seemed bewildered, stuck out here in the middle of nowhere at a telescope, and barely raised a flicker of interest when I spoke to him in Chinese. Jin appeared sad and lost and homesick, and talked of his wife and child in Beijing before subsiding into silence.

My brother was studying pulsars, the remains of massive stars created out of supernova explosions. They were small objects, about ten kilometres across, but with a mass greater than that of the sun, being made up of extremely dense material.

'One teaspoon would weigh millions of tonnes,' explained Simon in one of his rare moments of lucidity. 'They rotate, so we get flashes of radio signals, rather like a lighthouse emitting light.'

Simon was attempting, with others, to determine their form and evolution, as well as their distribution in the galaxy. 'About six hundred are known,' he said. 'More than half discovered in Australia.'

'How many by you?'

'Well over a hundred.'

'Surely once you've discovered one . . .'

'We have to find them all! Anyway, they're not all the same. Some are special. For example, binary pulsars are rather rare—pulsars with another companion orbiting them.'

'What kind of companion?'

'Another pulsar, a star or a black hole. Also of interest, of course, are very young pulsars, which glitch.'

'Glitch?'

'Like an earthquake on a pulsar, which causes a change in the rotation, which helps us understand what's inside the pulsar.'

'What is inside it?'

'A superconducting super-fluid liquid interior.'

'And how is knowing that of use?'

'It isn't.' My brother shrugged and grinned. 'It's just interesting.'

Later, over dinner in the canteen, the scientists were quiet, picking their way through their food, while Nicola, Mike and I babbled about our trip. Then I stopped: my travels seemed ridiculously Bohemian and indulgent in these surroundings. The table fell silent again and everyone scraped at the Commonwealth's mashed potatoes, Jin with a look of infinite misery on his face.

Suddenly Luciano, the Italian from Bologna, said out of the blue: 'Does the magnetic axis align with the rotation axis as the pulsar gets older?'

There was a scratching of knives and no one answered until Simon perked up: 'Well, observationally it appears to be the case. Because for old pulsars they have wider pulse profiles than younger ones, implying we are seeing them pole-on. But an opposite view is taken by Beskin, Gurevich and Istomin, who claim pulsars are counter-aligned with time. That's patently not true, I think. It's maybe true in theory, but when you look at observations it just isn't like that.'

'Does the pulsar rotation axis have anything to do with the galactic magnetic field?'

'No. It's too tenuous. The galactic field is surely too weak after the supernova has exploded. The planets' magnetic axes are in random directions without anything to do with the plane of orbit.'

Simon scratched his beard and Luciano didn't answer, apparently satisfied.

Then there was more silence, and the pioneers in the forefront of Australia's astronomical research went on with their eating.

Sydney was a stone's throw from Parkes, at least in terms of the distance we had already driven. I intended stopping there for a few weeks recuperation before flying to Tasmania, but I was not quite ready for urban life yet, and besides, a tangle of circumstances delayed my entrance to Australia's largest city. While there I was to stay with my brother, but he still had work to do at Parkes, and would not be home for at least a week. Nicola and Mike had become increasingly sullen with each other, and finally Mike had announced his intention of returning to England as soon as a ticket could be bought. He muttered about his visa expiring soon, and his lack of money, all of which was true, but I could not help thinking that it was also a fortuitous opportunity to escape my sister. Nicola took the news, at least in my presence, with relative equanimity, as if it were all for the best. Certainly she had no intention of going with Mike to England. To add to the complications of their disintegrating relationship was the practical realisation that her roots were in a different country —Switzerland—and that on a geographical as well as personal level they had reached a parting of the ways.

I decided to leave them to their own devices in Sydney, at least for a while: they would take a train back there while I took the campervan and meandered cross-country through the Blue Mountains and on to Canberra, both of which Nicola and Mike had in any case visited before my arrival in Australia. It was a melancholy parting, for despite our occasional differences, and the sometimes charged atmosphere between them, I had enjoyed their company. I had a suspicion I was not likely to see Mike again, though to each other we never admitted as much.

There was more science on the way to Sydney as we passed over the Blue Mountains: the blue haze here was caused by a phenomenon known as Raleigh scattering, in which dust and water droplets reflected light in wavelengths that appeared blue to the eye. As we ascended and descended the winding roads the brakes overheated, filling the van with an evil stench. I left Mike and Nicola at Katoomba railway station, standing together but sadly apart with their backpacks at their feet, before driving off to find somewhere to camp for the night.

Next morning brilliant sunshine and spectacular views restored my spirits. The Blue Mountains are 60 million years old, worn-out remnants of a vast plateau, and great swathes of the region are now national park, home to peregrine falcons, rock wallabies, koalas and tiger quolls. The name was rather a misnomer, since there were no peaks or mountains here: the top of the plateau was flat. But it was still a rugged and wild place, and long erosion had given it plunging cliffs and narrow, winding valleys. It was easy to see how this had long been an impenetrable barrier to the expansion of settlement westwards from Sydney. 'Beyond the Blue Mountains' was an expression indicating an unreachable, almost imaginary country until the ranges were finally breached in 1813. Development rapidly followed when the Anglo-Saxon inhabitants of the coast realised that the mountains were the ideal retreat from the summer heat. Like Sri Lanka's Nuwara Eliya, Malaysia's Cameron Highlands or India's Simla, Katoomba fast became a watering hole and relaxation spot for Sydney's colonial wealthy, who built their Anglo-Saxon cottages among the gum trees or came to stay in one of the hotels. Today democratisation had brought fast-food chains, day-trippers and international tourists, and along the highway there was a continuous strip of development that merged one town into another: Glenbrook and Springwood, Woodford and Wentworth Falls, Blackheath and Mount Victoria and Hartley, with their pretty British names and stone houses with English-style gardens.

At Katoomba the tourists gathered to eat in the Art Deco cafés before herding down to Echo Point, the most famous spot in the mountains, with its spectacular views of the valley and the columns of rock known as the Three Sisters. I herded myself there too, as if my sense of adventure had departed with my sister on the train to Sydney. This was a good place for a photo, and cameras whirred and clicked as people lined up by the retaining fences to pose with the view in the background. Groups of Japanese tourists milled around, conversing excitedly and bowing thanks to each other. Japanese tour organisers loved Katoomba. It was a day trip from Sydney—a long one that precluded any bushwalking or relaxation, but after all the tourists could still smell the gum trees and marvel at the rainbow lorikeets that screeched outside the visitors' centre, and they could still bring home their photos and say they'd been there.

I ambled round the path through the gum trees, towards the Three Sisters, past more Japanese in natty red and yellow anoraks and spanking-clean hiking boots that hadn't been anywhere near a dirt track. But who cared?—they were enjoying themselves anyway, it seemed. There were plenty of Australian families here too, up from Sydney and doing much the same thing, though they didn't seem half as excited about it all: the kids quarrelled with each other and were shouted at by their fathers, the mothers looked hot and harassed. There were four Taiwanese clambering over the rocks as well, one of them an elderly lady in baggy trousers and a long Vietnamese-style shirt to her knees. She wore a white cricket hat tied under her chin with a pink ribbon.

'I'll wait here until this foreigner gets out of the way,' she said to her daughter in Chinese as she saw me approaching.

'I'm not a foreigner,' I lied to her, also in Chinese. 'I'm Australian. Surely *you* are the foreigner!'

The old lady looked abashed and then cackled with laughter. '*Dui, dui, dui,*' she said. 'You're right. I am the foreigner. From Taiwan.'

I smiled back at her and we swapped courtesies. For some reason the interchange made me feel very happy, and I walked back to the campervan with a grin on my face. I drove on to the lookouts around Blackheath, then to the Jenolan Caves. These massive limestone caves had a superb collection of stalactites and stalagmites, tortured into gargoyle shapes. There were more tourists here, and plenty of them: caves were always fascinating. Their elemental attraction was a retreat to the womb, perhaps, or to the dawn of prehistory, when we lived in such places, lurking in the gloom to escape the terror of wild beasts and hostile weather. But the escape would have provided no comfort. Stalagmites or not, this is surely why most people like caves—they enjoy a vague feeling of angst. This is unfamiliar territory, a place of dark shadows and malevolent spirits. Bats live in caves, and dragons and warlocks and trolls.

There were more Japanese here, and some Chinese as well—what did they think of caves? Chinese dragons lived in caves too, but Chinese dragons were benign, harbingers of good luck, and the few Chinese caves I had visited did not seem sinister, but were garishly light by multicoloured spotlights. At Reed Flute Cave near Guilin one cavern had been fancifully named the Crystal Palace of the Dragon King, and gossipy tour guides had related stories to explain the wondrous collection of rock formations that dotted it. One large stalagmite was supposed to represent a scholar, who ventured to write a poem worthy of the cave's beauty. But after several weeks the poet had only managed to jot down a few lines that he thought suitable, and was eventually turned to stone for his trouble.

Here was a return once more to the personal relevance of tourist sites, not to mention their greater cultural relevance. Chinese caves seemed to evoke artistic imagination and a sort of innocent wonder that harked back to fairy tales and fabulous stories. To the Chinese, caves were also a source of powerful natural forces that required respect: like mountains or forests, caves were close to holiness. Western caves were the stuff that nightmares were made of, part of the underworld and close to the devil. At the Jenolan Caves there were no stories of poetic writer's block, only accounts of the local geology and shuffling tourists gazing at the dripping walls. Caves were dangerous places, and if you weren't careful (imagine if the lights went out!), you could get lost in them for ever, and die down here in the blackness, sealed into nature's own tomb.

I couldn't help but feel relief as I saw daylight appear through the passageway ahead. The rest of the group perked up too, and conversation resumed as we all emerged into the sunlight and open spaces. The Japanese were corralled into their tour coach and driven away, and I got into my van and drove away too.

Later, in Sydney, I would discover that more Australians worked in the tourist industry than on farms and outback stations. Tourism was a vital part of the national economy. As in many other economic sectors, it relied on the important Asian market. The Japanese were the biggest spenders among all foreign tourists, averaging some $700 per visitor, exclusive of the costs of their package deal. According to one study, 80 per cent of Japanese returned home carrying a stuffed toy (some of these were made in Taiwan). They also bought opals, other gemstones and jewellery, handicrafts, sheepskin goods and duty-free perfume, alcohol and chocolate.

The Japanese were the most numerous and therefore most noticeable of the visitors from Asia, but tourists also came from Hong Kong, Korea, Taiwan and South-East Asia. The Australian Tourist Commission advertised in those countries in the hope of achieving the same kind of success it had earlier achieved in the United States with Paul Hogan and his barbecue. The current 'Let the Magic Begin' campaign shown on the television channels of Asian nations featured Australia as a place to go for adventure-style holidays, a place of glorious nature, excitement and urban glamour.

'Though adventure to an Asian is not necessarily adventure to an Australian,' Greig McAllan pointed out. He was Asian regional director for the Australian Tourist Commission, based in Hong Kong, and I had contacted him to ask about marketing Australia's image in the region. 'They don't want forty-day camel treks across the Simpson Desert,' he said.

'It's golf, scuba-diving and the like, and for younger people perhaps bungee-jumping and white-water rafting.'

This was still a new departure from older campaigns, which had emphasised a more passive kind of tourism, with Australian wildlife and scenery observed from afar. 'Let the Magic Begin' built on the continent's reputation for nature but made the tourist's participation more active, and also introduced a new element, the city experience.

'The contrast between the active development of the nature experience with the stylish, cosmopolitanism of the city life experience—eating out, nightclubs, going to shows, fine wine. That is what we aim for,' said McAllan, before adding revealingly: 'We probably couldn't have promoted those things before.'

So here it was, Australia abandoning its cultural cringe and coming to maturity through the televisions of South-East Asia, now confident enough to go beyond the stereotypes. But marketing Australia still wasn't going to be that easy. Asian tourists today were no different from the Australians of twenty years ago: the social cachet of holidaying in Europe or America was enormous. Europe's culture and history were virtually impossible to compete with, while the United States was seen as being on the cutting edge of technology and glamour. Australia's advantage lay in promoting the juxtaposition of its unique nature and the urban life-style.

'Cosmopolitan, stylish, but relaxed in a typically Australian way,' as McAllan put it to me, his own cosmopolitan but relaxed Australian accent travelling down the wires from Hong Kong. Over the long term, he explained, it was hoped that Asian tourists, as they became more mature overseas travellers, would discover that Australia too could be exciting and that its big cities could offer some of the things available in London or New York, such as big shows like *Cats* or *Les Misérables*.

'It all depends on the market. With Korea we're still into pushing the cultural icons like kangaroos, the Barrier Reef and the Opera House—they're new tourists and that's all they know, so that's all we show them. On the other hand, Singaporeans, for example, are now more mature tourists, and many of them are repeat visitors to Australia, attracted to lesser-known regions, particularly in their case to Perth and Western Australia. They don't go on packages very much any more, they're independently oriented, they like to rent cars and drive themselves. They want to know what else Australia can offer. Hopefully that will counter the current assumption that Australia is a bit of a bland place.'

In Japan, where the Australian Tourist Commission ran a separate campaign and maintained another office, the 'Country of Surprises' advertisement was also doing its best to counter the perception that urban Australia was bland. While the Japanese often cited Australia as their most desired destination for an overseas holiday, it terms of actual visitors it ranked only in sixth place. The fact was that the Japanese had a very limited perception of Australia as a destination with fabulous wildlife and scenery, but with little else to offer by way of holiday experiences. In particular, it was identified as being too far away and lacking in good food, good shopping, and urban excitement. The 'Country of Surprises' campaign was at pains to point out that Queensland is closer than Hawaii, that sushi can be eaten in the outback, and that for variety you can sunbathe one day and ski the next.

And who was Australia competing against? The USA and European countries disdained to advertise their attractions—they had no need to, because of their cultural dominance and because airlines, hotel chains and travel agents advertised for them.

'Canada and South Africa promote "big nature" like us,' McAllan told me. 'But Canada tends to be winter-oriented and so not in direct competition. South Africa is spending a lot of money in promotions and has nature they claim is more exciting than cute koalas and kangaroos—it's hard to compete with lions or elephants!'

'But Australia is much closer.'

'Oh yes—which is why Indonesia is now emerging as an important market.'

'And China?'

'Well, China as you know is loosening travel restrictions for its citizens and has a boisterous economy that is being deregulated. There are a lot of wealthy people there—more than a million millionaires in US dollar terms. But at the moment only Singapore, Hong Kong, Macau, the Philippines, Thailand and Malaysia have been designated by the government as holiday destinations—the theory is that, since they have large Chinese populations, they are somehow suitable. But we are negotiating with the government to add Australia to the list.'

'How many visitors come from China now?'

'About sixty thousand. We're hoping it will be three hundred thousand by the end of the century.'

Eventually McAllan, friendly and helpful, rang off, leaving the taxpayer with a large telephone bill. But there was good money to be made from tourism, and this was how Australia was packaged and sold in the markets of Asia. The Australian Tourist Commission still relied on the old images of outback Australia, of its kangaroos and rugged landscapes, but they at least had managed to go beyond the stereotypes to portray Australia, too, as a land of urban sophistication, of high culture and fine cuisine. One day, perhaps, the rest of the nation would catch up.

And there would soon, it seemed, be a lot more Chinese in the caves around Katoomba.

After several days of meandering through hidden valleys I descended the Blue Mountains. Talk of adventure sport had obviously gone to my head. I might have refused to bungee-jump in Queensland, haunted by the thought of my knees springing out of their sockets in mid-air, or my head smacking on the ground by mistake like some dreadful cartoon injury. Now I decided to leap out of an aeroplane and plummet earthward, not on an elastic rope, but at the end of a parachute.

'It's the biggest adrenalin rush you'll ever experience in your life. I mean *ever*,' I had been told by a tourist in Katoomba, whose eyes had glinted at the very thought, like a junkie thinking about her next fix.

'It's changed my life,' said her boyfriend improbably. 'Mate, it's just awesome.'

Since I needed my life changed, I thought this might be as good a way as any, and one that actually absolved me from any thinking on the matter. On the approach to Sydney I therefore stopped at a ramshackle airfield that specialised in sky-diving, and before I knew it had committed myself to jump.

'Just sign this paper. It absolves the company from any liability in the case of injury or death,' said my instructor cheerfully, thrusting a two-page document in small print under my nose.

'Injury! I don't quite see how one can injure oneself. Death, yes. But if the parachute doesn't open, I'll hardly get away with just a sprained wrist.'

'Hm. People sometimes break their legs if they effect a poor landing. With the parachute open, of course.'

'And if it doesn't?'

'That's never happened at this airfield. There was a woman in America recently whose parachute failed to open, but she landed in a soft swamp and only cracked a few ribs.'

'I haven't seen any swamps around here.'

'Well, there have been half-a-dozen deaths in Australia in the last three or four years. I'm not pretending it's not a dangerous sport.' He didn't say it, but I knew what he meant: the choice was mine. Anyway, I had more chance of being run over by a truck, I reasoned. If Nicola had been here, *she* would have done it.

I was assured the safety checks were rigorous. The parachutes were meticulously inspected and folded away after every jump. As well as the main chute, there were also two back-up chutes that could be relied on in the event of an emergency. Besides, I was not jumping solo but in tandem with my instructor, who would be strapped to my back like an incubus.

'I pull the rip-cord and count to five. The parachute should normally deploy after three seconds. If we don't feel a massive jolt, it has malfunctioned. We immediately open the secondary parachute strapped to the chest.'

'And if that doesn't work?'

'There's a third one. It opens automatically at low altitude. It's also useful just in case you thrash around and knock me unconscious during the free-fall.'

Well, this seemed reasonable. What were the chances of all three parachutes malfunctioning? No one brought three oxygen tanks with them when they were scuba-diving.

'As you step out of the plane, you should cross your arms across your chest, bend your knees and lift up your chin. On landing, also bend your knees, holding them up high with your hands to break your landing.'

There was an old bit of plane beside the hangars, and we practised this manoeuvre. I felt like an idiot stepping into the dust in some kind of foetal position with a complete stranger pressed up against my back. This was easy: the ground was only centimetres away. We were going to jump from 3000 metres and career earthward at over 200 kilometres an hour. At around 700 metres our fall would be decelerated by a piece of canvas the size of a couple of bed sheets—would I be able to remember to bend my knees then?

The plane was tiny. I sat on the floor, wedged between my instructor's legs, with another aspiring parachutist wedged between my legs. I was extremely uncomfortable, and the harness around me was so tight it was cutting into my thighs and chest. Outside, the propellers were making a racket; I felt I would be glad to jump out and leave all the discomfort behind. I was still unexcited, and somewhat surprised by my lack of excitement. The other novice jumpers around me were chattering or telling jumping jokes or pretending they were terrified (maybe they were).

The instructor tapped me on my shoulder, a signal that the jump was almost upon us, and clipped his harness to mine. That was when I began to panic: not at the thought of the parachute not opening, because of course it almost certainly would, but at the thought that the only thing that connected me to the instructor (and thus the parachute, which he had wisely affixed to his own back) was a buckle, or so it seemed. My heart started pounding. Bodies were leaping out of the door in front of me. I shuffled along awkwardly with my human attachment and then, before I had time to realise it, I was out the door.

It took a matter of seconds to accelerate to free-fall velocity, but it seemed like minutes. My stomach was pressed up against my diaphragm as if trying to escape into my chest cavity, my heart had already fled up into my throat, and my cheeks felt as if they had migrated up to my forehead, so great was the force of the surrounding air whistling up around me. The wind was roaring in my ears and I got odd glimpses of scenery like a demented slide-show run in fast time: the corner of the aeroplane rapidly receding, a wisp of cloud against a blue sky, a vast expanse of green earth, another body that seemed to float near me, though my mind told me it was falling as fast as I was.

I was excited now; I was terrified. I thought I was going to be sick, and I was thinking: Oh god, I'm going to die, this is horrible. Let it stop, let it stop. And then I wasn't accelerating any more and the instructor indicated that I could uncross my arms. Then I was face down in a star shape, my arms and legs spread, and suddenly it was fun: we were swimming through the air and I was looking at the countryside spread out below, and it seemed very far away.

The fall lasted not much more than thirty seconds. Then there was a sudden jolt and it felt as if I was being hurled back upwards as the parachute opened. The harness dug into my thighs and I hoped the buckles wouldn't pop. Above me the chute billowed out like a massive green jellyfish. After that it was an anticlimax. I knew the chute was working and that everything was OK, and I drifted downwards, and it was only when I scraped the tops of the trees and came in to land that I realised how fast I was actually travelling.

That was sky-diving: several hours of waiting around an airfield, thirty minutes in a very uncomfortable aeroplane, thirty seconds of complete panic and exhilaration, ten minutes of drifting, all for $250. About eight dollars a second for the exciting bit.

The biggest adrenalin rush ever? Probably, but other adrenalin rushes had lasted longer: what about the Barrier Reef, the relief at getting the van restarted in Adcock Gorge—what about ripping open an envelope with a good exam result, or having a book accepted by a publisher, or finding a sublime piece of chocolate cake in Hong Kong after six months in China? Sky-diving is one of those things: you casually tell people, as you look calmly down at your finger-nails: Yeah, I've done that. Another of the thirty-second, short, sharp, prepackaged, expensive thrills that modern society seemed to thrive on.

Well, it didn't change my life. I was unemployed, homeless, without plans and lovelorn once more, and I still didn't know where I was going, nor what I was doing. But I had decided that not doing it and not knowing was, perhaps, a good thing. Tomorrow I was heading to Canberra, before going on to Sydney. Tasmania and Victoria lay ahead, as yet unknown, and who knew what I might find in those places?

Now *that* was an adrenalin rush; and, though I didn't know it then, it would change my life too.

tales of two cities

Canberra was the capital of Australia, and I felt I had to visit it, although everyone told me not to. It wasn't that far from Sydney, but Sydneysiders I met in the Blue Mountains had rolled their eyes and sneered at the idea of even spending a weekend there: the place was boring, they said, there was nothing to see, it was full of bureaucrats and diplomats and politicians—the last, along with New Zealanders, were the laughing-stock of the Australian people. Perhaps for this reason the national capital was something of a joke. More than anything, I got the impression Canberra was an embarrassment. It was provincial and conservative and stuffy, everyone told me. This was the reputation other cities in Australia had once had, I thought, though I did not say so.

Spend a weekend in any town and you can do little else than reinforce the stereotypes. Canberra to me on the first day seemed a collection of satellite suburbs lost in the bush, joined to each other by enormous highways, empty of cars, that apparently led nowhere. Urban laws prohibited billboards, telegraph wires, flashing neon lights—this was a good thing, but all one could see on the highways were planted shrubs and a distant smudge of hills, which unnerved me. Had I perhaps taken a wrong turning? Was there really a city behind the next clump of bushes?

Canberra was a small, insignificant town of almost Singaporean orderliness, pretending to be a world capital, full of extravagant embassies (the Thai Embassy looked like a

Buddhist temple with its upturned roofs, the American Embassy like a plantation mansion from *Gone with the Wind*) and centred around an improbable parliament building and a colossal war memorial. It was a clean and tidy Disney World built in the middle of the outback, inhabited (yes, the stories were right) by politicians and government workers. Canberra was Washington without the street crime, Beijing without the Forbidden City, Bern without the Swiss mountains, Ulan Bator without a through train. It was all the world's most boring and staid capitals rolled into one and deposited in the heat and hills of the Australian Capital Territory. Its only excitement lay in the suburb of Fyshwick, renowned for its pornography mail-order companies. The ACT had less stringent laws than the Australian States, and Fyshwick boasted the largest sex shop in the country, but it was clear its adventurous customers lived in other, more exciting, places.

Cruel? Why not. Foreigners and Sydneysiders could afford to be cruel, because they didn't have to live there, they didn't want to live there, and in any case, they hadn't been in the city for more than a few days, and that wasn't enough to pass beyond generalisation. It certainly seemed to me that Canberra was a city that had no right to exist: an artificial place without much soul or reason. It had come into being only because of rivalry between Melbourne and Sydney, when the movement towards federation had prompted discussions on where the seat of government should be. So antagonistic were the two main cities to each other that New South Wales threatened to withdraw from the new Commonwealth over the issue. 'Sydney never had the smallest chance of being the capital of Federated Australia,' fumed an editorial in the *Age*, the voice of Melbourne. 'In the first place the climate is not fit for the home of a progressive people.' Sydney's *Daily Telegraph* was quick to respond: Melbourne had hot winds in summer and fog in winter, and anyway its finances were a disaster.

A compromise was reached. The capital would be in New South Wales, but it would not be Sydney. In fact, it was to be at a distance of 'no less than a hundred miles' from that city, and built on land that New South Wales would be obliged to cede to the federal government. In return, Melbourne was to be the provisional capital until such time as the new capital could be founded. This was likely to be some while, as the proposed sites were nothing but bushland and farms.

In 1911 the new Commonwealth government took over the ACT and, through an international competition, chose an American, Walter Burley Griffin, to plan the town. He envisaged a city bisected by lines of roads into triangles of commerce, residential areas and government buildings, a significant departure in its day from the staid city planning of the Victorian era. Two years later work started on the new town, which was named Canberra, Aboriginal for 'place where people meet'. Myola had been the name favoured by the prime minister, and other offerings included Opossum, Emu, Bomballa and Kookaburra. Even Sydmeladeperbrisho had been considered, a name uniting the first syllable of the capital city of each of Australia's States. Sydbourne and Melbney were other conciliatory combinations.

Two world wars and the Great Depression gave Canberra a slow start in life. Parliament did not sit there until 1927. By the beginning of World War II the population was still only 13 000, and most government departments had just started moving into the town. Only in the 1960s did Canberra start to grow at a more rapid pace; now there were 300 000 inhabitants. From the top of Black Mountain, where I was standing, the city sprawled across the hills, far bigger than it was ever envisaged by Walter Burley Griffin, but I could still see his vision, with triangles radiating out from Capitol Hill, the roads like spokes of a wheel with the parliament at its hub. The New Parliament House looked directly across Lake Burley Griffin to the War Memorial, Canberra's other major landmark.

From my distance on the hilltop Canberra looked like a town made of Lego, with its neat shapes and red roofs. Its public buildings, such as the Supreme Court and National Library, seemed nothing more than big square blocks set down by an artificial lake. Even the roads looked toy-like: some of them were orange, and they were lined by regimented trees that all looked the same shape and size.

I should have listened to the voices of reason in Sydney, I thought as I stared across the valley: there was no need to come here.

I was staying with Laotian Australians who had come here in the 1970s—the family of Surit, a friend of my brother's who lived in Sydney. Surit, who was in Canberra for the weekend, had been very young when he had arrived in his adoptive country, and appeared very Australian. His elder sister and two brothers seemed less so, and their English was not as good, while his younger brother and sister, who had been born in Sydney, spoke pure Australian and refused to speak Laotian, even with their parents. There was a lesson here in cultural assimilation: a simple one, which was that it took time.

Not surprisingly, it was the parents who seemed the most isolated from the Australian community. They spoke poor English and seemed to know only Laotians, most of them extended family. But staying with them for a few days provoked my admiration and respect. They had come to Australia with nothing only twenty years ago and had built a new life here, with all the trappings of material success and university-educated children, all of whom had good jobs except the youngest daughter, who was still in high school.

While I was shown the sights of Canberra I was told stories of another world, as if caught between two dimensions, though they were different facets of the same family's history. In Laos, Surit's grandfather had been a wealthy businessman of ethnic Chinese background from the city of Luanprabang by the Mekong River, just across the border from Thailand. As a young man, Surit's father had been educated in a private Chinese school and had then travelled widely in Asia and enjoyed a cosmopolitan life. He married beneath himself, and to an ethnic Laotian, much to the disapproval of his parents.

'My mother came from a poor family. She was a country girl. She had no education,' explained Surit (we were in the Botanic Gardens, and the sun beat down on Australian flora, far away from this story of the tropics). 'She was brought up by her elder sister because her parents die when she was very young. I don't think she remember her parents. It is melancholy. She was younger than my father about eighteen years. She married at sixteen. My father was a cradle-snatcher! After married not even a year, bang! the first child was born, then the second and the third. It was in three consecutive years. My father was a very naughty boy. I don't know what he was doing at that time. But he must love my mother, to have married her.'

The family had lived with his grandmother in a two-storey house with four bedrooms—large by the standards of the day—in the area of Luanprabang where the Chinese congregated. They lived opposite the mansion of one of the royal princes, and not far from the palace itself. It seemed, as I listened to Surit, to have been a time of fun and games, like many childhood memories. 'Especially Laotian New Year. The parade was just fantastic. It was very colourful. Everywhere people are dancing in the street. Every year they have the most beautiful Miss Luanprabang riding the statue of a big tiger. The highest monks come out from the temple. The king and queen came too. The most fun game is the water bomb. My eldest brother was very naughty, we were on the second floor of my grandmother's house, we pour the water on to the people in the street. That was very childish and fun. We were so happy little children.'

Later we went to inspect the New Parliament House, an extravaganza that seemed inappropriate to this small town and thinly populated nation. Its construction had involved carting away an entire hillside, building the complex and then replacing the hillside over the top of it. It crouched under a smooth dome of grass like a nuclear bunker or science-fiction war station, its steel flagpole sticking up like an antenna testing the air for an alien invasion. It had cost a billion dollars, and I found its interior a wonder of marble and glass and wood, and crowded with paintings, tapestries and sculptures by Australian artists. An editor of the *Age* once wrote the entrance hall reminded him of Caligula's bathroom: it was certainly opulent. Official literature informed you that it recalled a forest of gum trees, with its white and grey marble pillars.

We wandered about, cooled by the marble floors, and peered out from its balconies over Lake Burley Griffin towards the War Memorial and the town centre on the other side. Here Surit picked up the thread of his life history once more. In 1975, when he was eight, the family's life was turned upside down. The communists took over Laos, the national anthem was replaced, the royal family imprisoned and murdered. 'A new flag was introduced. I thought it was quite boring, only three colours in stripes, red, white and blue. Before it was the head of three elephants,' Surit told me. Food became short, travel was restricted, ethnic Chinese were persecuted and the traditional culture disintegrated. Many middle-class and wealthy families began to flee abroad.

'My own family had been rich, I had an uncle who was a general in the royal army, we were half Chinese. There was no future for us. That's why we decided to escape. We left the house, our business, our land behind, we had to start all over again. Of course I was just a little kid. But I was awared of what was happening to our country. One of my friend told me he wouldn't leave Laos because he love his country. His family remain in Laos to this day.'

This, I thought, must be the eternal question haunting refugees, perhaps any immigrants: should they have stayed? Did they do right to leave? There was seldom sympathy for such immigrants among other Australians, who had little concept of what they had sacrificed as well as gained. Surit's parents had given up not only their country but their social positions and previous skills, and had been reduced to manual workers—Surit's mother a factory hand, his father a truck driver. On top of this other Australians, unable to tap into the social roles and differences of status that governed relationships within the immigrant communities, mostly saw all Asian immigrants as an undifferentiated mass. Not surprisingly, many immigrants experienced disorientation and even anger. Those of the older generation turned to family and fellow nationals for emotional and practical support, further isolating themselves from the Australian way of life and reinforcing other Australians' perceptions that they were different and exclusive—that they lived in ghettos.

If this latest wave of immigrants did not yet seem particularly assimilated into Australian society, Italians and Greeks had not been assimilated thirty years ago either; I had met one Italian Australian who remembered being spat at as a child because of her ethnic background. True, Surit's family spent their time mostly with other Laotians, and with them I went to Laotian social functions and the Laotian temple in a Canberra suburb. His parents did not seem too anxious about their isolation from Australian society and culture (or so it seemed to me), presumably satisfied at their material comfort and the upward mobility and success of their children, which they richly deserved. But they had welcomed me to their home unhesitatingly.

The younger generation were far less isolated. One of Surit's sisters had already married a foreigner, albeit a Thai, and his parents were actively encouraging their children to marry white Australians. Two of them had white Australian boyfriends, and their houses, jobs and ways of life seemed no different from any other Australians', except at mealtimes.

What was an Australian, anyway? If I had come to this country partly to find out, I still didn't know, though I remained convinced that Surit was one. It was hard to define an Australian, a nebulous concept anyway in a country where Western Australians talked of easterners as if they lived on another planet, where Sydney and Melbourne were bitter rivals, where Queenslanders considered themselves a breed apart. Perhaps Canberrans were the true Australians, though I supposed there were few real Canberrans. This made the city interesting: could it lead the way in defining the new Australia?

Australia was a small country, except geographically, but there was nothing wrong with having large visions. Canberra had been a vision of a world capital that would develop out of scrub-land, and most of its politicians promoted visions too, visions of a liberal Australia devoted to multiculturalism and tolerance. Who said Canberra was boring? Because of Surit's hospitable family I enjoyed my stay in Canberra more, perhaps, than I had enjoyed any other place in Australia. Surit too had made me realise anew that all places were unique, and nowhere was truly boring.

One only had to talk to people, and even Canberra became enlivening.

Sydney. Dusk was falling as I entered its outer fringes and crawled through the western suburbs, a tangle of multi-lane highways snarled with traffic and container trucks. I passed shabby houses made of weatherboard and peeling white paint, warehouses of corrugated iron, endless garages and petrol stations and drive-ins. Hadn't I read that Sydney was supposed to be one of the world's most beautiful cities? Parramatta, rendered poetic by its name (it meant 'place where the eels lie down' in the Eora language) seemed more of the same, at least from the highway. This was the geographical centre of Sydney, a good bit west up the Parramatta River from the harbour, which provided the city's real focus. It was also one of the sites of early settlement. Convicts frequently ran away from the farms around here, once deep in the bush, and sometimes their bodies were uncovered weeks and even years later, bleached by the sun. They believed China was not far away—some thought just over the Blue Mountains—and had thought to find refuge there among the hospitable inhabitants of the Celestial Empire. It was a persistent misperception among the convicts, resulting in escaped convicts being nicknamed Chinese Travellers.

It was benign, this view of the Chinese in those very early days; or would have been, if it had not caused the deaths of so many escapees. Things had changed since then. Asia was perceived as more threatening than welcoming, and anyway I was heading in the opposite direction, not towards the celestial land beyond the Blue Mountains but towards the sea and towards Sydney.

I stayed with my brother in the suburbs for a week before venturing into the city centre, where I had decided my first stop should be the famed Opera House. I caught a glimpse of it from the train as it crossed the Harbour Bridge—no more than scattered fragments of its white roofs through the grime of the carriage window and the cross-struts of the bridge's metalwork. At Circular Quay I rushed from the railway station and around the promenade as if about to be reunited with a lover, and there it was before me, a sight that, from the moment I drew near it, inspired me to poetry.

What was this building hanging over the edge of the water: soaring shells of mother-of-pearl, gusts of wind made visible, glacial peaks suspended in the Antipodes? A ship in full sail was the metaphor that sprang most readily to mind, perfectly complemented by the white yachts that skimmed past it on the blue waters of the harbour. Jørn Utzon, its architect, was satisfied with the analogy, though he had said he was inspired, more prosaically, by the peeled segments of an orange. Sydneysiders compared it to a concrete camel, or nine nuns in a rugby scrum (the denigration was typically Australian). The writer Elspeth Huxley in *Their Shining Eldorado* said the roofs were like palm fronds, then changed her mind and said they were 'the curved wings of bats or of cocked ears'— an odd analogy. To me they seemed more like the wings of a swan, but this was a European view, for swans in Australia were black. A Brisbane journalist had once written: 'From the front view it reminded me of Joan Sutherland, mouth open in the mad scene from *Lucia di Lammermoor*'.

On the ferries tourists had other comments: 'Like a shark's jaws,' said a small English boy.

'A pavlova.'

'Like clouds'—'No, clouds are not pointy.' (Two kids from Melbourne.)

'Like a ballet dancer's tutu.'

'A bishop's mitre.'

The metaphors grew increasingly odd and far-fetched as I scribbled them in my notebook, and then I came across Clive James' description—the Opera House to him was like a typewriter full of oyster shells. He thought it ugly—a misguided opinion. The Sydney Opera House to me was one of the most stunning edifices in the world, and certainly one of the twentieth century's greatest pieces of architecture. It was not only a public building but a work of art, inspiring and (as the metaphors showed) elusive.

I had read somewhere, though I no longer remember where, the observation that the Opera House, though designed by a Dane, was the only symbol of Australia created by white Australians—unlike Ayers Rock, boomerangs, koalas or

kangaroos. As such its construction was certainly a resound-
ing statement of Australia's slow emergence from the cultural
cringe and an affirmation that cultural life could indeed
exist—and flourish—Down Under. Yet some suggested that
this culture was elitist: its roofs pointed heavenward like a
cathedral and its hushed halls were devoted to an art that
few of the masses cared—or could afford—to enjoy. This
struck me as a very European observation on opera houses.
Sydney Opera House had been paid for by the public through
lotteries, and was actually a performing arts complex that
contained not only an opera house but a concert hall, a
drama theatre and a playhouse. Free musical events were
held in the lobby, shareholders' and board meetings (not to
mention Japanese weddings) conducted in its private rooms,
and buskers were encouraged to play in its shadows. Even
the opera here was not as elitist as elsewhere. Sydney had
proportionally the largest opera-going population of any city
in the world, twenty-dollar tickets were offered for standing
spaces with excellent views of the stage, and the libretto was
translated into English and displayed as electronic surtitles
during performances.

Nor was the building's exterior elitist, I thought as I gazed
up at it from every angle: it was surely resolutely modern,
positively brash, almost vulgar, like a pleasure pavilion in a
fun-fair. As such it was much more than an opera house, and
had become a national icon and a part of Australia's—or
certainly Sydney's—popular culture. At Circular Quay the
souvenir shops were cluttered with plastic models of the
building, and it adorned T-shirts, plates, mugs, pens, tea-
towels, address books, calendars and posters. The pointy
zigzags that recalled its roofs were splashed across corporate
logos and Sydney 2000 Olympics paraphernalia.

'Could you take a photo of me? Make sure the Opera
House is clear in the background.' I dragged my eyes away
from the white roofs and looked round.

He was a dollop of a man, his belly sagging, his face gone
soft with good living, his hair dishevelled. An attempt had
been made to comb long pieces over his balding head. His
clothes were untidy, his shirt tails escaping from his trousers,
his belt awry. But he was friendly, almost garrulous.

'I'm making a collage at home,' the man explained to me. 'Back in Los Angeles. All the places I've been to. I've got one with Trafalgar Square and another with Buckingham Palace.' He squinted at me in the sun and grimaced as I pressed the shutter on his camera.

'I've got one of me on a bus in Amsterdam, and on a ferry or whatsit, canal boat. And when I stopped over in Singapore on the way here I got one in front of that merlion thing. It's the symbol of Singapore, right?'

Amsterdam was famous for its bars where you could buy joints, its outrageous red light district, its Rembrandt and Van Gogh paintings, the house of Anne Frank. But when I asked the American what he thought of Amsterdam he was vague and seemed scarcely able to remember the city.

'I went on a canal boat,' he repeated. 'I asked someone to take a photo. It came out great.'

'Couldn't you have been on any boat anywhere?'

'You could see those tall buildings along the canal. When I put it in my collage everyone knew I had been to Amsterdam.'

The American was another of the trophy-hunters I had so often met when travelling. I recognised them instantly—I was one too. I was taking my own photos of the Opera House, though my dislike of posing meant I was not in them, and perhaps to the American this was not sufficient proof that I had been here. The Opera House, being such an icon of Australia, lent itself superbly to being photographed—and such obvious symbols were much needed by confused and disoriented package tourists in large cities. One should certainly have 'done' the Opera House in order to be accepted by the people back home. Imagine going to Sydney and saying you never went near its greatest symbol! Imagine going to Singapore and not seeing the merlion (a rather ugly concrete statue); imagine going to Paris and not visiting the Louvre and admiring the *Mona Lisa*! But the *Mona Lisa* was a small painting of a smirking woman and, to me at least, a disappointment. Never mind: these were the 'must sees' of the world. The tourist brochures advertised them, the guidebooks extolled them—the Michelin gave them four stars ('Worth a Journey')—and everyone talked about them. I remembered once writing to my mother from New York: 'I can't believe you brought us here when we were young and we never visited the Statue of Liberty. How odd . . .' And it was odd, more than odd—it was an insult, a deliberate revolt against the unwritten laws that governed the tourist culture.

All places had a certain value one way or another: objectively, a supermarket was no less interesting than Sydney Opera House, and perhaps more so, since it revealed much more of the daily life of Australians. The ideal tourist, of course, would be one who enjoyed travelling without minding too much about the destination. In any case, all destinations had a certain emotional relativism (as I had discovered in Perth and the Jenolan Caves) that had little to do with whether they were Greek ruins, famous waterfalls or opera houses. But in mass tourism the charm or interest of the place no longer mattered: travel had become a collective rite, and the tourist was but a collector of images. Releasing the shutter on one's camera was not an emotional response to a place but a cold and calculating acquisition of that place as one's own, in the same way as a collector of butterflies, pinning the lifeless, chloroformed creatures to a board, was hardly responding emotionally to the beauty of butterflies.

Anyway, who was I to talk? I still had not escaped from the tyranny of the camera, and I circled round the Opera House like a jackal round a carcass, scribbling notes, trying to pin its appearance down in words, trying to explain it.

After the first tourist views of Sydney from the Opera House, the city itself was inevitably a disappointment, full of ugly traffic-choked streets and sunless canyons created by unimaginative skyscrapers. I found it difficult to find a focus to Australia's premier city, where a fifth of the entire country's population lived. The Queen Victoria Building, perhaps, a nineteenth-century monstrosity as squat and shapeless as the empress portrayed by the statue at its portals. Inside there was a beautiful interior of mosaic floors and wood panelling and stained glass—but after all, the Queen Victoria Building was merely a shopping mall. George Street was usually designated as the city's central road. It was a curious mixture of the colonial and stately (the Bank of Australasia building, the General Post Office, the Town Hall) and the tacky. There was a Woolworth's opposite the Town Hall, several hideous cinema blocks, a host of fast-food chains, and in between the street was lined with cheap discount souvenir stores where men with microphones harangued passers-by in English and Japanese: 'Best quality Walkman, only fourteen dollars, T-shirts two for five dollars.' The contrasts continued in Martin Place, which I had vaguely assumed was the city's Tiananmen or Trafalgar Square. True, it had its war memorial and impressive colonial banking houses (ANZ, Westpac, Commonwealth, Reserve), but it also had a Ticketek and newsagents' stands and an underground railway station, and was a gloomy, cramped, unlovely place, cold in the shadow of tall buildings, where offices workers sat eating sandwiches or hurrying past to somewhere more attractive.

Meanwhile I gazed out the train window as I travelled to my brother's suburban house, and it seemed to me the places I passed had no true heart, seemingly all stamped from a similar mould, with their bungalows nestled among the gum trees and centred on a supermarket, video rental shop, barbecued chicken outlet and petrol station. Such unhappy mixtures were a feature of Sydney and I thought them uncomfortable, not quite successful. Sydney seemed to me not entirely a world city—and yet somehow it surmounted its drawbacks and still managed (although one could hardly say why) to be one of the most beautiful and livable cities in the world. The Washington-based Population Crisis Centre regularly placed Sydney in second place on its surveys of the world's top one hundred cities, based on quality of life. (Melbourne was first, Sydney losing the top spot thanks to its traffic congestion.)

Sydney Harbour was, of course, the city's greatest asset— here was the focus for an otherwise congested and muddled city centre, and its beauty made you overlook the ugly architecture on its shores. The harbour was convoluted into bays and indentations, snaking upriver as far as Parramatta, its topography confusing. Streets abruptly plunged down to-wards the harbour, and I found myself glimpsing unexpected views over the water, with the great humped back of the Harbour Bridge sticking up in the distance like the museum skeleton of a prehistoric creature. It was never in the direction I expected it to be, and I drove through indifferent Sydney suburbs that suddenly ended in expanses of glittering water and bobbing yachts, and that was when I drew my breath in and thought—this city is beautiful.

I often sat by the Opera House on Bennelong Point, named after one of the first indigenous Australians to be introduced to European society, where I could get the best view of all of this much-lauded harbour. Looking across the water there was Blues Point Tower, a high-rise apartment block, dwarfed by perspective under the arches of the Harbour Bridge; the brightly coloured clown's face that was a Sydney icon and entrance to the now defunct Luna Park; the North Sydney Olympic swimming pool right on the water's edge (surely the public pool with the world's best view); the elegant old apartment blocks in higgledy-piggledy architecture at Kirribilli; colonial Admiralty House on the headland, the suburbs of Neutral Bay, Cremorne and Mosman a pattern of white houses and red tiles, tumbling down tree-covered hills to meet the harbour in a scattering of expensive yachts and motor boats. On the southern shore there was the Harbour Bridge once more, the Overseas Passenger Terminal, the old buildings of the Rocks against the skyscrapers of the city; and, on the other side of the Opera House, Farm Cove where the first settlers planted corn, now the lush Botanic Gardens leading round to Mrs Macquarie's Chair, another good vantage point. I liked sitting at this spot, too. Here Japanese and Taiwanese tour groups congregated for the city views, descending from their air-conditioned coaches in the latest leisure wear and matching sun-hats. A photographer positioned them by a convenient bench in standing or sitting rows, plonking a stuffed koala and signboard in front of them for a group photo. After this they milled around, snapping pictures of their own, while the tour leader, in crisp white shirt and tie, looked at his watch.

Photographs could hardly do the cityscape justice, and nor could words. Nevertheless, much ink had been used up in attempts to describe Sydney Harbour. 'Inexpressibly lovely,' wrote Anthony Trollope in one of his rare moments of appreciation. 'I have seen nothing equal to it.' Later Joseph

Conrad, who arrived in the city as a seaman aboard a wool clipper in 1906, wrote that the harbour was 'one of the finest, most beautiful, vast, and safe bays the sun ever shone upon'. He was followed by D. H. Lawrence in 1922, who set the first four chapters of his novel *Kangaroo* in Sydney, although he only stayed in the city a weekend before moving on to Thirroul, a nearby mining town. Still, a weekend was enough to be captivated by the harbour's magic, though in *Kangaroo* the beauty is somewhat sinister: 'The sky had gone grey, and the low table-land into which the harbour intrudes squatted dark-looking and monotonous and sad, as if lost on the face of the earth: the same Australian atmosphere, even here within the area of huge, restless, modern Sydney.' Even Clive James, disappointed with the Opera House, had to concede that the harbour remained 'one of the Earth's truly beautiful places'.

If on a short visit the Australian landscape had had such a profound effect on Lawrence, its effect on Australians was so much the greater. The great spaces, the brilliant sunlight and the ubiquitous seascapes seemed fashioned for a hedonistic life full of optimism and *joie de vivre*. Yet underneath there seemed to be a streak of melancholy, even preoccupation with death, reflected in the eerie atmosphere of the landscape at sunset, a sad dwindling of the light in an ancient land. Now, aboard the ferry bound for Manly on a harbour sparkling with yachts, I was listening to an Australian father pointing out the sights to his small son, with a macabre sense of interest that seemed to me almost typically Australian.

'It's a 300-metre drop from that lighthouse down the cliffs into the sea,' the man said, pointing out over the suburbs of the southern shore, where a slim white lighthouse stuck up above the red-tiled roofs, standing sentinel over some distant ocean beach. 'That's where people commit suicide.'

'How many people?' asked his son, staring out over the railings wide-eyed.

'Hundreds a year,' replied his father rather fancifully (I hoped). 'They just fall down into the ocean and some of them disappear for ever.'

On the harbour shore bungalows with red roofs squatted at the water's edge under Norfolk Island pines, and closer at hand yachts skimmed past under a stiff wind. The ferry continued and there was a silence until we slid past a huge metal buoy in flaking orange paint, topped by a light.

'Marks the site of a sunken ship,' whispered the father. 'Went down with all hands.'

'What hands?'

'The crew—all the people on board.'

'But there's no waves here.'

'Not today, but sometimes the wind comes in strong enough to blow a dog off a chain, and the waves come roaring through the Heads.'

'Did they drownded?'

'Yes, every one of them. And that buoy marks where it is.'

'Are the people still on board?'

'Maybe their skeletons, Andrew. But the sharks would have got them by now. There are a lot of sharks in Sydney Harbour. If you fell off this ferry you'd be eaten up in a flash.'

This was a ghoulish litany to relate to a young child on a ferry ride in the sun, but to me it seemed part of the whole Australian fascination with danger and death, melancholia and deceptiveness. Australians might be hedonistic, but sometimes they seemed hardly happy: aggressive, resentful, with high rates of suicide and alcoholism and domestic violence that bewildered me. They upheld the image of the battlers, who struggled and ultimately failed; their national hero, Ned Kelly, was a criminal; and they took pride in the great defeats and slaughters of many wars: Tobruk and Pozières, Gallipoli and the Kokoda Trail. Even memorials to the nation's dead were not discreet edifices in streets but massive, monumental war memorials standing in central locations. Sydney's war memorial stood in the middle of Hyde Park in the heart of the city and was bigger than a house.

Later, on another ferry, as we sailed past the Heads that form the entrance to the harbour, I was told an Australian joke.

'A man is sitting up on top of South Head,' said the ferry passenger to me, pointing out at the spot. 'He's about to throw himself off the cliff on to the rocks below. A policeman comes by and asks him why.

'"The wife has run off with another bloke and my children have turned out badly—one's a bludger, the other's on drugs," says the man. "My business that I struggled with for years has finally collapsed and yesterday the dog was run over by a bus."

'"Look mate, why don't we talk it over?" says the policeman.

'And so they talk it over—and then they both jump off!'

As I contemplated the cruel humour of the tale we left the Heads behind and sailed up the harbour towards the city centre. A storm was brewing: the water was as grey as slate, the black clouds pierced by great shafts of golden light like a Doré engraving. Lightning flickered behind the sinister black steel of the Harbour Bridge (its pylons, I thought to myself, resembled the war memorial) like a melancholy *son-et-lumière*, and on the left the Opera House seemed to be newly sprouted like some exotic fungus in the rain.

It began to pour as we docked at Circular Quay. This was the harbour too: not just an astonishing beauty but a place of suicides and sharks, grey in the rain, as moody and enigmatic as the Australian mentality, and myself a stranger passing through, full of wonder at the mystery of it all.

Sydney was a Chinese city—or at least my Sydney was in those first few weeks as I tramped around, absorbing the sights. I haunted places my brother, who had lived here for years, had hardly even heard of, all the while disdaining to visit those better-known places that did not interest me: Bondi Beach, the well-heeled Anglo-Saxon North Shore, Centrepoint Tower with its circulating tourists eager to map out the city from above. My Sydney was Chinatown, with its multitude of restaurants and fast-food halls, where I was reminded of almost forgotten favourites from China: Grandmother's Beancurd, deep-fried *jaozi* with chilli sauce, spicy Sichuan chicken with peanuts. It was Paddy's Market on weekends with its customers from all the nations of Asia haggling over vegetables, prodding the melons as they might have done in the markets of China and Thailand; the Mandarin Club in the city, where Cantonese women with glitter in their hair screeched into the microphones in the karaoke lounge, and the Mandarin Centre in Chatswood, around which Hong Kong *émigrés* led their new lives; the back streets of Surry Hills, where I came across a church disgorging a congregation of Koreans. The Japanese hung out in North Sydney, the Vietnamese at Cabramatta, Shanghai immigrants in Ashfield, Taiwanese in Chatswood, Koreans in Campsie. Overwhelmed with nostalgia, I hunted with obsession (and it was an obsession—my sister, as usual, was right) for fragments of a past life, for glimpses of China in this alien city and perhaps, subconsciously, for a face I thought I would never see again.

The Taiwanese man on the aeroplane at the start of my journey had told me there were no Chinese in Australia, but he was certainly wrong, nowhere more so than in Sydney. Chinese free settlers and sailors who had jumped ship were already present in the city in the early 1800s, and by the 1840s the Chinese had started coming in significant numbers, filling the gap created by the dwindling supply of convict labour. They came as shepherds and farm hands, labourers and servants, furniture-makers and traders, and a few as convicts from the British territories of Mauritius and later Hong Kong. In 1848 a ship carrying 120 Chinese arrived from Amoy (now Xiamen), and only four years later the British Consul at Amoy reported that over 2600 Chinese had been sent to Australia to work as labourers. They also came from Canton, Shanghai and the British colonies of Hong Kong and Singapore. Already in 1849 the *People's Advocate* was complaining: 'These men—unrestrained by any moral feeling; unacquainted with Christianity: whose only God is the Devil—are to be let loose among us, to prey upon the very vitals of our community.'

To these early Chinese had now been added South-East Asians, Koreans, Japanese, Indians, Sri Lankans. They lived in every Sydney suburb and permeated virtually every facet of Australian life—indeed, they had changed the face of Australia in the last three decades. There were, however, still segments of the population who considered they preyed upon Australia's Anglo-Saxon society. Racism continued to lie just under the surface of Australia's apparent tolerance, and was sometimes brought into the open by any perceived wrong-doing in the immigrant communities. Examples frequently trotted out on the commercial television's current-affairs programmes included Asian students 'taking over' Australian universities to the disadvantage of locals; Chinese refugees suing the government over wrongful imprisonment; the high cost of rescuing some Chinese boat people who had been lost in the Kimberleys; fake marriages taking place in the Philippines in order to obtain residence permits; and even the use of live fish and seafood in Chinese restaurants.

'I find it quite hypocritical,' said a Chinese acquaintance crossly when I mentioned this last to him. 'So the Chinese keep their food alive until the last moment and have it killed in front of them, which is apparently distasteful to other Australians. But I admire their lack of hypocrisy. White Australians have their animals slaughtered out of sight and presented to them hygienically wrapped on supermarket shelves.'

The views of certain white Australians, however, were not based on rational thought but on ignorance and intolerance. Right-wing political figures occasionally gave voice to fears that Asian immigrants were taking other Australians' jobs; indeed swamping the entire country and its culture. Polls showed that many Australians imagined that Asians accounted for anywhere between 10 and 40 per cent of the population; in fact, not much more than 4 per cent of Australians were of Asian origin, hardly significant enough to 'take over' the 70 per cent or thereabouts who were Anglo-Saxon. In any case, there was not really any such thing as 'Asians' as a cohesive group, but merely a collection of peoples of different social, cultural and linguistic backgrounds who interacted little one with the other. It was extraordinary to imagine they could possibly have a co-ordinated agenda for the overthrow by stealth of white Australia.

Nowhere was the uninformed hysteria more marked than in attitudes to Cabramatta, a suburb that inspired a certain terror in Sydneysiders: it was the Bronx of Sydney, a place where few of the inhabitants of the pleasant eastern parts of the city had ever been, but which featured prominently in the urban lore. It had the highest crime rates in all Australia, and not a month passed without the newspapers featuring Cabramatta in a lurid tale of drug-peddling South-East Asian triads and crime syndicates, heroin smuggling, embattled police, teenage delinquency, shootings or assaults. To crown it all, a New South Wales member of parliament for the district had been gunned down outside his own front door, by persons unknown, although many assumed a Vietnamese gang was responsible.

Surit lived in Cabramatta, and since my time in Canberra he had become a friend. He had lived in Cabramatta for most of the Australian incarnation of his life, but it was his Chinese and Laotian ethnic background that interested me. His entire extended family had fled the country in small groups during the 1970s.

'I left with my aunt and two cousins. Normally the crossing point into Thailand was guarded, so we must walking six hours or so in the dark, barefoot, along the banks of the Mekong to where boat waiting to take us across the river. But boat was too small for all of us, we discovered.'

'So?'

'So my aunt putting in her own two children to the boat, and told me wait until it returned, and she climbed in, and off they went, leaving me sit there in the dark.'

'How old were you?'

'Ten. I don't remember being scared, I just sat there wait for boat returning, and eventually it return. But I never forgive my aunt, I don't think. To this day she least favourite of my relatives. It is not a good thing.'

The rest of Surit's family soon followed: his eldest brother swam across the Mekong to freedom, a feat which still filled Surit with admiration. The family spent ten months in a transit camp on the outskirts of Bangkok—longer than most because Surit's father had a lung infection and Australian immigration rules wouldn't let the rest of the family in without him.

'The only thing I remember, really, in Bangkok, is going to zoo and seeing two emus! I couldn't believe how big they are—legs like elephants, I thought! I couldn't believe bird was so huge—I suppose that was my first shock of Australia, before I even arrived here.'

Apart from a certain wonder at its wildlife, Surit's first reaction to Australia was one of disappointment. 'I hated it because there were no skyscrapers!' he laughed to me, having as a 10-year-old imagined Sydney as a wondrous place of towering glass blocks, futuristic monorails and planes swooping about overhead. Instead, the family spent months at a hostel for immigrants in the distant and characterless western suburb of East Hills.

'I wanted talk to others, and was very frustrated because all I could say is "hello" and "goodbye". But I start liking Australia when I learning some more English—and finally saw the skyscrapers of downtown Sydney! Hostel was out in suburbs, practically like the countryside in those days, with trees and bushes everywhere; I always live in a town, and I suppose I found it strange. We eventually moved out of the hostel to a flat in Carramar, which was when life really began.'

Surit now seemed very Australian: apart from erratic verb tenses he spoke near-fluent English, complete with Australian accent and idioms, had a flat where the only trace of Asia was the chopsticks in the kitchen drawer, and rarely spoke Laotian except to his parents. Only his taste in food remained resolutely Indo-Chinese. 'I'm afraid I having a lifelong dislike of Western food. Probably from the time when we live in hostel and got those appalling institutional meals. Vegemite, peanut butter and ham especially was, in my memory, all we got. Endless variations of the three in sandwiches for lunch.' He screwed up his nose.

But now Surit was cheerful enough, and Australia had been generous to give him another chance at life. Today, Australia had an exemplary record for unbiased immigration and social tolerance, and had become one of the least racist of Western societies. Periodic anti-Asian sentiment was maybe just a way of letting off steam—at least Australia did not erupt into racial violence, and there were none of the entrenched racial divisions one found in the United States. The Race Relations Cycle Theory proposed by the American R. E. Park outlined several stages of immigration: contact, competition, conflict, accommodation and, finally, assimilation. Australia was surely at the accommodation stage. The people had a right to be worried about whether assimilation could be achieved; it hadn't happened easily, if at all, in any other country.

There was no reason, however, why it could not be achieved; after all, Anglo-Saxon Australians had also been against the immigration of southern Europeans, Catholics and Jews, but these groups were now more or less integrated into Australian society. There was a huge experiment happening in Australia, and people had the right to feel uneasy about it. But if they pulled it off—peaceful multiculturalism. In a world where everything was increasingly internationalised and interdependent, surely this was something greatly to be desired. Australia might be too small a place to have significance in political and economic terms; but socially and culturally it could be a world leader. If multiculturalism could happen anywhere, I was beginning to think, despite everything, it could happen here.

I was stopping over in Sydney at the right time, for Sydney that summer was a city permanently in festival. There was Christmas under the blazing sun, complete with cards showing Santa in the snow, holly red with berries, and other trappings of life in a distant hemisphere. We went to the beach, and Nicola turned red as a reindeer's nose, and then we returned to my brother's house, where in the midsummer heat we sweated over a hot oven, cooking turkey and roast potatoes. Then came New Year's Eve, when a million people roamed the streets, shouting and littering, getting drunk and fighting, or coming out with their kids to see the fireworks explode over the harbour. I sat with Nicola and Simon on the steps of the Opera House with a bottle of Australian wine, watching the black waters of the harbour reflecting the red and purple blaze of fireworks, and wondering what the coming year would bring.

Then the Sydney Festival was launched, with its street theatre, circuses, concerts, literary gatherings and (to my pleasure) a vast number of buskers, who congregated around Circular Quay and the Opera House. A jazz ensemble (double bass, saxophone, drums) played to a gathering crowd while a man stood immobile as a statue with his face painted to resemble marble (or was it bird droppings?). Three kids in grubby yellow T-shirts played 'Rock Around the Clock' on trumpets and the self-styled World's Greatest Whistler piped out Gershwin music. Three men in silver body suits and Rollerblades, with space gloves to the elbows and bicycle helmets, mikes wrapped around their faces like Madonna in concert, moved around chanting about space and hyper-reality and totality. No one knew what they were on about, but everyone clapped enthusiastically. In a corner an Aboriginal man often sat in a loincloth, playing a didjeridu and shouting abuse at anyone who tried to take his photo.

No sooner was the festival over than it was Chinese New Year (fireworks and dragon boat races on Darling Harbour) and Australia Day (more fireworks), and then Sydney was gearing up for the Gay and Lesbian Mardi Gras. Begun in 1978 with a small-scale demonstration by activists campaigning for gay rights (which ended in a riot after police intervened), the Mardi Gras was now a full-scale three-week-long event of theatre, sports, art and other festivities culminating in a huge parade through the city and a party at the Showground. The parade now attracted half a million spectators and generated millions of dollars in foreign exchange from tourists (although the Australian Tourist Commission had long refused to include it in any of its promotional material, despite its world renown). As for the Showground, it was billed as the world's largest party, with nearly 20 000 participants.

What was once a demonstration had now become an outlandish and witty celebration, though still with a slightly political and activist slant for such concerns as greater funding for AIDS research. It was a fine example of urban Australia's tolerance, or at least acquiescence (homosexuality had only been decriminalised in New South Wales in 1985 and remained a crime in Tasmania): tourists, married couples, teenagers and families with their children turned out for the spectacle, cheering and clapping the participants. I found to my astonishment that this parade was the biggest annual event in Australia. It was television news headlines, it merited newspaper analysis and photos in the gossip magazines, entire city streets were cleared for the event and many Sydneysiders seemed proud of it. I was impressed—this was not the outback redneck Australia of history and the stereotypes, but urban sophistication and tolerance of the highest level, and when I found the Mardi Gras was broadcast live on national television I fell in love a little bit more with Australia.

'You have to go to the Mardi Gras,' people told me. 'I'm bringing my grandmother this year. It's fantastic, bring a milk crate to stand on, it's the greatest free show in the world.'

And what a spectacle it was: floats with stunning décors depicting underwater scenes (mermen, lobsters, oysters and swordfish in G-strings), Greek temples, pink Cadillacs, the Yellow Brick Road with Dorothy in drag. There were Mardi Gras costumes straight out of Brazil, with elaborate head-dresses of feathers and sequined gowns, people dressed as vampires and witches, army boys and majorettes, Egyptian slaves and Marilyn Monroe, the Statue of Liberty, skinny women in nothing but black miniskirts throwing condoms to the crowd, good-looking men with a year of gym work behind them, their naked chests sprinkled with glitter.

'What a waste,' lamented a woman standing beside me in the crowd to her friend. 'Aren't they gorgeous? I wish our men looked like that.'

There were a few Asians here, too, on floats marked 'Asians and Friends' with a telephone number, and another 'Long Yang Club'. An intelligent name: Long Yang was a warlord with a male lover in *Dream of Red Mansions*, one of the classics of Chinese literature. But the participants did not seem Chinese; some were dressed in traditional Thai costumes and others looked like Indonesians. They marched up Oxford Street, the 'Golden Mile' of businesses directed at the gay community (bars, nightclubs, saunas, restaurants, adult shops, discothèques) and disappeared in the direction of the Showground for a night of revels.

GOD CREATED ADAM AND EVE, NOT ADAM AND STEVE said a placard held aloft above the crowd by Fred Nile, Sydney's notoriously right-wing member of parliament, who wanted the Mardi Gras banned. I appreciated his wit if not his politics, but nobody else was paying any attention to him: the fathers with their babies ambled past, the groups of teenagers with their tinnies, the bare-chested men with their nipple-rings and swaggering assurance (this was their night, after all), the grandmothers and half a million other Sydney-siders.

I was shocked—my quiet upbringing had not prepared me for this. I had grown up in prim, conservative Geneva, studied at university in Presbyterian Scotland, lived in repressive China. But I was exhilarated too—here I was in a place where people could dance almost naked down the streets (and the police cleared the way for them), where they were given free symphony concerts in the park and busked in the streets, where they could indulge in Chinese food in every suburb. What a country! What a city!

There was no stopping a good show in Sydney.

the island of apples

Tasmania is an island, which seems obvious but says much. Like most offshore islands it tends to be overlooked by outsiders, and to retreat into insularity and conservatism in an isolation that is both geographic and intellectual; but an isolation of which the islanders are rather proud. 'I've never been to the mainland,' they say—and why should they? Tasmanians live in a tranquil place on the sidelines of world affairs, eating fresh cheese and full cream in houses by the sea among apple orchards and farms full of fat cows.

Tasmania's existence is all but forgotten by the rest of Australia, except when the island becomes a momentary embarrassment because of its refusal to adopt laws in line with liberal Australian thinking. Even corporate designers sometimes leave it out of company logos, in which maps of the country are otherwise conveniently rectangular. Tasmanians are remembered only as the Irish or Poles of Australian jokes. There are many reasons not to pay too close an attention to this island State, even though—or rather, perhaps, because—it is a place of significance in the country's history and culture. Many of the indigenous Tasmanians had been massacred; thousands of convicts had been sent here, a prison within the greater prison of Australia. Tasmanians are forgotten not only because they live on a small island, but because it reminds other Australians of the way they were thirty years ago, living on the edge of a wilderness, ignored by almost everyone else, reputedly redneck, probably inbred, and with a history best left unexplored.

Australians call Tasmania the Apple Isle, preferring instead to highlight its image of charming country wholesomeness—besides which, the place even has the shape of an apple, more or less, dented at the top and tapering down towards the South Cape. An apple means the rural life, crisp and clean and smelling like mother's cooking, and Tasmania is the sort of place where the Famous Five could have had a fabulous holiday. Tasmania is small, and therefore comforting. I could see half of it now from the aeroplane window, and one could drive across it in a day; coming from a mainland of daunting immensity, it was easy to see how Tasmania had a reputation for delightful cosiness. 'Tasmania. Be Tempted,' said the tourist brochures, which used the apple motif to invite you to this Garden of Eden. Here was irony indeed—as history showed, Tasmania was not an innocent place, and besides, it still had tracts of land virtually unexplored. This was no tamed garden.

Tasmania was misty too, a weather condition from my experience not common elsewhere in Australia. Even now, as I flew over it, clouds wreathed and writhed below the aeroplane, and peering out the window over Nicola's shoulder I realised Tasmania was also Australia reversed, turned inside out, its stereotypes shattered. Tasmania was not raw red and whisky-coloured but hazy blue and Donegal green and soft grey—comforting colours that suggested that water, not heat, was its defining element. While sun-seekers were basking on the beaches of the Gold Coast, snow capped the hills of Tasmania. The outback was flat, but Tasmania claimed to be the most mountainous island on earth, heaved into contours and cliffs, mountain peaks and plunging valleys, queer twisted pinnacles pointing out of the surf, the villages cramped into patches of level land. (Far below me now the sun glinted on the surface of a river like a secret signal, and the rocky mountains were a black smear against the horizon.) The mainland turned its back on the hostility and emptiness of the outback, huddling on the coastal margins as if to receive comfort from the gently lapping waves of the continent's shores, which had been urbanised, its beaches turned into a cultural icon. Here in Tasmania it was the sea that was hostile, infinite sheets of cruel grey that ended in the ice floes of the Antarctic, and the settlers had looked inland, to the lush pastures and hidden valleys that provided comfort and reminders of home.

We flew into Launceston, skimming country hedges and herds of cows standing pensive in tiny fields. I was travelling with Nicola again—I had coaxed her to come on her last Australian journey, for soon she would be returning home. Besides, she needed a distraction; since Mike's departure the inertia of the lovelorn had struck her, although I had seen her come to accept that their separation was all for the best. She had packed her backpack once more, almost with relief, stuffing socks and rolls of film into odd corners.

'God, I've been living out of this thing for a year and a half,' she had grumbled, an undertone of affection in her voice as she tugged at the straps and pockets.

We picked up a rented car at the airport and drove into Launceston. It was a Sunday night, and the streets were deserted, almost eerily so, traffic lights blinking and changing over empty roads. The shops were shuttered and one or two lone figures appeared occasionally on the pavements, their faces orange under the street lamps, their collars turned up against the weather.

'How peculiar,' said my sister, gazing out into the darkened streets under a light drizzle, bewildered after the busy energy of Sydney. 'Do you think something is wrong?'

'Wrong?' I shrugged. 'This is just Tasmania.'

'But this is supposed to be its second city.'

Maybe, but there were still only 70 000 people living in Launceston, although it was also one of Australia's oldest settlements, having been established in 1805 as a port at the head of the Tamar River. It had been the first city in Australia to use electric lighting (in 1895), but now it seemed to be reluctant to capitalise on this head start: the streets were dark and bare, and solitary lampposts glimmered out of the gloom, like soft-focus photography in black-and-white. Having checked into our bed-and-breakfast we had trouble finding anywhere to eat. We wandered around the empty streets, drifting past the odd solitary pedestrian scurrying in the opposite direction, eyes fixed on the pavement. Finally we found a pizzeria. We were the only customers, and sat dining in isolated splendour, hardly daring to talk; even Nicola seemed subdued. Pictures of the Italian Riviera, much faded, adorned the walls; Italy seemed much more than just half a world away, more like another planet. In the posters, gossiping Italians sat in crowds in street cafés, and rows of topless Scandinavian tourists adorned the beaches.

Next morning, skirting the town, I walked with Nicola out to Cataract Gorge, billed as a piece of wilderness on the edge of Launceston. There seemed to be little that was wild about these gorges. Cars parked in them, a suspension bridge spanned the river, a chair lift swung overhead and a trail allowed us to walk along the gorges themselves, which eventually opened out on a grassy area with clipped grass where peacocks strolled. There were gardens, a Fairy Dell, a bandstand and a pavilion selling ice-cream and afternoon teas. Small children splashed and giggled in an artificial pool. There were people here in this wilderness as there had not been in the town the night before. It looked thoroughly domesticated, but this was still Australia: signs warned against swimming in the deep black waters of the gorge, predicting hypothermia.

I sat in the pavilion and had an ice-cream while Nicola wandered off on her own up the hill to look for a view. A woman came in as I was scraping the last of some chocolate from the bottom of my glass and licking it off my spoon. She was wearing an immaculate, tailored suit—it had the cut of Armani, but surely Armani wearers, I told myself, would not be wandering around this place, nor seeking out a coffee in a styrofoam cup from a café with loud teenagers and discarded Mars wrappers. Her hair was elaborately coiffed, her nails polished—she looked like a CNN news presenter.

'May I?' she said, and sat down at my table when I nodded politely. She ordered a sandwich and a bottle of mineral water and began eating morosely, then caught my eye. We exchanged desultory conversation: she was from Melbourne, here on business actually, but she had the morning off. There was a meeting at one. She did not say what her business was, or what the meeting was about. We trailed into an embarrassed silence.

'Are you happy?' she said abruptly after a while.

I stared at her and finally shrugged. 'At this moment? Or in general?'

But the woman seemed suddenly to have lost interest in both the question and her food; the sandwich lay half eaten, the top slice of bread peeled back to reveal chicken and mayonnaise.

'Whatever,' she said, tapping manicured fingernails on the table, bored, so I wondered why she had asked in the first place.

'Generally, then—yes.'

'You don't look it,' said Armani Suit, I thought rudely.

'Well I'm not the cheerful, enthusiastic type. Not that kind of happiness, no. But overall I'm . . . content.'

'Oh.'

And I realised that I was. I realised that I had come to Australia restless and uncertain and, in the vast expanse of outback stars and hot red landscape, had found a kind of peace, a new perspective on life; not a huge change, just a quiet acknowledgement that this was a new country that I liked very much, that I liked travelling, I liked writing, I even liked being single, for the moment. Somehow in Australia you could be what you wanted: a slightly eccentric footloose China-obsessed bewildered foreigner always looking for answers and delighted when he couldn't find them—and you could still fit in.

I did not say this to Armani Suit—unless she had come for a psychologists' convention or a meeting of immigration department officials I doubted she would have been interested.

'Yes,' I just said, rather obscurely. 'I like collecting experiences. That's what makes me content. They don't have to be happy ones.'

'Oh.'

We lapsed into silence. Eventually the woman gathered herself together (handbag, folded newspaper, suit jacket buttoned) and stood up, extending her hand. For a moment I thought I was meant to kiss it. I stood up and shook it, feeling dry, slightly cold fingers and the most fleeting of pressure, bemused by the formality—bemused by the conversation. And then she was gone.

Not long afterwards Nicola came trumpeting back through the trees shouting about the photos she had taken of a peacock. With my contentedness and my sister I walked back into Launceston. By daylight it was a pleasant, quiet place, dotted with gardens and parks and squares filled with flowers and statues of royalty or colonial notables. It had a more historic feel than any Australian town I had yet been in, and numerous elegant old buildings attested to its early success. The Paterson Barracks were the oldest in the town, constructed in 1820, followed by St John's Church with its imposing stone clock tower with a rooftop weather-vane, and the Methodist Sunday School painted white, with prim railings separating it from the footpath.

With its town squares and old buildings and Victorian architecture, Launceston pandered to the illusion that Tasmania was a Little England. It was indeed much like an English country town, and even the street names were resolutely British: Elizabeth and Margaret, Balfour and Canning, Paterson and Edmund and Alice and Charles, like a congregation of middle-class Victorians out on a picnic. So too did the whole island confuse in its place names, I thought as Nicola and I plotted our Tasmanian route on a map. There was a Hampshire which was not a county, a Queenstown which was not a port, a King William that was not a monarch but a lake, an inland Brighton, a Tunbridge that had no wells and a Gretna with no green. There was also a Snug, a Crabtree, a Cygnet, a Grove, a Primrose Sands, a Golden Valley and even a Flowerpot to reinforce the island's idyllic rural image. (If one looked more closely, I noted later, there were other names more sinister: One Tree Point, Sandfly, Cape Grim, Savage River, Suicide Bay.)

Leaving Launceston early the next day, my sister and I travelled westwards through farming country to Deloraine, another charming town dominated by National Trust properties dating from the early nineteenth century, where we ate a picnic lunch by the river with its elms and willows transplanted from England by homesick immigrants a hundred years ago. Further west still we arrived at Cradle Mountain National Park, which looked not at all like England. The landscape here had been heavily glaciated, and was dotted with numerous lakes and tarns and mountain peaks that reminded me of Switzerland—I seemed for ever doomed, when travelling, to be reminded of home in the most curious places. But the vegetation was not Swiss: pandanus plants and massive King Billy pines and gum trees surrounded Dove Lake at the foot of Cradle Mountain.

We spent a couple of days walking in the national park, but this was not the Tasmania we had come to see.

'I can go home and do this,' said Nicola. 'This alpine walking.'

And so we left its beauty, rendered ordinary by familiarity, and headed west once more, towards the sea, which could not remind us of Switzerland at all. Nicola took the wheel. After months of chugging around in our elderly campervan she took advantage of the hire car and pressed her foot down on the accelerator. We hurtled through Rosebery, a company town, not leaving the highway: this place depended on the Electrolytic Zinc Company and the Pasminco Mine, names which did not inspire us to seek out its tourist delights. But we did stop at Zeehan, for petrol and supplies. Silver–lead deposits had been discovered here in 1882, provoking a boom: there had been a stock exchange, dozens of hotels, mining companies that had sprouted up and as soon disappeared with the profits, and Dame Nellie Melba and Caruso had once sung at the Gaiety Theatre. Not long after the turn of the century it had gone into a decline, arrested only recently by the reopening of a tin mine near by. This was still pioneering country—bushfires had razed the entire town in 1981. It seemed a strange place, strips of fresh tarmac in the middle of nowhere, bungalows with roofs of corrugated iron, hardly any trees.

Nicola accelerated away, and we sang ourselves down the road to the sea.

Tasmania was an empty place: almost the size of Ireland, it had a population of only half a million, and on the entire west coast there was but one town, Strahan, where less than 1000 inhabitants huddled against the elements. Huge seas battered the coast into rugged cliffs and convoluted inlets, an icy wind—the Roaring Forties—howled in from halfway round the world across the foaming ocean to crash on its shores, rain fell more frequently than anywhere else in Australia (silently, in countryside wreathed in mists, or screaming in fierce water-splattered gales), and the hostile forests kept a stranglehold on inaccessible valleys and mountain peaks. Water was Tasmania's defining element, never more so than here. The island's famous rivers flowed through the region, and dams held back immense sheets of water, the only calm among the teeming elements, which provided Tasmania with its energy—strange, the thought of this inhospitable wilderness permitting the production of electricity to supply the cosy homes of Hobart with toasters and washing machines, hair driers and televisions, domesticity wrestled from the wild waters.

Macquarie Harbour, on which Strahan sat, was one of only two safe anchorages on the entire west coast. Tourist blurbs liked to boast that it was larger than Sydney Harbour, but it had no Sydney. Strahan was a minute place, a busy port that had declined with the declining fortunes of the mining and timber industries and which was now little more than a fishing base and tourist centre—the latter the terminal fate, it would seem, of all once-thriving towns. The tourist thing to do was to take a tour by boat of the inlet, and so we did, with a tour operator whose package was as slick as the white lines of his powerboat.

Rain began to fall as we headed out to Hell's Gates, the entrance to the immense natural harbour. The entrance was only a couple of hundred metres wide, and the seas surged through it in a mighty current to form treacherous whirlpools. The place was scattered with the wrecks of ships that had been unwise enough to attempt the entrance during unfavourable weather, and ghoulishly many of the surrounding humps of rock and small islands had been named after them. We had a Tannoy commentary on our vessel, but I was reading Marcus Clarke's novel *For the Term of his Natural Life*, which was much more vivid. Set in nineteenth-century Australia, it was a tale of the iniquities of the penal system, and had become a classic.

> Once through the gates, the convict, chained on the deck of
> the inward-bound vessel, sees in front of him the bald cone

of Frenchman's Cap, piercing the moist air at a height of 5000 feet; while, gloomed by overhanging rocks, and shadowed by gigantic forests, the black sides of the basin narrow to the mouth of the Gordon. The turbulent stream is the colour of indigo, and, being fed by numerous rivulets, which ooze through masses of decaying vegetable matter, is of so poisonous a nature that it is not only undrinkable, but absolutely kills the fish that are driven in from the sea in stormy weather.

Further up the harbour we sailed past Sarah Island, a place of secondary punishment designed for convicts who had committed additional crimes either on the journey out or in the colonies. The first convicts arrived in 1822 and Sarah Island soon acquired a fearsome reputation as the harshest prison in Australia. The island housed dockyards, a jail, a guardhouse, barracks, saw-pits and forges; about 60 soldiers took charge of some 350 convicts. The commandant's house was at the centre of the island, and there was also a hospital and a chapel. On nearby Phillip Island vegetables were grown for the pleasure of the officers, while on Halliday's Island the dead were buried. The convicts spent the day in labour: felling timber, floating logs to the island, shipbuilding. Conditions were foul and the lash was not spared, and many convicts attempted to escape, though few succeeded owing to the treacherous currents of the harbour and the vast forested wilderness of its shores. The settlement was finally abandoned in 1834, overcome by its isolation and the expense and difficulties of supplying it. As the tour boat sped past, all I could see were ruined walls and piles of stones that said little about the life lived on this tiny hump of rock.

'She woke up one morning and found Billy Boy dead,' observed a voice in my ear as I moved along the boat's railings. I stopped, avid with curiosity: I had an unashamed love of eavesdropping.

'Yes, stone dead in the bottom of the cage,' said the voice. Only a bird! I relaxed slightly in disappointment, at the same time studying the couple. The man had white scruffy hair and a red checked shirt, taut over his pot belly, and was smoking an evil home-made cigarette shaped like a cornet, bulging with tobacco. The woman beside him was draped in

wooden beads. She was wearing a baggy sweater ravaged
with holes and had a pink band in her dishevelled hair. She
was clutching a bulging string bag to her chest: it contained
a jar of pickles, a large hunk of salami and several paper-
wrapped packages. She looked, compared to the small group
of other tourists with their expensive cameras and guidebooks, incongruous and rather sad, like a Balkan refugee.

'That reminds me of my sister, my younger sister years
ago,' the man was saying slowly, scattering ash on his shirt.
'She had a canary. Pride and joy that canary. One day it laid
an egg.' He paused as if considering the fact. 'Yeah. An egg.'

'Laid an egg? How could it?'

'Dunno. One morning there was an egg in the cage.'

'My neighbour has two finches,' sighed the woman. 'Lets
them out of the cage to fly around the house. I have a phobia
about birds. Hate the feathers.'

'Never mind.'

'We used to catch parakeets though, when I was a girl. Cut
the gum trees, got the juice out of them and rubbed it on our
hands, then on the wire of the fences, like. Birds land on
them, stick to them. My Uncle Bob used to sell them.'

'Yeah, my dad used to raise turkey and fowl, you know
. . .' The man began to cough. The couple were still talking
about birds—a disjointed conversation, neither of them
listening to the other, each intent on their own reminiscences
and oblivious, it seemed, of their surroundings—as Sarah
Island receded and we headed up the Gordon River.

It was hard to fathom the Mephistophelean imagination of
those who had sailed down this wild coast and founded a
penal settlement on a minute island in the wilderness; one
could not help but strangely admire the warped cruelty of
the vision. Convicts lived here in the most miserable conditions on earth, forced into hard labour, reduced to abject
submission by the lash, summarily hanged sometimes, sleeping in wet clothes covered in salt spray from the seas and
totally cut off from any outposts of civilisation, Caliban
figures on a small rock at the earth's end.

'The air is chill and moist . . . All around breathes desolation; on the face of nature is stamped a perpetual frown,'
wrote Marcus Clarke in another part of his book. His

imagination was Gothic, I thought as I read on, but accurate enough: I was cold, and rain was falling in an unhealthy, penetrating mist. But these days nature was to be admired, not endured or trapped with gum juice, and the region was a World Heritage area. The passengers watched the river banks slipping by, overhung with trees, and pointed out birds to each other. At a landing stage upriver we all disembarked and walked around a wooden pathway a short distance through the forest, admiring the dripping trees and tangled undergrowth. Then we got back on board and headed for Strahan once more, warming ourselves with cups of coffee.

If Hell had a capital it would look like Queenstown, I thought the next day. Here near the west coast, largely a wilderness area of great natural beauty and dense forest, the town was surrounded by hills denuded of trees, harsh mountains of rock and stone that were all that remained after a century of tree-cutting, sulphur pollution and bushfires. It rained here 320 days of the year, chilly, grey sulphur-smelling rain, and the winters were so wet and cold that grass did not grow. Its people were tough, and mean as the sunshine: they played football on a gravel pitch, disdained the use of umbrellas, and tore up the earth's innards looking for ore. Only in the evening did the surroundings take on a grotesque beauty as the declining sun set the hills on fire, so that they glowed pink and red and golden like something from the Promised Land.

There wasn't much mining in Queenstown now, and the inhabitants sought to attract the passing tourists, heading eastwards from Strahan along the Lyell Highway. The landscape was said to be a 'visual and psychological icon'—and so it was, but what a warped psychology, the icon of a culture seemingly bankrupt, a land laid waste by exploitation. Historic walking tours of the town were mapped out in leaflets, which Nicola rummaged through as I drove around the town.

'The Hydro-Electric Commission's Information Office is a major attraction,' she said to me.

'Hm.'

'And then there's Mt Lyell Mine, the Miners' Sunday Sculpture and a restored locomotive that, before 1932, provided the only access to Queenstown.'

'I see.'

We looked at each other, and looked out at the rain streaking the windows of our car, and left Queenstown behind us, driving on up the Lyell Highway. This was a beautiful region, but we were prevented from enjoying it by the weather. Crossing the Collingwood River, we stopped at Donaghy's Hill and stumbled forty minutes along a track to see a spectacular wilderness panorama, but saw only shifting mists that muted the contours of the landscape into a soft green. At the Franklin River we huddled in a picnic stall and ate our lunch, longing for the comforts of our campervan, with its handy stove that would have produced hot food and coffee.

The Lyell Highway was dotted with beehives, placed here over the summer, between December and March, to take advantage of the flowering of the area's leatherwood trees— leatherwood honey was unique to Tasmania and highly regarded in Australia. I spotted a woman tending to one group of beehives, and drew the car up behind her, and initiated a conversation.

The bee-keeper was none too keen to be identified, as if she were engaged in some kind of undercover activity. 'You seem to be making an awful lot of notes,' she said anxiously, peering into the notebook where I was scribbling illegible hieroglyphics in pencil.

'I have in mind to write a magazine article about Tasmania's honey industry,' I said. 'And you're the first bee-keeper I've actually met.'

'I wouldn't want my name mentioned in any magazine,' said the woman, making a vague pushing motion with her arms as if she desired to thrust me back into the car and see me on my way.

'Well,' I said mildly. 'I can always call you by a different name—in fact, since I don't even know your name yet, that's what I'll do.' Besides, whether I would actually write the article or not was open to question—I was always full of good ideas that fell by the wayside.

'Anthea Stonybrook,' said the bee-keeper.

'Pardon?'

'You can call me Anthea Stonybrook.'

'What a charming suggestion. But is subterfuge really necessary? All you're doing is producing honey.'

'It's the Parks, Wildlife and Heritage,' said Anthea Stonybrook crossly.

'Oh?'

'The department. The government! They have secret plans to undermine the honey industry in this State.' She poked a bony finger in the direction of my chest.

By this time I was wondering if Anthea Stonybrook was a madwoman; certainly my sister seemed to think so, as she tapped the side of her head behind the bee-keeper's back.

'Astonishing,' I replied. 'You can't keep up with meddling governments these days.'

'Too right. It's because all the leatherwood is in the World Heritage Area and that's what concerns them. They claim there may be significant impacts as yet unknown on the nature around here.' She snorted. 'Aren't bees nature?'

'Well—what kind of impacts?'

'Less nectar and pollen for native insects, increased hybridisation of native species. Competition with native pollinators, resulting in their decline. As if a few bees are going to destroy the whole habitat of the west coast! And the most ridiculous thing? They say our hives are an eyesore, that the tourists don't like them. "Detract from the natural views" I think they phrase it.'

I looked along the thin strip of tarmac that ran between the overhanging trees, dripping with moisture, and disappeared into the misty hills. The hives were little more than dots dwarfed by the omnipotence of raw nature, and I said as much to Anthea Stonybrook in order to placate her. Besides, I added, wouldn't tourists be interested in the hives?

'Hum. I don't often get stopped and quizzed by foreigners with notebooks,' she replied with a sudden twinkle in her eye. 'I tell you another concern. Apart from leatherwood, much of the rest of Tasmanian honey production comes from blackberry. We also use it to build up our bee stock before the leatherwood comes into flower. But that's an introduced

species too, a weed in fact, and efforts are under way to try
and exterminate it. If that happens, and access to the World
Heritage Area is restricted, there won't be much scope for
honey production in this State any more.'

'And you'll be out of a job?'

'Exactly.' She rubbed her hand over her eye and then,
unexpectedly, smiled at me. 'I love these bees, you know.
Being outdoors. Honey. It's in the Bible: manna in the
wilderness, the food the Son of God was supposed to eat so
he might know to choose the good and shun evil.'

'Of course.'

'St John ate honey and locusts in the wilderness. The promised land is flowing with milk and honey! The New Jerusalem!'

I had stopped writing now. I snapped my notebook shut
and bundled Nicola back into the car and we drove off,
leaving Anthea Stonybrook with a messianic glint in her eye,
leaving her mood swings and paranoias about government
plots and religious fervour.

No wonder she hadn't wanted her name in a magazine.

There is always a certain magic, for me, in taking a boat and
heading out to an unknown island: the magic of adventure
and travel, with the wind at your face, the seagulls wheeling
overhead, the hard slap of the waves against the hull and,
best of all, that beckoning island luring you on to discovery.
I have a photo in front of me now, taken by my sister: I am
leaning against the ferry's railings, splattered as they are with
bird shit, and the sea is a blue foam over my left shoulder, my
hair blowing in the breeze, and on my face an expression of
pure delight. The *Mirambeena* only took fifteen minutes, but
it was a fifteen minutes made in heaven.

Bruny Island. It was like those series of Russian dolls, one
inside the other. First there was Australia, an offshore
continent, then Tasmania, an offshore island of the offshore
continent, and finally Bruny, like the ultimate prize, an
offshore island of an offshore island of an offshore continent,
and just as one unpacks the final Russian doll and feels both
relief and disappointment, so I too felt conflicting emotions.
This was about as far south as I could possibly get, which

seemed like a relief (I could only head home from now onwards)—but heading home (where *was* home, anyway?) could bring its own tribulations.

Nicola and I had driven down to the south coast by way of several national parks. We had walked at Lake St Clair, looking to no avail for the platypuses that lived in the lake.

'We'll go on to Mt Field National Park,' I had consoled my sister. 'The wildlife there is vegetable and enormous, so we ought to be able to spot that.'

And we had. Charles Darwin, on his visit to the region, had likened the huge ferns of Mt Field to the elegant parasols of Victorian women. An absurd comparison, I thought, brought about, perhaps, through homesickness and want of female company. The ferns had hairy, gnarled stems thick as a man's leg (they were sometimes called manferns) and roots that writhed across the surface of the soil as though tortured. The undersides of the fronds were lumped and pitted and the leaves, though finely patterned, showed no fragility: these plants were survivors. Above them swamp gums draped ribbons of peeling bark, and white gums rose ghostly out of the gloom. The swamp gums were billed as the tallest flowering plants in the world and the second tallest plants of any kind after the Californian redwoods; the Department of Parks had set up a clinometer in the woods where, in the rain, we had measured one such tree for ourselves.

Now it seemed we had finally left the rain behind, for the sun was shining. Bruny Island was a small place with large historical echoes. Half the explorers in Australian history had been here: Captain Cook, Matthew Flinders, Bass, Franklin, Bligh (who planted what was reputedly Tasmania's first Granny Smith apple tree here), Furneaux and the Frenchman Bruny d'Entrecasteaux, who bequeathed his first name to the island and his surname to the channel that separated it from Tasmania. Being French, he did not merit much more, although there was a malodorous monument to his memory in the town of Gordon, sandwiched between a public toilet block and a collection of metal refuse bins.

At Neck Beach on the island there was, or had been, a memorial to Truganini but, almost appropriately, it had been vandalised. There was little left except the foundations, chipped and scarred, a sad relic, but somehow grotesquely appropriate for this woman born on Bruny, who was widely regarded as the last full-blooded Aboriginal Tasmanian.

'They roam no more upon this isle, so stay and meditate a while,' said Nicola, reading out the inscription. Then she rushed up a sand dune and began shouting about the views of the sea. I could not imagine my sister meditating, even for a while: she was far too sociable, and quietness irked her.

Ah, well. Genocide had carried the indigenous Tasmanians away into history, and it was too late to mourn them or meditate now. Meditation on Truganini did little for the reputation of the explorers or, perhaps more fairly, those who had come after them as settlers. After Truganini died in 1876 the Royal Society had her flesh carved off and her skeleton stored in an apple box, then displayed in the Tasmanian Museum ('The Last Tasmanian Aboriginal' said the label proudly), before being removed to storage until 1976, when her remains were finally cremated and scattered in the ocean off the island where she was born. Her husband, William Lanne, who had the dubious distinction of being the last Aboriginal man, had an even more grotesque fate. His body was exhumed from the graveyard and hidden in a hospital store-room, where it was later dissected, supposedly in the interests of science. The Royal College of Surgeons in London acquired his head, the trophy-hunting Hobartians cut off his feet and hands, which ended up in the Tasmanian Museum, and the Tasmanian Royal Society managed to hang on to what was left of his body.

Contemplating this at Neck Beach seemed almost absurd, I thought as I scrambled after Nicola: it was such a beautiful place, with the wind whipping in from an indigo ocean, and splendid views of sand dunes and mottled mud flats and dark hills. The Neck at Neck Beach was a thin strip of sand dunes that separated the two halves of the island: the north was pastoral and drier, and horses grazed in its paddocks, while the south was hilly and wet, with deep valleys hiding patches of rainforest. The sand dunes of the isthmus were the haunt of penguins and shearwater birds.

'Mutton birds,' screeched my sister against the wind (she had been studying her guidebook the night before, in preparation for the occasion). And then again: 'Otherwise known as mutton birds.'

'What?'

'Plentiful . . . flocks of flying sheep . . . sailors.'

'I can't hear you!'

My sister's mouth was still opening and shutting in a big O, like *The Muppet Show* without any volume, and all I could hear were the calls of flying sheep and the wind blowing fresh and salty off the white-capped waves.

Errol Flynn was born in Hobart. Was this fact of significance? Hardly so. It was difficult to imagine the swashbuckling movie hero of dubious sexuality but undoubted sex appeal coming from this Anglo-Saxon town on the edge of the known world. Hobart was a quiet little place of well-regulated streets with immaculate front lawns and carefully tended rose beds, with painted fishing smacks bobbing on the harbour and gulls screaming against a grey sky. It reminded me of Ireland: the same soft unpredictable weather and courteous inhabitants, the same muted green hills in the not-so-far distance, the same small corner shops and haphazard markets. And, like many towns in Ireland, it was built in a picturesque jumble between hills and sea.

Battery Point was the old heart of the town. Although the nineteenth-century municipal buildings (Government House, the Theatre Royal, the criminal courts, customs house) were located elsewhere, the jumble of residential buildings on the point had changed little in the last century and gave more of a taste of what Hobart was all about: a sprightly and well-regulated maritime air, with views of the harbour where yachts and fishing boats floated on the water; but a slightly raffish and disreputable air at the same time, with its narrow winding streets and historical secrets and pubs with buccaneer names—the Ball and Chain, the Drunken Admiral, Dirty Dick's, the Caribbean Room. (In the Maritime Museum were displayed models of whalers and clippers, steam ships and yachts in bottles, with old paintings and sepia photographs of Battery Point in its heyday, and the huge bones of a sperm whale's jaw.) A gun battery had been established here as early as 1818 and a signal station, still extant, constructed in the same year, from which tides were measured and messages relayed. The harbourmaster, who lived near by, kept an eye out for smugglers and escaped convicts.

The architecture on Battery Point was Irish too: grey pebble-dash houses with painted doors, pretty whitewashed cottages, Georgian and Victorian churches, barracks and houses of a grandeur almost out of place. A miniature Dublin, perhaps—and why not? The long arm of British colonialism had left its imprint on many corners of the world, leaving now a quaint charm that bore little reality to historical fact. But Battery Point was almost democratic: fishermen's cottages cheek-by-jowl with shipwrights' houses and Georgian mansions complete with stables and coach-house.

There were Georgian warehouses in Salamanca Place just under Battery Point, too, well restored. The warehouses, the old mansions, the important colonial municipal buildings were a constant reminder that Hobart was really a nineteenth-century town, its deep-water port attracting whalers (whales were once so abundant in the Derwent estuary that it was dangerous to cross by boat) and traders, and eventually mining companies, from all over the world. Grain and timber, wool and fruit, whale oil, tin and other metals were traded and shipped out of the town. Hobart had been a thriving place where fortunes had been made and industrial booms had taken place; the town had boasted Australia's first electric-powered trolley buses, its first brewery and its first public museum, opened in 1843 by Lady Jane Franklin, who aspired to make Hobart the Athens of the South. (She did not succeed, but Hobart today, in spite of its size, is renowned for the quality of its cultural life.)

Such businesses had mostly moved on, leaving Hobart in a quiet backwater. The warehouses of Salamanca Place now contained trendy cafés and craft shops selling hand-blown glass, intergalactic kitchenware and New Age candles. In the square in front a market was in full swing—everything from fresh cream with raspberries, Tasmanian honey and home-made jam, Canterbury bells tied in bunches, to cassettes and second-hand books. There was a family of Tibetans ambling around: I recognised them by their hard straight features and black eyes, and they seemed to add a touch of the exotic to the scene. They were among the very few non-whites I had seen in Tasmania; this was an Anglo-Saxon enclave still. In the harbour there were mostly yachts; the trade boom had long gone, and now the finish of the Sydney to Hobart Yacht Race brought only an annual buzz to the city's quay. At lunch time I prowled with Nicola around Constitution Dock, with its fish markets—crabs and scallops, stripy trumpeter and West Coast trevally, some of it cooked up there and then by the restaurants. (There was even a sushi bar: a harassed Japanese rushed about the tables, taking orders.) We nibbled at breaded fish and threw chips to the seagulls.

'I know where we might find Asians,' said my sister helpfully, for once deciding to collude in my search. She hurled a chip out into the bay and it landed on the deck of someone's yacht. 'The casino.'

This seemed like a good suggestion; after all, the Chinese in particular were determined gamblers. And the casino seemed worth a visit anyway: sitting out along the coast from the town, its glass-and-concrete tower dominated the landscape like an unwanted reminder of a world more sophisticated and modern. It was a famous place, once Australia's only legal casino, and still a major tourist draw-card.

There were Asians in the casino all right, a good many of them, who smoked and squinted at their cards and threw money on the table recklessly. A Hong Kong Chinese who lived in Hobart sidled up to me and started explaining how he made a living from playing blackjack by coming here two or three times a week and making $250 a time.

'Not every time, surely,' I said.

'I start with fifty dollars. If I lose the fifty, I leave, even if I've only been here ten minutes. When I win two hundred and fifty, I also leave, to ensure the money remains in my pocket.'

'So you earn between five and seven hundred dollars a week?'

'I'm trying. Last week I lost four hundred.'

'I thought you stopped after losing only fifty at any one time?'

'I was not disciplined.' He grinned at me. 'But for four weeks before that, I made about five hundred dollars each week.'

'If you keep winning they'll ban you anyway, or break your legs or something.'

'I think you watch too many movies,' he said. '*The Godfather*.'

'I don't think I've seen *The Godfather*.'

'Everyone has seen it!'

'Perhaps I resisted the temptation for that very reason.' The Hong Kong Chinese shrugged and shuffled his feet.

'How about some advice?' I asked, bringing the conversation round to safer topics.

'Play the same as the dealer. Stop if you have seventeen points or more. After all, if the dealer does it, it must be good, right?'

'Yes, but the dealer wins when it's a draw. So the casino is still ahead, in the long run.'

'You have to watch when to join the game. That's the difference. You see, the dealer has no choice, she has to keep going. But you can choose your table, see if you get good vibes from the other players. These things go in cycles. Join in when a winning streak starts for the players.'

'I see.'

I played blackjack for a while, but quickly lost $70—bad vibes, wrong cycle, what did I know? My Hong Kong acquaintance had already sidled away, which might have warned me. I stopped playing and slouched around, watching old Vietnamese ladies gambling at Club Keno and young Chinese men shuffling chips around the roulette table—piles of them, as if they were sweets bought by the bagful.

Nicola played blackjack for a couple of hours with the concentration and excitement of an amateur. By the time we left she had won $210 dollars, but she had lost $200 as well. Ten dollars profit.

The Hong Kong Chinese was nowhere to be seen. Hopefully he had pocketed more winnings than my sister.

We passed out of Hobart and crossed the Derwent River over the Tasman Bridge. Its supporting pylons were slightly out of line—in 1975 a freighter had ploughed into the bridge, killing a dozen people and, astonishingly, plunging the city into chaos. The bridge had closed; it took hours to reach Hobart from the other side of the river, a long detour on minor country roads to the nearest crossing at Bridgewater. The real-estate market on the stranded eastern shore collapsed, businesses closed for lack of road transport, and the crime rate rose by nearly half in the isolated suburbs. It was a reminder that Tasmania was still a frontier State, dependent on the vagaries of fate and nature.

We were heading towards Port Arthur, which stood testament to the fact that Tasmania was not the quaint and genteel offshore island of its current reputation but Van Diemen's Land—the name's pronunciation seemed fortuitous—a place of violence and repression that held some of Australian history's worst brutality. (This reputation was sadly enhanced some time after my visit, when a lone gunman named Martin Bryant opened fire here, massacring thirty-five people. His choice of Port Arthur was no accident; Bryant was later to comment: 'A lot of violence has happened here. It must be the most violent place in Australia. It seemed the right place.')

Van Diemen's Land was the last of the eastern colonies to halt convict transportation, and it was the only colony where the 'probation system' was introduced. In the last years of the convict era the British government announced that convicts were no longer to be distributed to individual masters under the assignment system, but would be subjected to 'formidable and certain' punishment in prisons, followed by work in labour gangs under direct government control. By dint of hard work and repentance a convict could move through successively lenient stages of the penal system, eventually earning a pardon.

The probation system, introduced in 1842 and abandoned after transportation was suspended in 1846, was an abysmal failure. By segregating the convicts from the general population, it increased degradation and failed to improve behaviour. (Homosexual behaviour—that 'unnatural crime' for which Victorians seemed to have a fascination—was particularly rife, and one wonders whether Tasmania's continuing homophobia has something to do with this historical memory.) As William Denison, the Lieutenant-Governor of the colony, remarked in 1847: 'The convict issues from the probation station a worse man than when he entered it.' The system also proved to be extremely costly. Mismanagement, lack of planning and lack of personnel willing to work in the penal settlements, as well as the remoteness of the colony, also added up to a disastrous outcome.

Such information seemed little more than a historical curiosity on arrival at Port Arthur; it was difficult to believe the convict system ever throve in such a setting, and time had removed the physical evidence of tyranny and misery. There were beautiful Tasmanian blue gums and park land, planted with elms and oaks and a nineteenth-century garden to remind the officers of home. Even contemporaries had described the penitentiary as elegant and imposing. Anthony Trollope, who visited Port Arthur in the early 1870s, noted the 'cleanliness and prettiness of the place', with its lovely bays and commodious buildings, and (astonishingly enough) enthused over the diligence and contentedness of the inmates.

'It looks like something out of Jane Austen,' said Nicola, as we wandered past the ruins of a church and down through flower beds towards a stone fountain.

It *was* a beautiful place, with its mellow sandstone buildings and seaside setting. I couldn't get away from that observation, although I kept reminding myself that the convicts would not have seen it like this. The protagonist in *For the Term of His Natural Life* certainly hadn't. 'Rufus Dawes had seen this prospect before, had learnt by heart each beauty of rising sun, sparkling water, and wooded hill,' noted one passage from the book. 'There was no charm for him in the exquisite blue of the sea, the soft shadows of the hills, or the soothing ripple of the waves that crept voluptuously to the white breast of the shining shore.'

The contrast between the beauty of its setting and the ugliness of its function made Port Arthur the Jekyll and Hyde of tourism. It was used as a working prison and a punishment station; after convict transportation was halted Port Arthur was a dumping ground for paupers and lunatics. This is historical fact. But the Lunatic Asylum was now a museum and gift shop. The museum had leg irons, flogging whips, lists of transportees and their crimes (the minimum sentence was seven years, the maximum given to one Joseph Parker, transported for life for stealing a silk handkerchief). These displays were almost knick-knacks; they appeared as irrelevant as the lip-plates of some distant Amazonian tribe.

The written evidence moved me more. The museum demonstrated that the settlement was controlled to the last detail; the Convict Department's regulations outlined the amount of food and clothing (two cloth jackets and three striped shirts) made available, when the convicts could speak, when they had to work. Between November and December labour was from five-thirty in the morning until six in the evening, with an hour's rest both at breakfast and lunch. The minute detail and rigorous organisation of such brutality could not but remind one of the Nazis' efficient running of their concentration camps. Punishments were also carefully categorised: twelve lashes for disorderly conduct, reduced diet for insolence, twenty lashes for insubordination, solitary confinement for a week for repeat offences of this nature.

But the gift shop seemed to negate the horror of the museum's information: such information was offered in coffee-table books with attractive Victorian etchings. There were tin mugs with convict arrows stamped on them, postcards, *I've been to Port Arthur* T-shirts. Spooky ghost tours were on offer. Even on our own, Nicola and I could hardly get away from the unreality of it all—the setting was too picturesque and peaceful to have any historical atmosphere. Perhaps the only eerie building was the Model Prison, no doubt because it was as yet the least developed, the most raw. It had chilly windowless cells with thick walls, endless barred doors and a dreadful quiet that impelled even Nicola to silence. The inmates here were deprived of any human contact, forbidden to speak and living in solitary confinement —even the chapel had individual compartments for each convict. This was a fashionable system of punishment in the 1840s, copied from Pentonville Prison in England and thought to be humane. It rapidly drove men mad.

'There are too many tourists here,' said Nicola. 'Of course, we are tourists too,' she added, just to be fair. But I knew what she meant.

'People call this a place of national pilgrimage,' I said. 'But it's a tourist pilgrimage, really.'

'You remember that Nazi concentration camp in Alsace? That was designed for tourists. But it wasn't *touristy*. I felt sick afterwards.'

'Yes.'

'This place is too enjoyable.'

That was the problem: you had no right to make an evil place attractive to tourists. Port Arthur managed to transcend its picturesque setting and its gift shops and tour groups, especially in the loneliness of the Model Prison's cells and the dark displays of the museum—but only just. Much later, when Port Arthur reopened to tourism in the wake of its modern-day massacre, I wondered anew about this difficult interface between daytripping and reality, and how it was being addressed.

We took a small boat out on to the bay. Tourists chattered and took photos and bought cups of coffee and Maltesers from the tiny galley. Loudspeakers gave us a commentary on Port Arthur's history, romantic stories of escapees and daring adventure. We circled the Isle of the Dead, where nearly 2000 convicts and 200 personnel were interred. Even here discipline had reigned: the military and civilians had been buried on high ground with imposing stone monuments, while the prisoners were buried, wrapped in sailcloth and covered with quicklime, several to an unmarked grave on lower, swampy land. Even dead the convicts were not entirely human—here was the lesson of Port Arthur as well as the lesson of concentration camps: the failure to remember that Jews, and even convicts, were people too.

The Isle of the Dead was a good place to take photos back towards Port Arthur, and the tourists did, as the boat chugged in circles and then headed back to the jetty. But the simple separated graves were also the embodiment of the whole site. And the lesson? Nobody deserved to be categorised, and then dehumanised because of that category. There was a modern message here too, I thought, for the racists who occasionally made themselves heard through the media.

I left Port Arthur feeling sad and despondent. I couldn't help liking the place, even though it was a symbol of all that was mean in the human spirit.

If Tasmania, and particularly Port Arthur, seemed like a place of contradictions, here was another contradiction, another symbol: the State's emblem was a fierce animal made cuddly. We stopped the car at a wildlife park not far from Port Arthur to see it. This symbol of the State had a fierce name—the Tasmanian devil—and it snarled open-mouthed out of government crests and letterheads, coloured black. In real life there wasn't much to endear one to this beast. Dark as hell, it had hard beady eyes and a drooling spiteful mouth filled with sharp teeth, with which it fought and ripped its prey, feeding noisily, screaming and snuffling like a pig among the slops. It had short legs and a truncated tail and a shapeless lump of a body and slept in holes and tree logs, coming out at night as if ashamed of its appearance, ugly and insanitary as a hyena, and a scavenger to boot.

At the entrance to the park they sold soft toys of the animals, a tourist absurdity. It seemed a strange beast to chose as a soft toy, still more as a mascot, even if it was Tasmania's largest surviving mammalian carnivore. But appropriate nonetheless, perhaps: uniquely Tasmanian and, like the cuteness of the State itself, hiding a virulent streak of nastiness. On the Tasman Peninsula the Tasmanian devil did not seem so incongruous after all.

Tasmania's east coast was benign compared to the west: here farms raised sheep and cattle and harvested grain, fishermen set out to a calmer sea, and local holidaymakers came to enjoy the sandy beaches and sheltered bays. At Orford there was a golf course, caravan parks and holiday flats, at Triabunna fishing excursions and a working horse museum, at Swansea water-skiing, bowling and (presumably a rarity in Tasmania, since the guidebooks all mentioned it) a full-size billiard table in the Community Centre. There were a few historic buildings too, Swansea being the administrative centre for the oldest rural municipality in all Australia. This was whistle-stop tourism now: our itinerary was lagging by days. We had lingered at Lake St Clair and Bruny Island, lingered in Hobart, as if this Apple Isle were an Avalon that would make us forget time and earthly considerations, and hypnotise us so we should never leave.

At Freycinet National Park wallabies hopped among the accommodation and we made the obligatory walk to the lookout over Wineglass Bay, where the sea frothed like blue champagne in a bay of golden sand and green, tree-clad hills —so photographed it has become a cliché. I took photographs too, of my sister squatting on a rock, and she took more of me, standing gazing out at this absurd beauty and pure colour. Freycinet was a place to rest, momentarily: to walk along the rippled beach at sunset and watch the mud burp and sizzle, to amble among the pink granite boulders. Then we drove on to Bicheno (a wildlife park and harbour) to turn inland at St Mary's and drive up over forested hills to the centre of the island, where we swung northwards towards Launceston.

We had a plane to catch.

twelve

through fields of gold

You part with people not knowing if you will ever be with them again, for you can never foresee the haphazard mischances of fate, nor where your own choices and those of others might lead. I said goodbye to my sister at Sydney airport, feeling bereft. Sometimes it takes a distant journey to make you realise that the best things have always been at home.

My own sense of identity was fluid and constantly changing. Who was I? This was a question I had been asking for years, and I knew I was a person much affected by the happenstances of my character, upbringing and choices. My view of the identity of others was much more rigid, and like most people I chose, most of the time, not to shift my mental parameters. Nicola was my sister: that was the framework in which I had wedged her, and which had prevented me from seeing a much more complex person. Beyond that I had hardly looked, but now after months of close companionship in Australia I was forced to reconsider. As I travelled around the continent, picking apart its stereotypes and myths, so too I travelled through the complexities of my sister's personality. She was generous to a fault, sociable and talkative, infuriatingly contradictory at times (no one had a right to be contradictory except myself), calmly tolerant, and one of those rare and valuable people with a truly giving spirit. She had no clear path in life, caught in indecision about her future, uncommitted and unsure of where her heart and best interests lay. In her I saw much of myself.

I had been sent to Australia (at least in my mother's eyes) to check on my sister's sanity and determine her plans for the future. Nicola was sane enough, but neither she nor I knew exactly what the future would bring. 'Better to live one day as a tiger than a thousand years as a sheep,' Nicola was fond of quoting—it was a Tibetan saying, meaning she was in no hurry to conform to expected patterns. The quotation hid rootlessness and lost relationships, yet we knew, too, that in it was excitement and challenge as well as insecurity. I watched her passing through customs, feeling deeply sad, realising too late that I had found a friend.

With Nicola gone my brother's Sydney house was quiet, Simon himself at work all day. Very well then, I would go on another journey. I loaded up the campervan once more, telling Simon I was heading for Victoria.

'Huh,' he said. 'I haven't had a holiday for a year.'

No, he hadn't, I thought: but he had a house and a career and a bank account, and had made his own choices.

Passing through Canberra once more, I headed south-west towards the Snowy Mountains, one of the few places in Australia I had actually heard about before coming here; I had studied its immense hydroelectric scheme in geography lessons in high school, and the Man from Snowy River was a famous Australian, though why and who he was I did not know. It was a long climb up into the mountains (little more than gentle rolling hills to my European eye) to Jindabyne, nearly 1000 metres above sea level, tucked into a pretty valley beside a lake. It was artificial, created by the hydro-electric project, and the original village was now under its waters. The new town was a tourist resort, advertising winter sports. There were posters of snowfields and brightly dressed skiers that seemed bizarre in the summer heat—it was late afternoon, and the temperature was still above thirty degrees.

There was a statue out near the lake shore, high on a granite plinth, the black metal figure pointing into the distance with one hand and holding a book tucked under one arm. I had seen such statues many times in China, but doubted this could be Mao Zedong. Perhaps my hunt for Chinese influences had spiralled out of control and I was hallucinating—but there was no doubt it had a definite communist stance to it, heroic and dramatic and a little bit intimidating. I walked over to it to find I was not entirely wrong: the statue had been presented to the town, on the occasion of Australia's bicentenary, by the Polish People's Republic, said the plaque. Its subject was not a revolutionary but the Polish explorer Count Strzelecki, who had been the first white to penetrate this area and who had named nearby Mt Kosciusko after a Polish hero.

I continued driving into the Snowies and stopped for the night at Thredbo, its premier resort. It had the rather depressing air of any deserted holiday town in the off-season, and seemed in any case a completely artificial village, consisting of little more than holiday apartments, hotels and restaurants. It had what passed for alpine architecture, though the attempt was rather half-hearted, consisting of hearts cut out of green shutters, and concrete buildings with wooden roofs and balconies. In the cafés there were rough wooden tables and the odd set of deer's antlers, the beer served in tankards. There was an Alpenhorn Restaurant, a Black Bear Inn and an Alpine Motel, and the holiday flats were named Wolf's Lair, Snow Goose, Tyrola and Sitzmark. In another mood and season it might have made me nostalgic for Switzerland (Nicola was back there by now, I thought), but in the heat of summer and in my present cynical mood it made me laugh. There seemed to be a confusion here: snow geese were Scandinavian, Tyrol was in Austria, alpine horns were Swiss, Sitzmark was what—a German peak, perhaps? Never mind, they were all European, and so lent a touch of glamour.

The next morning I took a chair-lift up the mountainside. From the summit it was a relatively easy, though long, hike across a metal walkway to the summit of Mt Kosciusko, Australia's highest peak at a little over 2200 metres. The alpine meadows were studded with bluebells, the yellow pompoms of billy buttons and the white stars of camomile sunrays, but I wasn't the only hiker among this natural beauty. 'Crowded like Pitt Street on a Saturday,' said one woman to me cheerfully, referring to Sydney's main shopping drag. At the summit a trigonometric survey plinth provided an ideal pose for a photo.

'Just to prove we made it,' explained one couple to me after asking me to take a picture of them.

After I had finished a child clambered up on top of it. 'I'm the tallest person in Australia!' he screamed delightedly.

I sat at the summit eating my sandwiches, a jumble of granite boulders near by, and in the distance views of blue ridges disappearing towards Victoria. There was a strong smell of Aerogard in the breeze, and flies buzzed about incessantly.

It was an accomplishment for these town-dwelling Australians, the top of Mt Kosciusko—possibly the nearest they would get to wilderness. Where were the stereotypes now of bronzed Aussies striding through the outback, a distant look in their eyes as if watching the endless horizon? Some of them had lugged their coolers up here, and one group had cracked open bottles of beer; they all had cameras and binoculars, and one woman even seemed to have brought her handbag. None of them was bronzed: they all looked rather pale, and wore sun-hats, and obsessively rubbed sun lotion into their cheeks and nose.

'We better be heading back,' said one lady to her husband anxiously. 'Before it gets dark.' And we all headed off down the metal track once more, towards the chair-lift. My own town-dweller's legs were aching with the unaccustomed exercise, and as I followed Pitt Street back to Thredbo I grinned to myself.

I wasn't feeling ironic today. I had enjoyed the walk, I had enjoyed eavesdropping on the people. I had even sat on the plinth myself, so I too could be the tallest person in Australia.

'Victoria: A Taste of Old England' said the heading in one of my guidebooks to the continent. In the finer print underneath it explained: 'It is the sort of place where you have to remind yourself that you are in Australia.' I found this extraordinary, though of course I had not been in Victoria for more than a matter of hours. I had followed the Alpine Way down the western side of the range and had crossed out of New South Wales just past the town of Khancoban. As I descended to the plains the sun had become stronger and stronger. The heat was beating down on the roof of the van and bouncing up from the road in front of me, causing me to squint even with sun-glasses. The tall brown grasses by the roadside crackled, and in valleys flooded into lakes the black skeletons of trees stuck up like pitchforks.

I still hadn't got used to the oddity of the Australian landscape, an oddity I knew I foisted on it from my outsider's perspective. From earliest times people had commented on the Australian scenery as alien, harsh, sad. 'The Australian mountain forests are funereal, secret, stark,' wrote Marcus Clarke. 'Their solitude is desolation. They seem to stifle in their black gorges a story of sullen despair . . . From the melancholy gums strips of white bark hang and rustle . . . Flights of white cockatoos stream out shrieking like evil souls.' He summarised the Australian landscape in two words: weird and melancholy. All this was surely a vision of the country through European eyes, or at least a European heritage. I agreed; I still saw Australia as hostile and frightening, as when I had first glimpsed it from the window of my aeroplane, but I had also come to admire it. It had its own beauty, and this corner of Victoria was beautiful too. It was not like Old England, and I did not want it to be. I had not come hundreds of kilometres to see something that looked like England.

I was intending to follow a route through the goldfields, for this I felt was the heart of Victoria—and fertile ground for my pursuit of the Chinese, who had played a major part in its development. It was hard to overestimate the significance of gold in the history of the State: it had influenced its early settlement, population growth, economy and political development.

Beechworth was my first stop on the trail of gold. Like many mining towns, Beechworth had begun its life as an expanse of tents and semi-permanent buildings that could easily be dismantled when the prospectors moved on. Beechworth had promised to yield a considerable amount, however, and so the town became more permanent, and wooden houses and weatherboard shops were built, and eventually stately stone public buildings. Like most mining towns, Beechworth had no doubt been a den of gambling, drunkenness, violence and impropriety, as indicated by its impressive jail, which had once been host to Ned Kelly and had the dimensions and appearance of a Scottish castle. Now Beechworth was a charming tourist attraction, thanks to its architectural unity and the preservation of much of the nineteenth-century town, including the court house, post office, railway station, school, and several hotels.

There had been plenty of Chinese in Beechworth—in the 1860s 7000 of them, in fact, half of whom had been miners. There had been four hundred Chinese shopkeepers, four hundred market gardeners, fifteen doctors, six barbers, five tailors, eight butchers, thirty-two carpenters, and a hundred street hawkers selling everything from needles to joss sticks for the temple. The Chinese camp had developed into its own section of the town, with Chinese theatres and boarding houses, eateries and temples. Today, to my disappointment, I found there was little left of this impressive presence except the cemetery, dotted with hundreds of Chinese graves and the distinctive towers, with their pyramidal caps, used for burning prayer papers and offerings.

In a café, however, there were echoes not of history but of modern life. There were three Taiwanese women sitting sipping at lemon tea and eating apple danishes. They had come up for the weekend from Melbourne, where they were studying, and I asked them why they wanted to learn English.

'Because our husbands screwing their secretaries,' answered one of the women. Her two friends giggled as I stared at her in embarrassment, caught unawares by this fresh-faced, carefully dressed Chinese woman who was so forthright (I might have said, so un-Chinese, except that this observation was patently absurd).

'Oh?'

'Yes. You know, a lot Taiwanese men screwing their secretaries,' she said matter-of-factly. 'Having affair with younger lady, usually employee.'

'That's terrible.'

'Chinese proverb say, love like lemon. Sweet to look at, but bitter to taste.'

'So we wives left at the home, doing our housework,' contributed another of the ladies. 'Our kids growing up, we feel boring, nothing to do.'

'So you learn English for an interest, a distraction?'

'We learning English for spending husband's money! Is only benefit coming from marriage, so why not? And only way revenge.'

'We choose most expensive course,' added one of her companions. 'Now we go study tour of Australia, I think very costly.'

'So now you have lunch with us, no worry about it, choose big cake, my husband pay bill!'

So I sat and had lunch at a philandering husband's expense, and was entertained by three Chinese ladies, and eventually they gave me their phone number in Melbourne.

'You arrive Melbourne, give me tinkle.'

And I drove out of Beechworth smiling to myself.

As I travelled westwards the landscape of the goldfields had none of the vast flatness that I had seen on most of my trip around mainland Australia—here there were rolling hills and fenced fields and grasslands that were on a much more human scale. There were no reds and oranges here, either; the landscape was mostly green and yellow, and other splashes of colour intruded into the scenery. I noticed them as I drove along, distracted momentarily from the road: a white horse standing in a green field, three men in bright yellow shorts cycling along the grey road, a black bull resting in the shade of a blue car abandoned in the tall yellow grass, a red-and-white train on a hill.

Arriving in Bendigo, I stopped at Central Deborah Gold Mine for a mine tour—after all, this was what the goldfields had been all about. Inside the mining compound there was a group of boy scouts running around, making all the usual hullabaloo of 12-year-old kids. A loud overweight woman in a floral print dress was yelling at them and looking dishevelled.

'Daniel, *Daniel*. Down here. DANIEL! Mark, tell Karen to send Daniel down here.' She wiped the perspiration from her forehead and sat down on a bench across from me, looking at me as if inviting sympathy. I stared back at her coolly: I found Australians always seemed to be yelling at their children, telling them what to do, what not to do, harassing them.

'Andrew, are you afraid of heights?' the woman was now screaming at one of the boys clambering happily about on the poppet legs that supported the mine lift.

'No,' replied Andrew.

'Well hurry up then, what are you standing there for, come down.'

Another boy came and sat down beside me. He had an open, freckled face and bent over a tourist brochure of Bendigo, spread on his knees.

'Don't sit there! Over in the corner!'

'But why?'

'Just sit over there! In the corner! Go.'

The boy got to his feet and moved over to the other bench, where he sat sullenly swinging his legs. Luckily at that moment the tour guide came, and I scurried off in her wake. I was willing to listen to a mob of 12-year-olds, but not to this mean-mouthed woman with her petty tyranny.

The tour guide was petite and soft-spoken. We stood at the entrance to the mine shaft and she told the assembled group that the Empire State Building would fit down it and not be seen—it was 410 metres deep, on seventeen levels. This was meant to be an impressive statistic, and there were murmurs of approval, but after all it was hardly surprising—mines were supposed to be deep. Perhaps this added glamour and a certain cosmopolitanism to the Deborah Mine; people in this country were certainly fond of such comparisons.

'There are three mines,' the guide was saying as we descended below the earth in the cage. 'Central Deborah, Deborah and North Deborah. And even the mine cat here is called Deborah,' she added, without the faintest trace of humour in her voice. I felt a sinking feeling as she added: 'The cage takes ninety seconds to descend the mine shaft.' I knew then she would be one of those guides who was full of useless information.

'A ton of gold was taken from the mine over a fifteen-year period from 1939 to 1954, which would form a cube about the length of a school ruler. Only half a teaspoon of gold could be recovered from every ton of rock—about 60 000 tons of rock were excavated in all. The closure of the mine heralded the last gold operation in Bendigo, although there are now plans to reopen it.'

We were ushered into the crib room where the miners ate lunch and played cribbage, as during their eight-hour shift they were not allowed to return to the surface. There were examples of miners' hats here: they were made of felt dipped in wax, or from layers of cardboard that merely provided protection from dripping water, not from rock falls. The hats were not compulsory, and had to be paid for from the miners' wages.

'Many miners went deaf from the noise of the machinery, or died of silicosis, the result of inhaling quartz dust into the lungs. My husband watched his father die of silicosis. Coughed his lungs up, a horrible way to die,' said the guide before passing on to other things. But she did not make it sound horrible, and the blandness in her voice was irritating me. Undoubtedly she had given the same explanations many times; but still, a mine tour depended on the interest of the tour guide—after all, there was a limited visual interest in tunnels dripping with water, old pieces of machinery.

The rest of the tour group was very quiet. They talked in low voices as if they were in a cathedral. Just as in caves, in mines there is awe and perhaps an element of fear; or maybe it was just because there was no other background noise, and so normal voice levels seemed unnaturally loud. When the guide demonstrated the bogger used to load the ore into trucks, and the rock drill, the roar of the machinery in such a confined space was positively terrifying.

While the woman uttered more statistics, I trailed around and thought my own thoughts. This was Narnia country, it was *The Lord of the Rings*, and I imagined goblins and trolls and dwarfs; and then I thought of the Chinese and other immigrants and their pursuit of gold, the horrifying miners' lives, of soulless drudgery in the pursuit of material gain. There were stories to be told here, enormous social and cultural resonances, but the tour guide was talking about faults and compression and north-south quartz lines and pyrites.

The toilet in the mine was known familiarly as the Taj Mahal, Buckingham Palace or the thunder box. There was a deliberate crack in the toilet seat; it was uncomfortable, so the workers didn't sit there too long on management time. I wrote it down in my notebook, a small detail with, I thought, a larger significance.

It was just about the only interesting thing I learned in Central Deborah Mine.

In its heyday, much before the operational years of the Deborah Mine, Bendigo had been a grand place. Its main street was named Pall Mall and its chief intersection Charing Cross. In the middle of Charing Cross there was a fountain in mustard and cream. It was surrounded by nymphs, each with one arm upraised as if dancing an Irish jig, and at their feet were horses with mermaids' tails. Across the road there was a white statue of a suspiciously slim Queen Victoria—but even Victoria, I supposed, was young once.

Bendigo was built on the grid pattern much favoured by Victorian town planners, but its architecture seemed to have burst out of these inhibiting confines like an exotic plant from a garden trellis. There was a wild mixture of the Italianate and the Gothic, grandly imposing, the town dotted with statues of enrobed royals that looked like splendid figures in drag, with fountains of cavorting goddesses and ornate bandstands. The opulent buildings were cluttered with Indian stupas, delicate scroll work, icing-sugar balconies, urns garlanded with stone vines, decorated pillars, Greek columns, turrets and chimneys.

Curiously enough, the first public buildings of any permanence to emerge in Bendigo, in the 1850s, were a chapel, the Masonic Hall and the Roman Catholic church. These were followed by grand Victorian buildings, including the Town Hall, Post Office and law courts. These symbols of spirituality and urban order must have belied the true nature of the place: a rough masculine mining town where men flocked to search for gold, where racial tensions were high and frequently flared into violence, and where most of the buildings were impermanent structures of wood and canvas. The town had been founded on gold and greed, and gold and greed remained for long its defining element. In the Shamrock

Hotel, another notable nineteenth-century edifice, the dirt floor had been swept nightly after the departure of the rowdy miners, and sieved for the gold flecks that had dropped from the miners' boots; nothing was overlooked. Today the town still lived on gold, although miners had been replaced by tourists. The sandwich board outside the Shamrock Hotel invited me to 'Discover the style and charm of a past era'. Inside the hotel there were crisp white tablecloths and polished wood, and a green salad was five dollars fifty. The style and charm that never was made plenty of money these days.

There had been Chinese in Bendigo from the beginning, though none had seen them as part of its charm. The discovery of gold in Victoria in the 1850s had prompted massive Chinese immigration. Newspapers likened their arrival to the biblical plague of locusts that had descended on Egypt, and called them the 'Tartar horde' or, more unkindly, 'moon-faced barbarians'. Cunning and deceit were loudly proclaimed as the characteristics of the race, and the Chinese were regularly accused of idolatry, disgusting manners and unsanitary habits, homosexuality (known as the Chinese Vice; there were few if any Chinese women on the goldfields) and even infanticide. Opium abuse was another sin associated with the Chinese. 'A more degraded life it is hardly possible to imagine. Gambling, opium-smoking, and horrid dissipation seemed to prevail among them constantly,' tut-tutted Anthony Trollope in *Australia and New Zealand*, before going on to accuse the Chinese of all the usual litany of crimes. (Ironically, it had been the British East India Company that had introduced opium-smoking to the Chinese, in order to correct their balance of trade with China, from which the British and Australians bought huge quantities of tea.) Of more serious concern was the fantasy that the Chinese would 'breed like rabbits' and take over Australia, even though only a minute proportion of the immigrants were women.

Still, there were over 40 000 Chinese in Victoria by the end of the 1850s (though as the gold rush declined many returned to China or migrated to fresh finds in New South Wales and Queensland). There was widespread alarm that the Chinese had a nefarious influence on the morality of Australia, that they were responsible for the introduction of new diseases to the country (smallpox and leprosy were frequently cited), that they would make the continent an outpost of the Celestial Empire, that they worked too hard and this was unfair competition on European workers. A £10 tax was introduced, payable by all arriving Chinese immigrants. Many Chinese avoided the tax by landing instead in Guichen Bay in South Australia and passing into Victoria overland, along routes that were only haphazardly policed. They carried their tents and supplies with them, journeying some thirty kilometres a day, digging their own wells for fresh water and buying sheep along the way for fresh meat. In 1857 a party of Chinese from Guichen Bay stumbled across one of the richest of the goldfields at Ararat, but the following whites who rushed there to stake claims soon forced the Chinese miners out, burning their tents and stores. Eventually the colonial governments legislated to restrict Chinese immigration, and in 1901 the new Commonwealth parliament passed the Immigration Restriction Act. These measures had a decisive influence on the Chinese in Australia. Their numbers declined sharply, and by 1940 there were only some 7000 in the entire country.

As a matter of fact, most of the Chinese immigrants in Australia had been highly educated—more than a third of those in Victoria had had a classical training of at least six or seven years. They were diligent workers, often fossicking for gold in poor-yielding or exhausted goldfields, and they had well-regulated townships with tightly knit communities which looked after the interests of the old, the poor and the unfortunate. The organisation, prosperity and value of the Chinese community could be glimpsed in Bendigo's Golden Dragon Museum, which depicted the history of the Chinese in these parts. It was home to the longest Chinese imperial dragon in the world, which made a sortie every year at Easter, supported by fifty-five volunteers. The museum also had a collection of burial figures, Chinese dominoes in a velvet-lined box, coins, teacups with lids decorated with Chinese scenes, ceramic jars, plates decorated with the Chinese zodiac and Taoist trigrams, and numerous other articles highlighting the richness of this culture so reviled by the uncouth European miners of the day.

Just outside Bendigo was the area's last remaining Chinese temple dating from gold-rush days. It was built in the 1860s from handmade bricks, and was saved from demolition twenty years ago by the National Trust. Dedicated to the god of war, Kuan Kung, it was the oldest Chinese temple in use in Australia. There was an elderly woman watering the plants as I wandered up to the site. She swept me inside and sold me a ticket, then hustled me into the temple itself.

The guide did not linger to indulge in small talk but launched straight into her set piece. 'The altar has a pair of dragons and a pair of oil burners,' she informed me abruptly. 'There are three wine cups, three incense sticks and a candlestick with seven lotuses—note that these numbers are odd. Also displayed are prayer sticks, offerings of fruit and flowers. An incense tablet burner, though they do not use this any more, they are content to use the more convenient sticks. This is the cabinet they use in association with fortune telling, here the sword of Kuan Kung, panels on the altar read "Loyalty, utter devotion, benevolence and courage", "May the merciful people spread to every corner of the world".'

'If the merciful people are the Chinese, then they certainly have done,' I remarked.

The woman did not respond. Barely pausing for breath she hustled me into an adjoining room. 'Front entrance chamber. As you can see, this is the figure of Confucius in the centre, on each side two wooden panels bearing poems in ancient Chinese. Beautiful lanterns. This is the door guardian Mun Dei, this is not normally part of their temple but is a household shrine, a house god was usual in their homes, we put it here so visitors could see what it was like . . .

'Now, if you'd just like to come this way, the Ancestral Room. This is dedicated to the memory of their ancestors, the three tablets are memorials to the deceased, originally there were hundreds of memorials, but they were smashed by vandals during a break-in.'

'Ah—I was wondering why there was such a large fence around the compound,' I interrupted. The fencing was two metres high and had three strands of barbed wire on top of it.

'That's always been there. The place next door is a munitions factory. It wanted to raze the temple in the seventies and take over the land for expansion, but the National Trust stepped in.'

'What do they make in the munitions factory?'

'I don't know.' She paused. 'Probably better not to ask!'

After this little sign of humour the woman seemed to recollect her mission to tell me as much as possible about the joss house without saying anything of interest. 'Panels on the side say "Buddhism brings you luck and eternal good fortune" and "The spirits of the dead bring you good omens for ever". On the side altar is Kuan Yin, goddess of mercy. The women like to come in here to pray to Kuan Yin, the men usually remain next door in the main room, where they like to play with the fortune sticks. They shake the sticks out of the holder to determine the omen. Of course, it is a very simple religion really, not like ours—they are very superstitious.'

I woke from my lethargy at this extraordinary pronouncement. Later the guide said: 'The term "joss house" is derogatory in China. It comes from the Portuguese *deos*, meaning god. But overseas in European countries that is what we call them, and that is what it is called here, though they call it the Big Gold Mountain Temple.'

This spiel astonished me. It was delivered in a monotone; either the guide had said it so many times before she was hardly conscious of the fact, or she was uninterested in what she said. This is not a European country, I felt like saying to her, and all religions are superstitious. I hated the way she repeated *they, they, they*, as if talking about some alien beings.

I said nothing. I listened to the lengthy tour in puzzlement, trying to figure this woman out: she worked in this place, one had to assume she appreciated it—and yet her choice of language seemed to deny admiration. Now she was talking about a 'little Indonesian monk' who once came here (Asians are always little to some Australians), and a 'lovely little

Vietnamese family' who had donated a statue and some lanterns to the temple. As I was about to leave she said unexpectedly: 'It must have been wonderful in the gold-rush days. Imagine the men, with their pigtails and mandarin's robes, coming in here. Wouldn't it have been wonderful? I have a great imagination.'

She said it in a flat voice which seemed to contradict the statement—but how should I know? I was just a stranger, why should she reveal her imagination to me? And what did I really know about what she thought of this temple, of the Chinese? Possibly she loved the place. In spite of myself I smiled at her, and fleetingly she smiled back at me.

'I came here for only two weeks, to help out,' she confided. 'That was eleven years ago. My name's Joyce Pellew. I only learned about the temple gradually, little by little, from the people who came to pray here. I tried asking about it all— they wouldn't tell me. It would have been like boasting for the Chinese, revealing all this information.'

'Hm.'

'Of course, they have a very close community, keep themselves to themselves. But help each other, too. Very good to the family. I rarely see my own children, you know. That's what it's like for us.'

This seemed to open the way for reminiscences in Joyce Pellew. Her transition from objective monotonous recital to personal recollection was sudden and, as far as I could judge, without any provocation. She sat down on a little red stool near the temple's altar and told me about her father back in England, whom she had loved despite his being a strict disciplinarian, beating her. When he had taken ill it had devastated her. With five children to look after as well, she recalled wandering the streets of Manchester in search of calves' foot jelly, as this was supposed to be good for sickness.

'I found some, but my father took one sip and wouldn't drink the rest. He died . . . I thought I would never get over it, I wanted to die too . . . Not long afterwards I immigrated to Australia with my family. After three months in Melbourne my husband met another woman in a pub and left me with the five children. In court I refused to take any support from him, wouldn't touch a penny.'

Joyce had married again, to another man with whom she had spent ten wonderful years, until he had suddenly contracted a brain disease similar to Parkinson's, that had resulted in his losing his memory and requiring constant care. He was now in a nursing home.

'I have him at home for a few hours every Sunday, but I don't think he knows where he is, who I am.'

I listened to the story, aghast and fascinated, not knowing what to say, except that I was sorry, I was sorry, over and over, as she related one tragedy after another. Joyce didn't see her children that often; too busy with their own lives. All five of them were divorced, she was in touch with only six of her twelve grandchildren.

'Don't get married until you're forty,' she advised me as I left. 'You have plenty of time after that to meet the right person and have children. Meantime, enjoy your life.'

I promised that I would, and said goodbye. I felt sorry now that I had distrusted her, thought her uninteresting, had given way to irritation at her spiel about the temple. Joyce Pellew sat here day after day, with her loneliness and her memories, and in the end had given me a precious glimpse into the personal corners of her history. I wanted to hug her.

Most Australian towns were flat places—this, I suddenly realised as I drove into Ballarat, was actually the most striking thing about them. The buildings were low, many of them had flat roofs, and only a few were more than a couple of storeys high. Most Australian houses were bungalows—why not, with so much space? In the country towns they almost seemed to crouch down in sympathy with the flat countryside, hiding under the trees as if to escape notice. The churches, with their pointy roofs and clock towers, appeared immense by comparison.

Ballarat had been an important place once, and some of its buildings were larger than the norm. Gold had been discovered here in 1851. Tradition has it that James Esmond, a prospector, was travelling through the region and took shelter under a tree during a storm. Idly digging in the ground with his boot, he unearthed several pieces of gold. The first short gold rush was on, which brought more than 1000 people into the region. When later, larger discoveries were made, the flow increased until there were as many as 60 000 hopeful immigrants searching the goldfields of the surrounding area. There had been fifty-six churches and nearly five hundred hotels, and Sturt and Bridge Streets had been lined by shops and businesses doing a roaring trade. By 1918 the last mine had closed and the town sank into somnolence.

Ballarat was another Bendigo, with its churches and public buildings, banks and hotels from the last century. It was a nice place, which suffered only because I had seen so many, similar nice places right across the goldfields. I crawled through it in my campervan, peering out the windows at the notable buildings, feeling like a cheat. But I stopped just outside, at Sovereign Hill, where an outdoor museum portrayed the way of life in the goldfields in the 1850s. The township included diggings, an underground mine, an Edinburgh Boot and Shoe Mart, a confectioner, blacksmith, coach builder, a bank, a reproduction of Ballarat's first post office. There was a grocer's (Clarke Brothers) and a bakery advertising meat pies with tea or coffee for only threepence. Inside there was a real bakery, but the prices had risen sharply. There was also a Chinese village, a tiny place with a minute joss house—quite inaccurate, given the large numbers of Chinese miners who had worked the fields, I thought. The staff who worked here walked around in Victorian costumes. Like all such reconstructions, Sovereign Hill was immensely successful, and I enjoyed wandering about, watching a woman making old-fashioned sweets, visiting the apothecary. This was a tidy and picturesque place reeking with nostalgia for a more gentle time that never was. This was entertainment, I thought to myself as I left; not history.

Towards the Grampians on the Western Highway, which ran all the way to Adelaide, I passed through another former gold town, Ararat, now a centre for the surrounding wheat and wool farms and wineries. 'DON'T HANG ABOUT DOING NOTHING,' said an advertisement I had picked up, its commanding capitals like something from a war recruitment poster. 'VISIT ARARAT'S J WARD HOME FOR THE CRIMINALLY INSANE.' This seemed grotesque, and without pausing I skipped along the highway to stop the night at Stawell. Next day I headed into the Grampians, part of the Great Dividing Range which swept down through Queensland, New South Wales and Victoria to end here in dramatic cliffs and jagged peaks of rock. I camped once more, at Halls Gap, its tourist centre. It had a scattering of caravan sites, motels, swimming pools, crazy golf, pony rides, craft shops, postcard stands, scenic flights, tennis courts and all the usual trappings of the Australian wilderness experience. Koalas squatted in the gum trees, and one couldn't help imagining they had been placed there by the wily locals.

I had become fascinated by my tourist brochures. 'The splendour and beauty of the Grampians have been 400 million years in the making. With sheer slopes, dense forests and crystalline lakes, these ranges are truly spectacular. Majestic waterfalls roar over rock formations, and tumble into mist shrouded valleys abundant with fern growth and lichen encrusted rocks.' It sounded cool and idyllic, but the heat had been building up steadily since I had left Thredbo, and now even the locals were calling it a heat wave. Temperatures in Victoria and South Australia had been in the high thirties and low forties for several days running. School children had been sent home, shops had sold out of electric fans, electricity consumption had soared (causing blackouts in some places), people had been taken to hospital and fourteen old-age pensioners had died from heat exhaustion.

I decided to climb up a mountain. I saw no plunging waterfalls, only burning rock surfaces, and no trees, although there were plenty of lichen-encrusted boulders. The sun felt as if it were penetrating my eyes and searing right through to the back of my head, and my sun-cream, smeared across my forehead, felt as if it were deep-frying my skin. Greasy perspiration ran down my shirt. I made it to the summit and squinted out at the spectacular view shimmering in the heat haze.

Then I walked back down again, and was sick.

On the way to Melbourne I found a conversation, in a roadside McDonald's where I stopped for pancakes with maple syrup and (more importantly) refillable coffee and a newspaper. The place was crowded with travellers, the noise was almost deafening, and I stood in the queue for minutes on end—the staff had run out of change. Grasping my tray, I finally fled to the only empty table to find I had sat down beside an uncouth family with a horrible little boy. The family laughed and encouraged the boy to spit down his straw into his Coke. Finally he threw the drink on the floor, which was apparently considered funny by the three adults who were with him.

When they were gone the teenage girl who came to clean it up was phlegmatic.

'This is the second spillage in ten minutes,' she told me. 'At least it's not a milk shake.' She shrugged. Amiably we discussed the relative merits of mops and spilt liquids.

'Some kids decided to have a food fight earlier this morning. If it was adults, you would call the police,' she said as she trailed away with her mop.

When she was gone the empty table was taken over by an American. He was from Seattle, here on holiday, and was driving from Sydney to Adelaide by way of Victoria.

'Of course, it's not so different from back home,' he said to me. I was astonished, and said so.

'Well, look,' he answered, waving his hand around the McDonald's, as if it were Australia's fault he had chosen to breakfast here.

There were many American things in Australia: fast-food chains and television programmes, Hollywood movies and shopping malls, fashion and pop music. These were outward trappings, I thought, that hid a rather un-American society.

'How so?'

'Well, Australians are materialistic, but they don't seem interested in the status material possessions bring, they wouldn't defend it with a gun. They don't worship wealth in the way of Americans,' I said.

'Because they don't have as much of it,' said the American sourly.

'Because they're more easygoing. They don't think work and money are all-important. I think Australians are more truly hedonistic than Americans. The puritans never got much of a foothold down here. At the end of the day Australians prize enjoyment above achievement.'

The American was not about to concede anything. 'Australians are just lazy,' he said.

I bridled in annoyance, feeling defensive. 'Another myth. You can't call a different attitude to life laziness. Actually, I think a lot of Australians work pretty hard, but they have the sense to want more than two weeks holiday a year.'

The American slurped at his coffee. It was no use talking to him of other values, different cultures: he couldn't see beyond the American way of life, in which he had the unshakeable self-assurance of his countrymen.

'But they shared a similar pioneering spirit, didn't they, in history. A kind of survival against hardship,' he said. 'A mentality that they are somehow blessed, have made something of themselves.'

Did Australians think they were blessed? I wasn't sure. The Americans had looked west and found new pastures and new land to cultivate, had opened up a new continent before them like a promised land. In Australia that land had only become more and more barren the further the settlers had moved towards the interior, and so they had forever turned across the sea for support and guidance.

'But Australia does call itself God's Own Country, right?'

I thought about this a while. I had never heard the expression, and it certainly sounded more like an American idea— Americans often claimed that God blessed their nation, that they were especially chosen.

'I don't know. I've heard Australia called the Lucky Country far more often. I think that's more accurate. I think Australians probably believe they have achieved their blessings quite by chance, as if they don't really deserve them. These days I feel they're beginning to panic a bit as their luck runs out. Americans have far vaster problems, but they never seem to feel abandoned by their God or the American Dream.'

I ate a pancake, and then I said: 'Americans are far, far more certain of themselves. Australians aren't sure about anything too much.'

The American I was talking to looked pleased, as if I had complimented him. I could have added: that's why I think I like Australians better. But I didn't. I just drank my coffee and asked him about Melbourne ('Great art museum, nice food'), and then I went on my way.

'When I think of Melbourne, I vomit,' wrote Robert Louis Stevenson mercilessly. 'Its flatness, its streets laid out with a square rule are doomed to have a detrimental effect on those who are condemned to dwell by the yellow waters of the Yarra River.' The people of Sydney would no doubt have agreed. Rivalry between the two cities had been a source of contention for well over a century. Sydneysiders had warned me of Melbourne in just the way they had warned me of Canberra. It was a boring place, the people were conservative and worked all the time, and the weather was awful: it always rained. The conservatism of the city seemed true enough—it did not take me long to discover that Melburnians talked in whispers, and they seemed quiet and considerate and old-fashioned in the best sense of the word. In Sydney the citizens yelled at each other on the trains, and on the beaches you could overhear the most intimate details of sunbathers' relationships. They were loud and brash and not very sophisticated, materialistic and probably depraved, at least in the eyes of Melburnians.

To myself as an outsider this rivalry was quite extraordinary and deeply institutionalised—much more serious than the bickering that went on between Edinburgh and Glasgow or the conflicting purposes of Beijing and Shanghai. The two Australian cities had been antagonistic since their founding, and had long feuded over political influence, railway gauges, international airports, rights to hold the Olympics, the attracting of overseas investment and company headquarters. There were even arguments over whether Captain Cook had first sighted Australia on the coast of what was now New South Wales or Victoria. Melbourne scored a coup in 1934 when the city was presented with Captain Cook's cottage, relocated from Yorkshire to the Fitzroy Gardens. Sydneysiders were incensed: what had Melbourne got to do with Cook anyway?

To Melbourne it was a triumph, obtaining this cottage associated with the man that history (which likes clear-cut answers) had decreed discovered Australia. Of course he hadn't—and the leaflet handed out with my entrance ticket merely claimed cautiously that Cook 'did more to clarify the geographical questions in the Southern Hemisphere than any other before him'. Nor was there any conclusive evidence that he had ever lived in the cottage, although he was believed to have spent some time there between voyages. Never mind. The acquisition infuriated Sydney, and it was also a little bit, however tenuous, of the history that white Australia barely possessed.

For my three dollars I didn't spend much longer than ten minutes in the cottage, which was a minute two-up-two-down with a former stable extension out the back, now housing a souvenir shop and a few panels on Cook's voyages and the cottage's history. The articles inside the house (oak table and chairs, kitchen utensils, grain measures, pewter dishes) were of the period but had no connection at all with Cook, and there was no indication of the character of the man, and hardly even of the Yorkshire life of his times. The American I had met at the Sydney Opera House would have appreciated the photo opportunity, perhaps, but the building served little other purpose. With its red brick and tiled roof, its chimney and ivy (grown from cuttings from the original site), it was picturesque, but it was sterile too: another Sovereign Hill, another sanitised Port Arthur. Where had the great man gone to the toilet? I asked myself.

Captain Cook's cottage was a dull place, and I did not see why Sydney wanted one too (they had looked around York-shire for a suitable candidate, just to annoy Melbourne, but none had been available). Anyway, I was determined not to become embroiled in the antagonism between the cities, especially as my perspective would undoubtedly be skewed towards Sydney, where after all I had stayed for months, enabling me to develop a feel for the place, not to mention a fondness. I would be staying in Melbourne little more than a weekend, and in that time I knew it stood little chance in comparison. Yes, it rained when I was there, and it did seem a little dull compared to Sydney—but staying in a hotel room was dull (I had temporarily abandoned the campervan), and I knew no one in this city, nor even where to go for excite-ment. Sydney was my own Sydney, one in which I had the time to make it what I wanted it to be. My Melbourne was the Melbourne of other people, of guidebooks and leaflets and instantly accessible city centre streets and sights.

And yet I liked Melbourne immediately. Perhaps it was only because it was the weekend, but it seemed more civilised, less hectic than Sydney—the traffic slow and courteous, the buildings stately, the boulevards wide and tree-lined. It had more flavour than Sydney, the architecture and the streets grander but at the same time somehow more intimate, more lived-in. I liked the trams—they were a Melbourne institution and a delight. How could I not like a city with trams, which reminded me so much of my childhood, for Geneva had trams too. The hot smell of metal wheels, the hanging straps, the rattling windows and swaying of the carriages from side to side and the way they suddenly lurched forward—this was an experience from the past, a ride through nostalgia. Other cities got rid of trams as anachronisms and replaced them with air-conditioned buses or soulless, claustrophobic underground railways. Trams were full of character and life, and in Melbourne passengers sat down beside you and started to talk (or mostly complain, usually about the State government) as you rattled up streets of plane trees and restaurants.

Melbourne seemed the most European of Australian cities, with its nineteenth-century architecture, pretty parks, grey pigeons, fashionable dressers, street cafés with their endless cappuccino-drinking newspaper-reading clientele. The east end of Collins Street, in the heart of the city, had traditionally been the quiet and dignified part of town, the location of gentlemen's clubs and doctors' surgeries, with a few exclusive hotels and shops and theatres. It was supposed to look like Paris, and at first glance, not surprisingly, it did—because I knew it ought to, and I noticed things that seemed Parisian. There were news kiosks splattered with pigeon droppings, plane trees, green metal benches, and even the McDonald's on the street corners were Parisian, too. There was a small dirty building called Le Louvre and a Cartier shop. But the shop next door sold Waterford crystal, and no one said Collins Street looked like Dublin. The churches on Collins Street certainly did not look French. St Michael's looked faintly Byzantine with its patterned brickwork, which was almost vulgar; the Scots Church across the road was dour Presbyterian grey somewhat enlivened by a roof cluttered with miniature spires.

Collins Street was not really Parisian, and Melbourne was not really European—to me this was no criticism. Australians were fond of comparisons, which seemed to reassure them and lend a certain second-hand sophistication. Melbourne did not, to me, seem European exactly—more colonial European, perhaps, with its impressive public buildings, grand statues and immense boulevards (space was not an issue if you could snatch your land from other people). Melbourne reminded me of other colonial cities—Mexico City, say, or Buenos Aires. Why compare, anyway? Melbourne had a charm that was all its own, a very Australian blend of many places and many people.

On Collins Street there were well-dressed women with too much lipstick who blew evil cigarette smoke over my face with contempt as I stood waiting for the traffic lights. That could have been Paris, at least, I thought to myself.

Sydney was identified by suburbs: Cabramatta (ethnic and crime-ridden), Balmain (well-heeled and arty), Newtown (scruffy and bohemian). Melbourne, in contrast, seemed to be defined more by its streets, at least for me as a visitor— Lygon and Collins, Brunswick and Chapel, Toorak Road.

I had tinkled the three Taiwanese ladies as promised on arriving in Melbourne. 'You meet us Chapel Street, good place go shopping,' one of them told me on the phone. (I did not know which one, and felt it impolite to ask.) I arrived there to find the street a strange mix—an antique shop beside a used fridge bargain centre, a Salvation Army store beside a flash women's gym ('Gym and Tonic'), a tailor with Greek lettering on the door and old-fashioned men's suits in the windows beside a clothes shop with a rack of skimpy dresses outside in lime green and shocking orange. There was a Polish restaurant with coloured plastic strips hanging in the doorway to ward off the flies, and beside it The Temple of Isis, whose specialities included Scandinavian healing, reiki and sekhem (whatever they were), emotional counselling, tarot and meditation classes. The window displayed purple crystals and books on Egyptology. Across the road was a pawn-broker. 'Cash for everything: we buy and sell gold, diamonds, silver, gemstones,' it said hopefully, but the windows showed a basket of old watches, a dusty row of stereo sets and an old circular power saw.

I soon realised that I had arrived at the wrong end of Chapel Street from the good shopping so fondly mentioned by the free-spending Taiwanese wives. It was hard to know where the transition began. The Greek names became Italian and pseudo-Japanese, and there were suddenly clothes shops that called themselves boutiques and design houses. They had polished wooden floors and black shop assistants with rippling muscles. (There were few blacks in Australia, and they all seemed to be working in trendy clothes studios.) The old Greek men with two-day stubbles, nicotine-stained fingers, and worry beads had gone, too, and instead in the cafés young men sat in T-shirts a size too tight, with earrings and mobile phones.

The shops on this end of Chapel Street had obscure names: hOWard shOWers, pto, Witchery, Mono, Hound Dog, Hot Tuna, moos spc, Tequila Blues. You had to be an initiate to know these were fashion labels and clothes boutiques, and their difficult punctuation and spellings were out to trap the unwary. 'Get the Look' said a huge advertisement hoarding for a clothing chain, the lettering in yellow, the latest trendy colour. It was a black-and-white photograph, of course, mostly out of focus, showing bright young things with slick hair and astonishing eyelashes.

I hated yellow and I didn't have the look. In fact, I was wearing a baggy old sweatshirt, and I had earlier that day sat down on a wet bench—the back of my jeans was damp. I slunk off into an almost deserted shopping mall. A young Australian was coming out as I went in. He had a briefcase that looked as if it had been carved out of steel. His face was tanned, he had a gold ear stud in one ear, he was wearing black jeans and a tight black top with very short sleeves, which went well with his Chinese features. He was gorgeous and he knew it; he walked with a slinky insolence and when he saw me staring at him he looked straight through me with eyes of ice. I felt old and overweight and dowdy. It was one of those moments in time, those brief glimpses of enlightenment that come upon one suddenly in the most unexpected places—and I knew then that I wasn't young any more.

The Taiwanese ladies, on the other hand, didn't seem concerned about my lack of style and youthfulness. They giggled at me and swung their bags of shopping.

'You enjoy Bendigo? It not fun place, I think.'

'I went to the Chinese temple there.'

'Chinese temple? I don't know Chinese temple in Bendigo.'

'Just outside, about three kilometres from the centre of town.'

One of the ladies sucked in her breath. 'Wah! Too far, we go Bendigo in train, can't walk so far. We strolling around, eat lunch in nice hotel.'

We arrived at the Jam Factory, a cinema complex and shopping mall on Chapel Street. It looked like a cross between a Las Vegas casino, a 1950s American milk bar and Cleopatra's palace. There were Assyrian-style reliefs on the wall (warriors in chariots and rearing horses), palm trees, Greek columns made of neon lights, a floor like a circus arena and a tasteless mix of fashionable colours on the walls—tangerine and salmon, fuchsia, bronze and aquamarine.

'We take photo for souvenir, OK?'

The mall was full of grotesque statues—a human figure with the skin markings and head of a leopard, riding on a horse; an alien monster; a Marilyn Monroe in wax with a billowing skirt. These were good backdrops for our photos, and I stood there with varying selections of Taiwanese ladies, feeling foolish.

'We return back, tell husband this Australian lover,' giggled one of the ladies raffishly.

'Wah! Chen Ling, you too bold, get big trouble.'

'I'm not Australian anyway.'

'You hear? He not Australian.'

'Where you come from then?'

'Maybe from Ireland,' I said.

'Oh, very far away place.'

What could I say? Throughout my childhood Australia had always been the epitome of the far away place, an almost mythical country you could only get to by digging a hole in the sand and popping out at the far reaches of the earth. Travel upset such casually acquired cultural norms. Now Ireland was far away, and Australia was right here, under my feet. And as the camera flashes popped and the ladies chatted, I thought to myself, sometimes the reality is better than the myth, after all.

Brunswick Street was more my style, a scruffy, Bohemian road that was slowly becoming more trendy, though in a more humane way than Chapel Street. There was a laundrette ('Bundle drop by arrangement') that was a survivor of another era, with its massive steel washing machines and linoleum floor and tattered posters peeling off the walls. There was an old-fashioned butcher's shop in white tiles where slabs of beef lay bleeding, and restaurants with laminated tables cluttered with salt cellars and vinegar bottles, where generous helpings and traditional hearty meals were offered. But in between, shops had tarot and psychic readings, bold sofas in tiger stripes and chairs that looked like instruments of torture. There were New Age shops full of baskets and wind chimes, restaurants that served focaccia or sushi, and sometimes both. The hairdressers on Brunswick Street looked like dental clinics or art galleries, the art galleries like cafés, the cafés like Italian peasant kitchens.

The people here didn't look through you as if performing a surgical operation. They sat on the street, drank coffee and ate enormous breakfasts of bacon and scrambled eggs and talked to you, like Jack, down from Canberra.

'I came to block traffic with my bicycle,' he told me carelessly, shovelling huge forkfuls of hash brown into his mouth.

'How do you do that?'

'It's a sort of pressure group, called Critical Mass. Cyclists get together to ride through the city. Sometimes we block off entire intersections for several sequences of traffic lights. We did it in Melbourne yesterday.'

'What does that do, apart from annoy motorists?'

Jack sniffed. 'It's a statement about how cars have taken over the urban living space, you know. Like, to remind people

of road safety for cyclists, and environmental friendliness?'
He had a hesitant uplift to his sentences, as if asking questions
himself.

'Why don't you do it in Canberra?'

'We do. Also in Brisbane, Sydney. It originated in the
United States, I think. Our slogan is "We're not blocking
traffic, we are traffic".'

I said: 'That's pretty cunning.'

'We had a good party in Edinburgh Gardens afterwards,'
said Jack gleefully, describing the occasion. He was a university student, and these things counted: any good cause had to
have beer and girls in it somewhere.

This was Brunswick Street, a place of people with quirky
ideas and plans to save the world, a place where you could
talk over breakfast to a woman who had lived in a small
Moroccan village for five months, or over dinner to someone
with an evangelical look in his eyes, relating how he had
travelled in Egypt and found an oasis he had seen in dreams
since childhood. These people were alive, they had ideas,
they had character and warmth that seemed a long way from
the steely-eyed fashion clones of Chapel Street.

There was a Chinatown in the heart of Melbourne, and
despite my limited time in the city it was one place I was
determined not to miss. The Chinese had come to Melbourne
in significant numbers during the gold rush, and by the 1850s
had established their enclave on Little Bourke Street between
Russell and Swanston streets. Most of the Chinese there were
transients, passing by on their way to the mining towns, but
around fifty took up permanent residence, supplying provisions—meat, opium, tools, clothes—to the miners. With the
decline of the goldfields Chinatown became significantly
larger, occupying several more city blocks than it does today,
and by the turn of the century there had been over 1000
Chinese living there. 'I do not suppose', lamented one newspaper, 'any city in the world can show such foul neighbour-
hoods centred in its very heart.' Few white Australians entered
the area, which was assumed to be a cesspool of all the vices
typically associated with the celestials. In fact, the diligent

Chinese here were operating wholesale groceries that did much to supply the State with fresh vegetables and tropical fruits, as well as labouring in other businesses such as cabinet-making and tailoring.

By the 1930s such trade had almost vanished with the decline of the Chinese population under the White Australia Policy. There were few of the original Chinese buildings left (many of the old clan buildings and temples were now car parks), but Chinatown, which claimed to be the oldest in the Western world, was undergoing a revival. While Asian influences in Australia were still strongly resisted in the fields of culture, religion, life-style and the arts, they had been accepted in the realm of cuisine, and there were close to a hundred restaurants operating in the area. There were a few reminders of the grocery businesses of old: Louey Hin's ('Importer and Bean Sprout Specialist'), Hong Oriental Food Company, Kwong Lee Lung's beancurd business. In the middle of Chinatown there was a gateway in Chinese architectural style, a replica of a gateway in Nanjing, capital of Victoria's sister province of Jiangsu. There was also a Chinese Methodist Church and a Chinese Masonic Society in a curious (though apparently successful) blend of east and west. The blend did not extend to the Chinese from different clans and origins in mainland China. Many of the shops and restaurants here were rigorously divided along clan lines, and the Chinese would frequent only those operated by owners from the same background—which might be no more than a hundred kilometres apart in southern Guangdong Province. Unnoticed by white Australians, such divisions were testimony to the inability of 'Asian' immigrants to form a cohesive group that might threaten white culture.

There was a museum in the middle of Chinatown, concerned with the history of the Chinese in Australia. It was very quiet; I was the only person in the whole building. The attendant selling tickets said there were seldom more than ten people on a Sunday, maybe twenty or thirty on other days. When I asked him, he ventured there were more Westerners than Asian visitors, though quite a lot of overseas Chinese. He seemed disappointed with the lack of interest among Chinese Australians. Behind his desk loomed the snaking, multicoloured figure of Dai Loong, the dragon used during the Chinese New Year festivities in the city.

'I'm not Australian. I'm from Sarawak,' said the attendant shyly when I asked him. 'Malaysian. I like it in Melbourne because of the fresh weather.'

As it was pouring with rain, I glanced out of the window and grimaced.

'Yes, I like even the rain. Not too hot. My family lives in Darwin, but I hate that sticky weather. I feel too sleepy!'

He had been here more than a decade, but had not yet become an Australian citizen. 'Too many problems in Malaysia. You must lose your property or investments if you take a foreign nationality.'

Yes, I thought: and you will have to remove your earring if you go back to Malaysia, too. He seemed to me like Mark in Darwin: no longer entirely of his home culture, not exactly Western either, an Australian hybrid.

'I like it here. Of course I will remain here. It's my home now,' he said to me.

Inside the museum, there was a series of scenes depicting Chinese involvement in the exploitation of gold. The first was of Hong Kong harbour, and then one passed through the dark hold of a ship (the floor rocked and creaked) to arrive in Australia to the sounds of cockatoos in the trees and a vast landscape across which a line of Chinese struggled with their belongings on shoulder poles. Then there were vignettes of life in a Chinese mining village on the goldfields—Ah Chang's cookshop, a temple, Poon Toy's Cantonese Opera ('New Play Every Night!'), and a Chinese lottery shop.

Other parts of the museum did not hesitate to show the uglier side of the story of the Chinese in Australia. 'White Racism' said the title on one information board bluntly. Fear, envy and economic competition had had a profound effect on the Chinese community in Australia. They had been forced out of their businesses, which in some cases they had actually set up and developed themselves—banana-growing in Queensland, pearling in Western Australia—and restrictions and higher taxes had made them increasingly uncompetitive in market-gardening, furniture-making and other fields of endeavour. Discriminatory, bigot, racist—these were words used throughout the commentary on the audio-visual show, a fast-moving and upbeat, though not terribly detailed, romp through the history of the Chinese here. Of course, the supreme irony was this: that it had been the British who had caused much of the economic chaos and hardship in China which had forced the Chinese to look overseas for other opportunities; and the authorities in Australia who had invited them to this country as hired labourers after the abolition of the convict system.

On the top floor there were black-and-white photos from the first half of this century showing young girls at a debutante ball arranged by the Chinese Youth League, a Chinese football team in Melbourne in long baggy white shorts, a well-known boxer of the time. There was one enlarged photo without a date or caption, showing four women in elaborate head-dresses and traditional costumes embroidered with bamboo leaves and blossoms. They were holding a papier mâché dragon's head which a young man was putting on. He looked out through the gaping mouth and was the central focus of the picture. He glanced sideways with a slightly cheeky expression and was giving a big grin, his whole face alight with fun and good nature.

I stood and looked at the photo for a long time, and thought: Anyone who thinks there should be no Asian immigration to Australia should come and look at these photos, and especially this one.

Yes, I thought as I looked at the displays. I am obsessed with the Chinese. But I had reason to be—I wanted everyone to share my enthusiasm and my passion, to shake them and shout: Can't you see? Isn't this wonderful? I stared and stared through the glass of a display cabinet at an embroidered tunic. The robe was that worn by a mandarin in the imperial government. It was deep blue and heavily embroidered with gold thread, with a writhing central dragon with jaws agape and spread claws. There were various attendant dragons with finely detailed scales, and embroidered flowers and swirls that might be stylised clouds or waves. And I thought: this is a beautiful thing. And I felt a deep longing that was almost like love; and I surprised myself at my overwhelming sentimentality.

Fall in love with an alien culture and it influences you for the rest of your life. My whole vision of Australia had been seen through the prism of its Asian immigrants, and everywhere I went I still searched for the Chinese and never quite found them—how could I, when I was not Chinese? But I liked Australia, I liked its multicultural population. I liked Australia's sense of confusion over identity, its uncertainties, its muddled visions of the future. I had loved China, a place that had profoundly changed my outlook on life; and now I found I loved Australia too, though for different reasons. China had been the shock and challenge of the different. Australia was myself, with all my split views on the world, my inability to reach conclusions, my uncertainties that were really a form of positive energy, my difficult adaptations of various cultures and backgrounds that caused me so much trouble but, I hoped, made me a better person.

I was sitting in a museum in Melbourne, and suddenly I knew, then, that I would make Australia my home.

Journeys end emotionally before they end physically. I still had some of Victoria to see before travelling up the south coast of New South Wales and back to Sydney. But my journey was over, I thought, here in this museum, and I was going—where? Home? But I didn't know where home was any more, and I had decided to apply for residence in Australia, and live in Sydney. It has been said that travel is an escape from the self, from one's normal preoccupations and problems, even a flight from all responsibility. Sometimes I thought travel was just the opposite: an immense complication, a gigantic reassessment of one's whole life and culture in the light of the lives and culture of others. And so perhaps I was leaving just to come back again, to a new life, new friends, new job, new meaning.

It was the past that was easy, for the past was an old life, as withered and unchangeable as the body of a Stone Age man preserved in the British Museum. The past was a meandering line that circumnavigated Australia on a map, while the future was the unknown, and a new start.

Perhaps this was not the end of Australia, I thought gleefully. Australia was really only beginning.

epilogue: in a town hall

Sydney. Leichhardt Town Hall. I enter its main doors with an Australian friend and we walk down a gloomy corridor lined with black-and-white photos of councillors past and present. They scowl or smirk down at us, their brows creased into furrows of worry, or perhaps laughter—how can one tell? The faces have been frozen into caricatures of themselves: gaunt and horrified, or heavy-jowled and small of eye, all with the white, sad look of bureaucrats with a lifetime of offices behind them. The corridor walls are pale green, a colour I loathe. There are a couple of chairs pushed back against the wall, the occasional wooden table from some long-gone drawing room: an unimaginative, institutional look. From a room at the end of the corridor wafts a doleful tune played by a solitary trumpet.

'Sounds like a funeral,' I whisper. The carpet smells like death, dusty and at the same time mouldy.

'Leichhardt—Italian style,' my friend answers, for the area is renowned as a centre for Italian immigrants. 'More like a tune from *The Godfather*.'

As we enter the hall I see there is not only a trumpeter but an entire band, the Leichhardt Municipal Band, no less. They liven up into a merry ditty as I scan the room, taking in the rows of uncomfortable chairs and the gathering of people, who are standing around in small clumps and not speaking, as if they have just been informed that their relatives have been involved in some terrible airline disaster. The brass ensemble are wearing yellow jackets and dark blue ties and are sitting behind a row of potted plants, while behind them is hanging the Australian flag, flanked by the flags of the Aboriginal Australians and the Torres Strait Islanders. Banners with the flags of all nations are hung overhead like gay bunting at a wedding reception. Almost unconsciously I hunt out the Chinese flag, then the British and Irish ones, then the Swiss one, in that order. The Swiss one seems to be missing, but that is OK: Switzerland seems a long way away. The band starts 'You're just too good to be true, can't take my eyes off of you'—an American pop song from the seventies, though I can't remember who sang it— Donna Summer? As I settle down on a chair they proceed to massacre the 'Ode to Joy' from Beethoven's Ninth Symphony. The musicians look resolutely Anglo-Saxon to a man (and one woman), I note, and say as much to the friend sitting beside me. No, you wouldn't think of Italians looking at the Leichhardt Municipal Band.

I am here as the result of a letter. 'I am pleased to tell you', it told me, 'that your application for the grant of Australian citizenship has been approved. On behalf of the Government and people of Australia, I would like to congratulate you on your decision to become an Australian citizen.' This seemed nice, to congratulate me on something as if it were the result of some physical prowess or an astonishing examination result. Actually, I had done nothing except pay fifty-five dollars and avoid a police record during my residency in Sydney.

'Australian citizenship is the common bond which unites all Australians,' the letter had continued. 'Today Australians come from more than two hundred different cultural back-grounds. Becoming an Australian citizen means that you have adopted as your home a country that respects the diverse cultural inheritance of all its citizens.' I liked this too—this was a clever way to win me over. Then the letter wished me happiness and prosperity (very Chinese, I thought, almost like a fortune cookie), and was signed: 'Yours sincerely, Philip Ruddock, Minister for Immigration and Multicultural Affairs'. It is a good title, Multicultural Affairs. I wouldn't mind being the minister for that; I've had a few myself, I think as the band plays on.

Now, in the crowd in Leichhardt Town Hall, there is a scattering of people from various parts of Asia. There is also a girl with a nose pin, knee-length black boots and a dress that seems to be made of little more than knotted string. There are several people in suits and ties, and others in jeans. There are people with kids, and an old man with a wild eye and scraggly white beard, with the looks of a biblical prophet. He has a knitted woollen tam-o'-shanter on his head in green and red. There are all sorts of people here, and I know I have made a good decision.

We are invited to stand. Mayor Councillor Kristine Cruden enters and the trumpeters from the band blare out an approximation of a processional march as she wanders in, looking faintly bemused. Her chain of office hangs round her neck but is almost camouflaged by the busy gold pattern on her dress. As she walks towards the front of the hall she looks around her benignly, as if surprised and gratified to see so many turn out for the occasion. She laughs nervously into the microphone so that it snorts and hisses, echoing around the room.

The mayor begs for indulgence. 'This is my first citizenship ceremony, so do shout out if I go wrong,' she says.

This is my first citizenship ceremony too, so I doubt I will be of any help, but there is a po-faced official in a black suit hovering over the mayor, who looks as if he could take control in a crisis. Anyway, it is a nice signal—this is going to be pleasant and relaxed and Australian, I can see that. Soon Mayor Cruden gets into her stride, and gives us a clear and elegant account of the rights and responsibilities of being an Australian, with a passing nod to the wonders of multi-culturalism and the simultaneous irrelevance (for citizenship purposes) and importance (for cultural purposes) of one's ethnic background.

Certain people in Australia have been known to complain that immigrants have divided loyalties, that they are not really 100 per cent Australian, as if this is something to be lamented. I do not think there is anyone, anywhere, who can actually tell me what an Australian is: this is exactly why I want to be here. Thoughts go through my head as I watch the people assembled in the room. I despise categorisation and stereotypes, which are deeply inimical to the individual human experience. Do I have divided loyalties? I cannot answer this question. I can only say I have a European heritage of which I am immensely proud; I have an upbringing that cannot be wrapped up in a bag and disposed of like an unwanted take-away. I have a passion for China too, which I am not prepared to throw out either. But I have chosen to become an Australian, something that people who are born Australian never do. That, to me, shows commitment enough. And the choice is not easy; it involves sacrifices of another life, other countries, my family. I have not seen my sister for more than a year.

We all stand up and swear the allegiance together. 'From this time forward, I pledge my loyalty to Australia and its people, whose democratic beliefs I share, whose rights and liberties I respect, and whose laws I will uphold and obey.' Then we file up one by one to get our certificates, issued by the Minister for Immigration and Multicultural Affairs, stating that we have undertaken to fulfil the responsibilities of an Australian citizen. The names are read out: Korean, Chinese, Filipino, English, Spanish, Arab, Indian. I shake the mayor's hand and an official photographer blunders round in confusion, trying to get the best angle. I wait, glued to the mayor's hand, while he changes his roll of film. The mayor keeps muttering congratulations in my ear and shaking my arm like a water pump before she releases me.

Electoral officers are present and we are immediately enrolled so that we can vote at the next election (always the foreigner, I have never voted in my life, and look forward to the event). We stand to sing the national anthem and the mayor is beaming—she has to read the words, just like us, from a sheet of paper. 'Our land abounds in nature's gifts / Of beauty rich and rare / In history's page, let every stage / Advance Australia Fair' I warble, out of tune.

Then we all repair to the back of the hall for a glass of wine and (surely this seems fitting, this most Australian of snacks) a sausage roll.

Or is it, perhaps, a large spring roll? Have the Chinese even influenced the palates of Leichhardt Municipal Council? You never know in this country, I tell myself, peering down at the flaky pastry in the gloomy light of the hall.

I pick it up and bite into the taste of Australia, smiling.

afterword

While I was working on the final manuscript of this book, Australia was overtaken by a political and social furore as a result of a maiden speech given to parliament by an independent Queensland MP, Pauline Hanson. In her speech and in the months that followed, during which she formed her own political party, she outlined her view of Australia's future: a withdrawal from the United Nations and all its bodies, a cancellation of any overseas aid to developing nations, the abolition of gun-control laws enacted after the Port Arthur massacre, and huge restrictions in funding for Aboriginal Australians, who she claimed were among the most advantaged groups in Australia. Her scaremongering played on the vague fears of white Australians. I was reminded of the anxieties that I had encountered in people such as Martin and Sarah, the retired couple with the shotgun whom I had met on the road out of Katherine.

Ms Hanson also made reference to the supposed practice of cannibalism among Aboriginal people. Her purpose was undoubtedly to dehumanise and revile Aboriginals. There is not a shred of serious historical or sociological evidence that cannibalism has ever been practised by Australia's native peoples. There is, however, much evidence to prove that Aboriginal Australians have the worst living conditions and health problems of any group in the developed world.

Pauline Hanson also favoured restricting Asian immigration, claimed that such immigrants could never adequately conform to Australian society, and warned that Asians were taking over Anglo-Saxon Australia—by 2040, she estimated, more than half of Australia's population would be of Asian ethnic background. In fact, reliable estimates suggest that the Asian component of Australia's population will still be less than 10 per cent in forty years time. Once again, wildly inaccurate claims fed on a general unease among Australians.

Pauline Hanson's opinions unleashed an unprecedented media and public debate over these issues, and particularly the issue of Asian immigration. Whether her views are shared by large numbers of the Australian public is a matter that has not been resolved, but she certainly gathered significant support, and the row unleashed suggested that there were many others in the community who were in agreement. At the same time, there were also many voices raised in opposition to her views, as well as public rallies in support of multiculturalism.

One notably reluctant participant in the debate was the Prime Minister, John Howard, who refused to condemn the new member of parliament's speech directly and said little about the immigration issue until obliged to by public and media reaction—and eventually by defections of his voters to Pauline Hanson's One Nation Party. By that time, however, Australia's reputation had been damaged in Asia, Asian Australians were feeling humiliated, and occurrences of racist abuse had risen in the country. And once again the perennial question was being asked: what is an Australian anyway?

In the light of all this, the themes of my book seemed fortuitously relevant. The reader need not be told of my opinion on the question of Asian immigration. After all, I am an immigrant myself, just like every other Australian, for that matter, since the First Fleet landed at Botany Bay—so I could hardly oppose immigration. What I do oppose is the careless labelling and categorisation of groups of people, and discrimination on that basis. For a start, there is no such thing as an 'Asian' immigrant; there are Malaysian immigrants or Hong Kong immigrants, perhaps—or maybe just Malaysian Chinese and Malaysian Malay immigrants—or maybe they are all individuals with as much right as anyone else to a decent life, to their own dreams and aspirations: like Mark, whom I met in Darwin, or Surit and his Laotian family in Canberra. The race debate also uncovered an astonishing ignorance of Australian history. Many people appeared to assume that 'Asians' had only come to Australia since the 1970s. They can hardly be blamed for their lack of knowledge. Pick up a general overview of Australian history in a library and look up 'Chinese' in the index; you will be lucky to find any mention at all. This is not just ignorance but the deliberate slanting of the story of Australia, in which the Anglo-Saxon male must always take centre stage. Yet, as I discovered in my travels, people from many parts of Asia in fact have a long and rich history on the continent; though they have frequently been reviled and discriminated against, they have contributed significantly to Australia's development.

Pauline Hanson is a very unintelligent person, frighteningly so given that she is a member of the federal parliament. She is unintelligent because she understands little about the significant historical role people from Asia have played; or about the diversity, complexity and immense value of their societies and people; or about the inevitable relationship Australia must have with its northern neighbours if it is to have a viable future. Most of all, she is unintelligent because she is profoundly lacking in human sympathy.

Common as it is, I will always find it deeply shocking to come across people who are so sure of the superiority and unquestionable value of their own way of life and culture that they imagine it should not be changed or influenced, let alone improved, by the culture of others. It is equally disturbing to dehumanise people and races. To accept others as humans, not only on a logical level (most of us can do that), but on an emotional level too—surely that is one of the truly valuable realisations of any travels, whether literal or spiritual?

This book is dedicated to my sister Nicola, for without her I would not have succeeded in travelling so widely in the outback, nor had such pleasure in doing so. However, I would also like to dedicate this book to all the people from every part of Asia who have come to Australia, whether they be Australians, residents, refugees, students, business people, tourists or others. I thank them for their contributions, and for the patience they have shown in waiting for certain white Australians to come to the hard realisation that they are not, after all, at the centre of the known world.

And I ask the reader's indulgence for this Afterword, which is merely an excuse to get on my soapbox and shout; but I hope you will agree with its necessity, and appreciate my anger and frustration. Ms Hanson's policies lead only backwards to a shameful past. What next? A return to the White Australia policy, perhaps? Or why not go the whole hog and bring back Pine Creek's tubs of cyanide? Racism has nothing to do with freedom of speech, and should be resisted vociferously.

Anyone who enjoys travel must surely seek out not just the uniqueness of each place and culture, but also the similarities that bind us all together. The Australia I had travelled was a country with a sometimes inglorious past, but its people were striving to overcome its history as they travelled towards a more civilised and tolerant future: for this I admired and respected them. Pauline Hanson's Australia is not the Australia I chose to be a part of, and I have confidence that it is not the Australia the majority of its citizens wish to live in.